FREUD FOR HISTORIANS

Books by Peter Gay

The Bourgeois Experience: Victoria to Freud, volume I,
Education of the Senses (1984)

Freud, Jews and Other Germans:
Masters and Victims in Modernist Culture (1978)

Art and Act: On Causes in History—Manet,
Gropius, Mondrian (1976)

Style in History (1974)

Modern Europe (1973), with R. K. Webb

The Bridge of Criticism: Dialogues on the Enlightenment (1970)

The Enlightenment: An Interpretation, volume II,
The Science of Freedom (1969)

Weimar Culture: The Outsider as Insider (1968)

A Loss of Mastery: Puritan Historians in Colonial America (1966)

The Enlightenment: An Interpretation, volume I,
The Rise of Modern Paganism (1966)

The Party of Humanity: Essays in the
French Enlightenment (1964)

Voltaire's Politics: The Poet as Realist (1959)

The Dilemma of Democratic Socialism:
Eduard Bernstein's Challenge to Marx (1952)

FREUD

FOR HISTORIANS

Peter Gay

OXFORD UNIVERSITY PRESS
New York   Oxford

Oxford University Press
Oxford   New York   Toronto
Delhi   Bombay   Calcutta   Madras   Karachi
Petaling Jaya   Singapore   Hong Kong   Tokyo
Nairobi   Dar es Salaam   Cape Town
Melbourne   Auckland

and associated companies in
Beirut   Berlin   Ibadan   Nicosia

Library of Congress Cataloging in Publication Data
Gay, Peter, 1923–
Freud for historians.
Includes index.
1. Psychohistory.   I. Title.
D16.16.G39   1985   901'.9   85-10665
ISBN 0-19-503586-0
ISBN 0-19-504228-X (pbk.)

Printing (last digit): 9 8 7 6 5 4

Printed in the United States of America

To
ERNST PRELINGER
and to one other

for talking, and for listening

Acts and examples stay
WILLIAM JAMES

Preface

This book is the concluding volume of a trilogy I did not intend to write. When, in 1974, I published *Style in History,* I thought I had paid my tribute to historiography. In that expedition of discovery among the stylistic devices of four master rhetoricians—Gibbon, Ranke, Macaulay, and Burckhardt—I attempted to locate history among the human sciences. My conclusion, less banal, I trust, in the extended argument than in bald summary, was that, for history, the old sharp division between art and science is untenable: in ways I attempted to demonstrate in the book, it is both.

Although there is at first glance nothing very startling about such a judgment, my particular formulation raised questions about the fundamental intentions of my craft that *Style in History* could not address, let alone resolve. The historian's art, I proposed, forms part of his science; his manner is neither decoration nor idiosyncrasy but is inextricably bound up with his matter. Style, in short, helps to bear the burden, and define the nature, of substance. This quite naturally propelled me from the way that the historian expresses himself to the issues he is bound to find most critical. "In the course of his work," I wrote two years later, "the historian does many things, but his most difficult and, I think most interesting, assignment is to explain the causes of historical events." I found that to think about cause is to enter an uninterrupted professional debate in which historians engage with great gusto, and in which the stakes are the highest possible. And it is to encounter the insistent claims of psychology on the historian's attention.

Like *Style in History,* its sequel about causation, *Art and Act,* was steeped in concrete experience: in the company of most historians, I have always been most comfortable among specific instances. While, in the earlier book, I constructed my case by examining the work of four great historians, in its successor, I focused on three influential artists—Manet, Gropius, and Mondrian—to urge a pluralistic but confident stance toward historical causation. In an introductory chapter I spelled out the theory informing these exercises in cultural biography, and diagrammed the relations among three clusters of causes, those springing from the private domain, from craft, and from culture. It is in their subtle interplay, their jostling for supremacy, that psychology asserts its special rights.

The intellectual kinship of these two books lies on the surface. Both are explorations in historical epistemology; both, while arguing for the overpowering variety of possible ways of expressing historical truths and of reaching them, are relatively optimistic about the historian's reach and grasp. It is curious: when historians settle down to reflect about their business—a self-conscious, not always felicitous venture into philosophical rumination they are often seduced to undertake after they have reached the age of fifty—they are apt to profess themselves pronounced subjectivists. They will likely insist that every historian's personal demons or social aspirations dictate a severely limiting perspective on the past, and that no amount of self-awareness will ever let him escape these inescapable pressures for partisanship. The historian's style, on that view, is a repository of biases

and his perception of causes is bound to be compromised by
the same crippling ideological burdens. In dissent, I argued
that style can also be a privileged passage to historical
knowledge and that the historian's particular vision of what
made the past world move, however distorted that vision
may be by his neuroses, professional deformations, or class
prejudices, may yet assist him in securing insights into his
material that he could not have gained without them. Gibbon's stately irony, for one, a kind of magnificent nastiness
that pervaded his character, was the perfect instrument for
dissecting the dominant political motives of Imperial Rome,
with its high professions and low motives; Burckhardt's repressed bachelor existence, for another, gave rise to luxuriant fantasies of cruelty and power supremely adapted to
appreciating the mentality of the outsize condottieri conducting the wars of the Italian Renaissance. I had no taste
for joining the camp of historians who judge attainment of
reliable knowledge about causes a chimera, or those who
reduce the glittering, multicolored costume of historical experience to the drab uniform of a single dominant set of
impulsions. The two books were at once a warning against
the facile pessimism of the skeptics and the equally facile
simplifications of the dogmatists.

My plea for history as an elegant, fairly rigorous aesthetic
science was, as I have already hinted, powerfully assisted
by my commitment to psychology, in particular to psychoanalysis.[1] I saw it then, and see it even more now, as a re-

---

1. I should emphatically make plain from the outset that by "psychoanalysis" I mean more than the body of work done by Sigmund
Freud and his immediate disciples alone. I include that of their successors who, though in some respects going their own way and attending to clinical experiences not available to Freud, securely belong
into his camp. I stress this here because the title of my book, and the

warding auxiliary discipline that the historical profession
has so far inadequately trusted, and certainly far from mastered. The much canvassed disasters of psychohistory, on
which its detractors have fastened with a kind of unholy
glee, are ground for caution rather than for despair—or for
disdain. A reliance on psychoanalysis, after all, need not entail a naive, reductionist, monocausal theory of history. My
intention, in those two volumes, and in this one, has not
been to propose that historians substitute Freud for Marx in
their monotheistic rites, or that they celebrate any rites
whatever. The study of religion, politics, culture, technology, geography, those great standbys of historical explanation, retains, for me, all its independent validity, for all invade, and help to shape, men's minds. I said in *Art and Act*
that "all history is in some measure psychohistory," but I
immediately added the disclaimer that "psychohistory cannot be all of history," and offered a sketch of reasons why

---

necessary centrality of Freud's ideas throughout the text, might prove
somewhat misleading. Certainly the ego psychologists, such as Heinz
Hartmann, Ernst Kris, and Rudolph Loewenstein, never thought that
they were doing anything other than to elaborate those ideas on mental structure that Freud had begun to explore in the early 1920s. Their
self-appraisal strikes me as essentially correct. The English object-
relations school, most notably W. R. D. Fairbairn and D. W. Winnicott, presents a somewhat less clear-cut case. Especially Fairbairn dis-
sented from some of Freud's formulations. But in concentrating on
the pre-oedipal relations of the infant with his intimate world, particularly with his mother, the object-relations analysts extended, and
further complicated, Freud's range of vision without materially alter-
ing it. I have no intention of reading a psychoanalytic historian like
Judith Hughes who heavily draws on the English school, or a Kleinian
biographer like Phyllis Grosskurth, out of the club. Apart from the
essentials about which no compromise is possible, psychoanalysis is
not a fixed body of doctrines but an evolving discipline of research
and theorizing.

psychology could not enjoy a monopoly in causal explanation—on principle. In this book I am developing these terse, apodictic pronouncements into a full-fledged argument.

Freud for Historians completes business left unfinished by its two predecessors. In the introductory chapter of *Art and Act* I offered a brief, rather unspecific critique of psychohistory as then practiced. Uncharacteristically, I offered no concrete instances, only noting that while psychohistory has spawned unwarranted reductions and extravagant speculations, offering vulnerable targets for reviewers to shoot down, it has also suffered from a certain timidity. While its practitioners, I said, "explain too much by too little," they, at the same time, "claim too little rather than too much." They have by and large confined themselves to psychobiography or to outbreaks of collective psychosis. Instead, I called for "a psychohistory of a kind that has not yet been explored, let alone practiced," a history that, "without compromising Freud's biological orientation, genetic explanations, or radical propositions about infantile sexuality and psychological strategies" would nevertheless be heavily invested in reality, sensitively registering the pressures of the outside world that so forcefully impinge on all individuals. I have written this book to address in detail issues I first raised in 1974 and adumbrated as a program two years later.

Unlike *Style in History* and *Art and Act,* in which questions of historical method continually encountered and drew on historical substance, the present volume is a sustained argument in which I have taken contemporary practices rather than past realities for my principal materials. But I have conceived and written it in close conjunction with a large-scale historical enterprise on which I am now engaged: a study of nineteenth-century bourgeois culture from a psychoanalytic perspective. Its first volume, dealing with sexuality, has already appeared; companion volumes on love, aggression, mastery, and cultural conflict are in preparation. I want them to be taken as applications of a method and an ambition that I am here simply commending and trying to justify theoretically.

My interest in psychoanalysis as a system of ideas and an auxiliary discipline goes back three decades, long before I published *Style in History,* before I even started my career as a historian. Around 1950, while I was still a graduate student and beginning instructor in political science, I projected a book to be called "Love, Work, and Politics." I never wrote that book—cannot, for that matter, remember just what I planned to say in it. All I can recall is that in those years I was a devotee of the revisionist psychoanalytic views of Erich Fromm, of his attempt, as I then saw it, to synthesize Marx and Freud. That was long ago. I have come to recognize that any effort to unite Marx and Freud could only lead to a shotgun marriage with calamitous consequences for both. Moreover, Fromm's critique of Freud, which grew more strident with the passing years, came to seem less and less cogent to me. Still, these controversies encouraged me to pursue a course of reading in Freud, unsystematically and informally. The attentive reader can find traces of those studies in my work from the late 1950s on, faint as they still were at the outset. But then in those days I was developing another dimension of history, one I christened the social history of ideas.

From the perspective of the years in which I pursued the social history of ideas most intensely, mainly in my books on Voltaire and on the Enlightenment, my current preoccupation with the uses of psychoanalysis for history may seem a long journey and a drastic displacement of interests. Actually, it has not been that at all. It would be plausible to object that I am only, in the manner of autobiographers, smoothing away the obstacles and straightening out the detours on the paths I have taken in order to present a spurious sense of consistency and continuity. Freud once said that the biographer is bound to fall in love with his subject; the autobiographer, I suspect, is only rarely exempt from this infatuation. But while I cannot pose as the final judge of my personal intellectual history, I think it registers no drastic break, only a slow and organic evolution. The two decades or so in which I was engaged in the social history of ideas, the mid-fifties to the mid-seventies, were attempts to break out from what I perceived as the intellectual historian's self-constructed prison in which one isolated thinker wrestles, looking neither to the right nor the left, with other thinkers, equally isolated. I wanted to discover, following Ranke, how things had really been, how mental products— ideas, ideals, religious and political and aesthetic postures— had originated and would define their shape under the impress of social realities. It was my sense of the debt that the mind owes to its worlds that enabled me to read Voltaire as a passionately political animal, and to place the principles of the Enlightenment into their natural environment: the scientific revolution, medical innovation, state making, and the impassioned political debates of the eighteenth century.

My interest in the still largely unappreciated rewards of psychoanalysis for the historian simply turns inward my old program to grasp ideas in all their contexts. A moral imperative, an aesthetic taste, a scientific discovery, a political stratagem, a military decision and all the countless other guises that ideas take are, as I have said, soaked in their particular, immediate, as well as in their general cultural surroundings. But they are also responses to inward pressures, being, at least in part, translations of instinctual needs, defensive maneuvers, anxious anticipations. Mental products in this comprehensive sense emerge as compromises. Hence the psychoanalytic history of ideas is the counterpart of the social history of ideas, the one complementing and completing the other. Actually, as will, I trust, become plain in the course of my argument, the two are really the same kind of history glimpsed from different vantage points, steps taken in tandem on the road to total history, the science of memory.

In 1976, the year I published *Art and Act,* I entered the Western New England Institute for Psychoanalysis as a research candidate, to undergo my didactic analysis and take the full complement of courses that would, I hoped, turn me from an informed amateur in the Freudian dispensation into something of a professional. It proved a fascinating experience, laborious, painful, and exhilarating in about equal proportions, and immensely illuminating. It would be impossible for me to draw up a list of lessons that I, as a historian, learned from my years as a candidate; psychoanalytic insights work far more deviously than that. But I am satisfied that it taught me much: new, more instructive ways of reading diaries and dreams, letters and paintings, novels and medical texts. It sharpened my sensitivity to the unconscious shared fantasies that underlie cultural styles, and to the potent, largely concealed currents of sexual and aggressive drives that give energy to action, invade and distort objective perception, and make rationalistic interest psychologies appear naive, downright helpless. More, I found that psychoanalytic techniques like free association or dream interpretation, and psychoanalytic discoveries like the family romance or the Oedipus complex, paid out unanticipated dividends in the study of seemingly familiar material, and in addition turned puzzling, opaque artifacts into usable material in the first place. I am not intimating that psychoanalytic training acted on me like a series of luminous conversion experiences. I was not, when I entered that training, on the road to Damascus. My analysis and my courses did not generate whatever historical imagination I possess, they stimulated it. The profits of Freud came unexpectedly, undramatically, building on what was already there. After a time they became, not exactly addictive, but comfortable, easy and natural.

It is only fair to add that in the years of my training, I acquired not merely a healthy respect for the diagnostic instruments my profession could borrow from psychoanalysis but also a fairly well-defined sense of its limitations. Some of these limitations, I am persuaded, stem from the almost unrelieved clinical preoccupation of its practitioners, from their principled, I am tempted to say, passionate inwardness. I do not want to overdramatize the resistance of psychoanalysts to qualified outsiders mining their ideas. On the contrary, I must gratefully record that my reception in my own institute, as a guest of the New York Psychoanalytic Institute or, for that matter, of the parent organization known for short as the "American," was unfailingly cordial and never condescending. Still, psychoanalysts are as likely to be impatient with "objective" realities in which the historian revels as historians are wary of the analyst's mysterious and elusive materials. And most psychoanalysts can scarcely repress their suspicions of what they think of, a little grudgingly, as "applied analysis." The psychoanalytic historian must be prepared to face skepticism from Freud's followers almost as much as from his denigrators.

The learning process the historian undergoes while mastering the psychoanalytic dispensation should therefore go more than one way. The social psychology that Freud left largely implicit in his papers has far-reaching explanatory power. But neither Freud nor any of his disciples have ever fully developed it, and it seems to me that the historian is peculiarly well prepared to make that social psychology work for the study of culture, of its origins, its course, and its irrepressible conflicts, a study to which Freud devoted much energy and many hours. I shall elaborate these points at some length. But an exploration of just what psychoanalysis could learn from the historian, fascinating though that would be, lies beyond the scope of this work. In these pages I want to generalize, and tease out the implications of Freud's observation about totemism: its explanation, he wrote, should be "historical and psychological in one, to give information under what conditions this peculiar institution developed, and to which mental human needs it gave expression." Historical and psychological in one: this states my program with admirable economy.

I had thought to leave the matter here. But the old controversies swirling around Freud, as old as psychoanalysis itself, have reached such a pitch of excitement and vituperation in the months that I was preparing this book for publication that I cannot ignore them.[2] The attempt to discredit

2. In some measure, the flurry of the mid-1980s is the "fault" of Janet Malcolm's brilliant pair of essays for *The New Yorker,* later made into books (*Psychoanalysis: The Impossible Profession* [1981], and *In the Freud Archives* [1984]). In the first, Malcolm combined a lucid and informal introduction to psychoanalytic theory and therapy with a telling, though far from unsympathetic, profile of politics in the New York Psychoanalytic Institute; in the second, she acquainted a wide public with two extravagant characters, both disappointed lovers of Freud: the first, Jeffrey Moussaieff Masson, for a brief and

psychoanalysis by questioning its uses as a therapy is not new. Nor is the effort to blacken Freud's reputation. But since the early 1970s and, even more, the early 1980s, both have been pursued with unprecedented vigor and some imaginative twists. The effectiveness of psychoanalysis as a therapy, as compared to doing nothing, resorting to other therapies or to placebos, remains a matter of strenuous debate. Plainly, the cures that psychoanalysis may claim are highly resistant to quantification. But the empirical and experimental evidence offers no good reason to accept the devastating verdicts of Freud's most uncompromising opponents, welcome though they might be to those anxious to erase Freudian ideas from our culture. In fact, they strike me as far more vulnerable than the Freudian claims they seek to discredit. But even if it could be shown that psychoanalytic treatment deserves no privileged status, it would by no means follow that the central tenets of psychoanalytic theory—psychological determinism, the dynamic unconscious, infantile sexuality, the workings of defense mechanisms—have thereby been compromised, let alone refuted. (I will be dealing with the issue at some length in Chapter 2.)

The same important point holds for Freud's character. In some ways, the current wave of denunciation may be an inescapable, if unpleasant, response to the idealization, even idolization, in which Freud's admirers have indulged in the past. (See Chapter 2.) According to Freud's most intemperate adversaries, he was a liar, a coward, a fraud, a plagia-

stormy period Projects Director of the Freud Archives, the second Peter Swales, an amateur researcher passionately doing detective work on Freud and his world, and their encounter with Kurt Eissler, the guardian of the Freud papers. Malcolm's treatment of psychoanalysis and its spectacular vicissitudes is as genial as it is informative, but it roused the barely dozing hounds of the anti-Freudian contingent.

rist, an authoritarian, a male chauvinist, a slipshod researcher, an adulterer, and (at least in his dirty mind) a
pedophile though probably not a pederast.[3] I do not recognize Sigmund Freud in that caricature, and in view of what
we reliably know about him, I doubt that it will ever be
substantiated. To be sure, the cleverest of polemicists have
tried to link his character to his theories, and seem to believe that if they can ruin the first they have ruined the
second. But even if Freud should turn out to have been a
consummate and consistent villain, his work stands on its
own. In any event, the program I am developing in this
book does not depend on the demonstration that psychoanalysis is the best possible cure for neurotic disorders, or
that Freud was an impeccable gentleman.

P. G.

---

3. See, Malcolm, *In the Freud Archives,* passim, reporting on Masson
and Swales; and especially Jeffrey Moussaieff Masson, *The Assault
on Truth: Freud's Suppression of the Seduction Theory* (1984); Frederick Crews, "The Freudian Way of Knowledge," *The New Criterion*
(June 1984), 7–25; Frank Cioffi, "The cradle of neurosis," *The Times
Literary Supplement,* No. 4,240 (July 6, 1984), 743–44. "There is an
understandable reluctance," Cioffi concludes his reviews, "to credit
the extent of Freud's opportunism, so it will be some time before we
stop hearing of 'Freud, the indefatigable seeker after truth.' (Although some of his more sophisticated admirers are already preparing
an alternative niche—Freud, justified perjurer in a noble cause.) Those
who believe neither in Freud's integrity nor in the nobility of his cause
can console themselves for the short-term futility of their attempts to
set the record straight with a reflection from the Master himself: The
voice of reason is soft but it is insistent" (p. 744).

Contents

FREUD FOR HISTORIANS

List of Abbreviations

Int. J. of Psycho-Anal.	*International Journal of Psycho-Analysis*
J. Amer. Psychoanal. Assn.	*Journal of the American Psychoanalytic Association*
PSC	*Psychoanalytic Study of the Child*
S.E.	*Standard Edition*
St. A.	*Studienausgabe*

The Argument: Defenses Against Psychoanalysis

Historians like to reject psychoanalysis as an auxiliary discipline with one sweeping, summary denial: you cannot psychoanalyze the dead. To make the attempt would be to introduce inappropriate techniques into historical inquiry, allow baseless speculation to subvert the explanatory process that has served historians so well for so long, and reduce the beautiful, variegated bouquet of thought and action to drab, depressing psychopathology. Historical individuals, groups, classes, nations, are not patients on the couch, not even an imaginary couch. Other charges round out this dismissal: students of the past informed by psychoanalysis violate good sense, strain credulity, disregard the weight (or disrespect the paucity) of evidence, trample on the demands of style. Some historians, offended by claims for Freud, have even stepped outside their accustomed sphere to wonder out loud whether, beyond being unable to psychoanalyze the dead, one can really psychoanalyze the living. But irrelevance, irresponsibility, and vulgarity remain the principal counts in the indictment against the psychoanalytic historian.

I intend to take these aggressive defenses against psychoanalysis seriously, organizing them in a logical and, I hope, lucid sequence. I am visualizing the historian's defensive maneuvers as six concentric rings of intellectual fortifications mobilized against the Freudian assault. If he is obliged to surrender the outermost wall to the enemy, he can fall back on the second set of bulwarks to offer further resistance; if the second falls, the third remains, and so forth, right down to the fortress in which the historian nervously awaits the invader.[1] Why, to begin with, should the historian trouble himself with any formal psychology whatever if, for centuries, good sense, honest scholarship, and mature experience have been enough and if, more recently, certain psychoanalytic notions have become so commonplace that one may safely pillage them like a text in the public domain? Then, if the need for psychology, and for some precision in its employment, have been conceded, why should the historian resort to technically difficult Freudian notions rather than drawing on competing psychological systems that appear much more plausible and much more palatable? Next, suppose the credentials of psychoanalytic thought have been credibly established. Is psychoanalysis not in its very essence unhistorical, with its postulate of a stable human nature that runs counter to the historian's commitment to development and fundamental change in human nature and which, unhappily, seems to slight the one apparently

---

1. I have adopted in this book the old standard generic usage, employing the pronouns "he" or "his" and the nouns "man" or "men" to denote all of humanity.

stable element in human experience, self-interest? And even if Freud should have been vindicated, both for his treatment of self-interest and his perceptiveness in human affairs, is his vision of humanity not at best a transcription of a purely local type—the turn-of-the-century Viennese?

Fourth, assuming that psychoanalysis is not quite so unhistorical, and history not quite so hostile to the idea of human nature, as we have long supposed, does it not remain true that psychoanalysis, overpowered by its clinical preoccupations, can at best illuminate a narrow segment of historical experience, that of irrational conduct or neurotic distortion? Fifth, suppose psychoanalysis proves to be a general psychology, little less informative about reason than it is about unreason, is the historian not justified in restricting its employment, since Freud's is the most incurably individualistic of psychologies? It is only after the historian recognizes that psychoanalysis has the potential of explicating group behavior, and the continuous interaction between world and mind, that he may feel ready to incorporate it in his tool kit of investigative methods and integrate it into his view of the past. Even then, one more defense remains, that of impracticality: however credible, however instructive psychoanalysis may be, is it really useful to the practicing historian? *Can* you psychoanalyze the dead? These are final and formidable questions I dare not evade and intend to address in my last chapter.

1
✦
Secret Needs of the Heart

1 | PSYCHOLOGISTS WITHOUT PSYCHOLOGY

The professional historian has always been a psychologist—an amateur psychologist. Whether he knows it or not, he operates with a theory of human nature; he attributes motives, studies passions, analyzes irrationality, and constructs his work on the tacit conviction that human beings display certain stable and discernible traits, certain predictable, or at least discoverable, modes of coping with their experience. He discovers causes, and his discovery normally includes acts of the mind. Even materialist system-makers like Karl Marx, who subject individuals to the ineluctable pressures of historical conditions, have given room to the play of mind, and professed to understand it. Among all his auxiliary sciences, psychology is the historian's unacknowledged principal aide.

But it remains, by and large, unacknowledged; as devotees of common sense, historians have been reluctant to canvass the place of psychology in their discipline. Indeed, their uneasiness has visibly mounted in the last few decades, ever since psychoanalysis has insinuated itself into the profession and become the psychology of choice for a brash, isolated, but irrepressible minority. For the overwhelming majority of historians, the emergence of Freud as a possible guide to the mysteries of past minds has become an occasion for reasoned skepticism, ill-concealed anxiety, or cold rage. It would be a characteristic old Freudian tactic, tempting but illicit, to interpret historians' emotion-laden acts of rejection as resistances, and to welcome them, wrily, as unintended demonstrations of Freud's ideas. Certainly his ideas need stronger arguments than this to commend themselves to the serious scholar: the days are gone when the followers of Freud can discredit rational criticism by psychoanalyzing the critic.

In the early 1940s, Marc Bloch underscored the historian's obligation to explore what he called men's "secret needs of the heart." But he intended the exploration he envisioned to remain on the surface of awareness: "In the last analysis," he wrote in his unfinished, posthumous *Historian's Craft,* "it is human consciousness which is the subject matter of history. The interrelations, confusions, and infections of human consciousness are, for history, reality itself."[1] Although few historians would care to deny that man is the true subject of their discipline, they grow nervous before those "secret needs of the heart"—more secret even than

---

1. Bloch, *The Historian's Craft* (1949; tr. Peter Putnam, 1954, ed., 1964), 151. Curiously, a rather different historian, Richard Cobb, has employed a strikingly similar metaphor. There "must be a wide element of guess work in social history. It is like attempting to sound the unsoundable and to penetrate the secrets of the human heart." *Paris and Its Provinces, 1792–1802* (1975), 117.

Bloch imagined. Nor has the guide to these needs that Freud offered been calculated to reassure them. Many historians who celebrate Marc Bloch as a master have found his proposal too rash. I want to show that it is, though beautifully stated, too circumspect.

The nervous historian I have invoked and will continue to invoke is a construction, but not a straw man. He is a condensation of many anxious and therefore hostile practitioners who embodies the consensus in the historical craft. Most professional historians have not committed to print their views on psychology in general or on Freud in particular, yet I am safe in surmising that even those, in the United States and elsewhere, who might acknowledge that they could profit from a sophisticated psychology, would reject the Freudian dispensation as ill-equipped to supply it. "Historians in general," Stephen Gottschalk, a student of Christian Science, had noted in reviewing, negatively, a psychobiography of Mary Baker Eddy, "tend to be extremely wary of the application of psychoanalytic concepts to history and biography."[2] His voice is the voice of my profession. Now and then some prominent historian has displayed a measure of sympathetic interest in psychoanalysis, but his commendations, normally vague and condescending, are likely to be more damaging to the claims of Freud than the straightforward disparagement that is typical for his colleagues. The late E. H. Carr, in his widely read, resolutely trivial *What Is History?*, assigned to Freud a twofold relevance to historians: he focused attention on their biases, and he discredited the "ancient illusion" that men's ostensible motives

---

2. "Mrs. Eddy Through a Distorted Lense," a review of Julius Silberger, Jr., *Mary Baker Eddy,* in the *Christian Science Monitor* (July 2, 1980), 17.

are "adequate to explain their action." This scarcely seems a heroic contribution to a science of man on which historians could draw; appropriately enough from his perspective, Carr appraises Freud's work as a "negative achievement of some importance."[3]

This sort of grudging concession has evidently struck most historians as too generous. Reflecting on how students of the past cope with the influence of nonrational impulses on historical actors, G. R. Elton warned in 1967 that "some historians, and above all biographers," have come to believe "that a knowledge of psychology (especially of morbid psychology) is indispensable, with the result that one too often encounters some pretty awful bits of Freudian or post-Freudian commonplaces in the analysis." That seems fair enough; I shall, after all, be citing some pretty awful bits of that sort in the following pages. Elton, though, is no Freudian anxious to protect a precious and delicate legacy. "We are still enjoined occasionally," he comments, "to call in Freud when studying people in history, at the very time when psychologists are poised for a mass-flight from Freud"—thus mistaking the shifting moods of the general public for the serious convictions of academic psychologists who, if anything, have been growing rather more hospitable to psychoanalysis.

Indeed, it seems that when man's mind, especially his unconscious mind, is at issue, some historians seek refuge in a deliberately cultivated philistinism, and parade their ignorance as a badge of professional wisdom. "Thirty years ago," Kenneth S. Lynn recalled in 1978, approvingly, "Arthur M. Schlesinger, Sr. informed me—with considerable testiness—that he had never read Freud and did not intend

---

3. Carr, *What is History?* (1961), 185.

to." He was far from unique. "Although years ago," J. H. Hexter has told his readers, "I read most of the pieces by Freud in the old Modern Library Giant, I skipped a few, and I have not gone back to them." Those unidentified pieces in the old Modern Library Giant, in the faulty renderings by A. A. Brill, have long since been superseded by better translations, but plainly Hexter has refused to go back to them because he found Freud himself rather than Brill's versions wanting. Yet if history, as Elton has put it, justly enough, "is concerned with all those human sayings, thoughts, deeds and sufferings which occurred in the past and have left present deposit,"[4] the historian is entitled, in fact obliged, to inquire how those sayings, thoughts, deeds, and sufferings can be most effectively investigated and most sensitively understood. Established craftsmen like Schlesinger and Hexter apparently take pride in not knowing Freud, having persuaded themselves that he has nothing to teach them.

Perhaps we should be grateful for this willful innocence; other historians, after a rapid tour through the country of Freud, usually without a compass and ignorant of the language, have been far more destructive. A few have mounted what they, at least, consider to be definitive refutations of any reasons why historians might go to school to psychoanalysis. In his self-confident papers on historical science and psychohistory, the German social historian Hans-Ulrich Wehler, who is usually receptive to innovations in method,

---

4. Elton, *The Practice of History* (1967), 81, 25; Lynn, "History's Reckless Psychologizing," *The Chronicle of Higher Education* (January 16, 1978), 48; Hexter, *The History Primer* (1971), 5; Elton, *Practice of History,* 24.

has dismissed psychoanalytic history as a "blind alley rather than a promising path."[5] David Hackett Fischer's foray into historians' fallacies presents a list of "five substantial failings" in Freudian theory, and judges that "the failures of Freudian historiography" probably "derive in some degree from limitations in psychoanalytic method." And at least two historians have tried to shame psychoanalysis so thoroughly that it would never show its face among historians again. Jacques Barzun, in an amusing and vigorous essay, *Clio and the Doctors,* attempts to rescue Clio, his muse, from quacks of all descriptions; and among the gangs of faddists and technocrats the "doctor of psychology" prescribing for the "patient, History," makes a menacing figure when he is not being ludicrous. For his part David E. Stannard in *Shrinking History* moves, with a kind of stately rage, from the failures of psychoanalysis in history-writing to its failures in therapy, in logic, in theory-construction, and in cultural perception to conclude that there is nothing to be said for psychohistory because there is nothing to be said for psychoanalysis. Stannard invites the historian to look elsewhere: "The time has come to move on."[6]

---

5. Wehler, "Geschichtswissenschaft und 'Psychohistorie,' " *Innsbrucker Historische Studien,* I (1978), 213; see also his "Zum Verhältnis von Geschichtswissenschaft und Psychoanalyse," *Historische Zeitschrift,* CCVII (1969), 529–54, somewhat revised in Wehler, *Geschichte als Historische Sozialwissenschaft* (1973), 85–123. Though famous for virtually drowning his readers in footnotes, Wehler on Freud is quite defenseless.
6. Fischer, *Historians' Fallacies: Toward a Logic of Historical Thought* (1970), 189; Barzun, *Clio and the Doctors: Psycho-History, Quanto-History & History* (1974), 2; Stannard, *Shrinking History: On Freud and the Failure of Psychohistory* (1980), 156. For more details on Stannard, see the bibliography, pp. 213–14.

Although the texts I have been citing date from the late 1960s and after, my own experience, in no way untypical, suggests that the injection of psychoanalysis into history aroused massive opposition practically from its very beginnings a decade and more earlier. The opening words of this chapter, in which I called the historian an amateur psychologist, closely paraphrase the first sentences of a paper I delivered before the Society of French Historical Studies in 1960. "As historical personages parade" before the historian, I said, "he can see their acts but he must infer their motives." I then proceeded to survey how historians of the French Revolution have treated the speeches of Robespierre, Danton, and their fellow orators in that oratorical time, and briefly analyzed the speeches themselves. My paper was a modest attempt to ground the expressive activities of Jacobins and their rivals in their reality, in their tradition of rhetoric and the pressure of events far more than in their convictions, their idiosyncrasies, or their unconscious needs. Most of my remarks hugged the coastline of manifest experience: the speakers' verbal conduct, their religious metaphors and classical allusions, their quotations from Plutarch and Rousseau, their sincerity, and their bombast. Only toward the end did I venture out, "playfully," into the high seas of psychology. I speculated that the notorious anxiety and suspiciousness Robespierre displayed in the Spring of 1794 might have been an acting out of the deadly sequence in which frustration is translated into rage and assuaged by revenge. And I suggested, labeling my suggestion "still more frankly speculative," that we might see the succession of events leading from the King's flight to Varennes to his execution as bearing the lineaments, and producing the guilt feelings, of parricide. To forestall misunderstanding, I underlined that "the answers to such psychological questions cannot be found in psychology alone," but must also be sought "in politics, in day-to-day events."[7]

My disclaimers went unheard; my precautions were an exercise in futility. A quarter of a century later, the paper seems to me downright conventional in its method and in its presuppositions. There was very little psychoanalysis in it. And I intended my concluding sentence to soothe rather than to alarm: as Sigmund Freud once said, I told my listeners, "there are times when a man craves a cigar simply because he wants a good smoke."[8] Yet my presentation caused what I can only call a genteel riot. One distinguished historian rose to denounce historians as flighty beings, susceptible to fads among which, he thought, psychoanalysis was only the latest. "I have seen them come and go," he said. "It used to be anthropology. Then it was sociology. Now it is psychoanalysis. But this too will pass." Another indignantly wanted to know whether historians would in future have to study psychology as their second field—apparently an ominous prospect. The debate I unwittingly provoked was not over the substance of my presentation but over the threat that an alien and esoteric discipline posed to historical studies. I felt like a witch doctor who, by some ghastly social gaffe, had been invited to address the meeting of a medical society.

Psychoanalysis had just burst upon the profession with a spectacular conjunction of events two years before, in 1958. It was the coincidence of William Langer's widely quoted presidential address to the American Historical Association and Erik Erikson's *Young Man Luther* that gave Freud in-

---

7. "Rhetoric and Politics in the French Revolution," *American Historical Review,* LXVI, 3 (April 1961), 664, 674–75.
8. "Rhetoric and Politics," 676.

stant high visibility among historians.[9] Langer's address, which called on his colleagues to employ psychoanalytic ideas in historical inquiry, was all the more unsettling since its author had made his reputation with volumes on diplomatic history, impeccable in their documentation and conservative in their technique. And Erikson's book, which presented itself as "A Study in Psychoanalysis and History," generated some impassioned debates. Together they resulted in some well-endowed conferences and a fervent clan of imitators. By now, as everyone knows, psychohistory has secured all the stigmata of permanence in the historical profession: appearances on the annual program of the American Historical Association and in the pages of its official review, no fewer than two quarterlies, and, of course, its problematic name. In 1973, Fred Weinstein and Gerald M. Platt, two optimists among scholars who have welcomed the Freudian dispensation, thought it evident that "both historians and sociologists intend to make systematic use of psychoanalytic theory in their work."[10] Indeed, to judge from the ferocity of Barzun and Stannard, many articulate historians fear that the "systematic use of psychoanalytic theory" is only too much at home in historians' work.

In actuality, I think, not much has happened. Inevitably, those most hostile to psychoanalysis have been those most alarmed at psychohistory. To them, it is nothing less than a disfiguring, perhaps incurable epidemic that has invaded their craft. The "reckless psychologizing" of the "woolly-

---

9. William L. Langer, "The Next Assignment," *American Historical Review*, LXIII, 2 (January 1958), 283–304; Erik Erikson, *Young Man Luther: A Study in Psychoanalysis and History* (1958).

10. Fred Weinstein and Gerald M. Platt, *Psychoanalytic Sociology: An Essay on the Interpretation of Historical Data and the Phenomena of Collective Behavior* (1973), 1.

minded men and women who call themselves psychohistorians," Kenneth S. Lynn wrote in 1978, has grown into "a cancer that is metastasizing through the whole body of the historical profession."[11] But three years later, Marcus Cunliffe appraised the situation rather more genially and far more perceptively. Reviewing two psychoanalytic biographies, he listed the predictable names from Erik Erikson to Christopher Lasch to exemplify psychohistorical activity, only to add that he saw a pronounced retreat from "Sigmundian arrogance." Psychohistorians were beginning to concede that the Oedipus complex is largely dated, the reputation of Erikson was on the wane, prominent one-time believers were publicly turning apostate, and, most telling of all, "respected historians" like Jacques Barzun and Geoffrey Barraclough had voiced "sharp criticism," while Lawrence Stone had called psychohistory "a disaster area." From this perspective, Cunliffe concluded, sounding a little—only a little—like David Stannard, "psychohistory begins to appear as an idea whose time has come—and gone."[12]

---

11. "History's Reckless Psychologizing," *Chronicle of Higher Education* (January 16, 1978), 48. We may gauge the depth of Lynn's affective engagement by his unpleasant metaphor, and by the intemperate attack he launches in the same one-page diatribe against the American historian Richard Hofstadter who had, according to Lynn, descended by the mid-1960s to "unconscionable" manipulations of "psychological jargon," though he ventured to hope that Hofstadter would eventually get over all this nonsense—this to one of the most perceptive and sensitive stylists in the historical craft. What particularly aroused Lynn's displeasure was Hofstadter's application of the term "paranoid style" to describe the convictions and rhetoric of some angry men in American politics, a vivid and telling coinage that Hofstadter from the outset surrounded with elaborate cautions. This, according to Lynn, did nothing more than to "besmirch the reputations of certain groups of Americans whom he either distrusted or feared." 12. "From the Facts to the Feelings," a review of Joseph F. Byrnes,

This, to my mind, defines the dominant and enduring mood of the historical profession with fair adequacy. The competent, at times impressive, publications by historians openly acknowledging their debt to psychoanalysis have made few dents in the armor of their colleagues. In fact, all these wistful endorsements and frantic repudiations cannot conceal the essential imperviousness of the craft to Freudian psychology, an imperviousness even more striking outside the United States among historians in Britain or France, Germany or Italy. In 1967, G. Kitson Clark had already warned his fellow historians eager to borrow ideas or methods from other disciplines, that while in earlier time, zoology and anthropology had supplied some "rather dreadful examples" of "ugly nonsense," now "psychology has probably taken their place as the science most open to abuse."[13] That he had psychohistorians in mind is beyond question.

The response to John Demos's book of 1982 on witchcraft in seventeenth-century Massachusetts may serve as an instructive instance of all this triumphant defensiveness. An ambitious and well-thought-out study that attempts to surround its fascinating subject by calling on the resources of traditional biography, sociology, social history, and psychoanalysis, *Entertaining Satan: Witchcraft and the Culture of Early New England* had a highly appreciative reception—except for the psychoanalytic section, an integral, indispensable element in Demos's argument, which the reviewers found either bewildering or unfortunate.[14] In short, psycho-

The Virgin of Chartres: An Intellectual and Psychological History of the Work of Henry Adams, and Charles K. Hofling, *Custer and the Little Big Horn: A Psychobiographical Inquiry,* in *The Times Literary Supplement* (October 23, 1981), 1241.

13. G. Kitson Clark, *The Critical Historian* (1967), 21.

14. Thus Alan Macfarlane, reviewing *Entertaining Satan* in the *Times*

history is highly visible, but mainly as a target. Some of its notoriety, no doubt, is the unwelcome results of the defects that compromise much of its work—its pressure toward reductionism, its often barbarous language, its cavalier way with the evidence. Critics of what passes for the Freudian way of writing history can find ample supporting materials in the way it has been written. But whatever its performance or its possibilities, psychoanalysis has remained a stranger in the company of historians ringed, like an exotic and probably contagious newcomer, by distrust. The psychoanalytic penetration of the historian's defensive fortifications remains marginal; the unflagging ardor of the counterattacks is therefore a symptom rather than a necessary response. The Freudian invasion has been contained.

That the psychoanalytic vocabulary has become common coin in our time, even among historians who would be shocked to find themselves in any way indebted to Freud, in no way compromises my conclusion. For the currency is debased. The less technical among psychoanalytic terms—*conflict* or *projection* or *repression,* even *ambivalence*—have almost acquired the status of platitudes. With that, the radical insights and sharp, precise meanings they embody have been smoothed down or conveniently forgotten. No one can dispute Keith Thomas's observation that psychoanalytic concepts "have become part of ordinary educated discourse,"

<hr>

Literary Supplement (May 13, 1983), 493, calls it "an interesting, thought-provoking and readable book," but wonders whether Demos's "talk of affects and defences, of anality and orality, or narcissism and projection really helps. It takes us away from the individuals and their contexts into obscure and ultimately unsatisfactory abstract speculations." My point, of course, is precisely the opposite: projection and defenses, and the rest of the Freudian armamentarium, seriously and delicately handled, take us away from obscure or abstract speculation into the heart of psychological dynamics.

and that Freud's ideas, "often vulgarised beyond recognition no doubt, have entered the collective consciousness and become part of what most of us regard as 'commonsense.'" Even a historian as impatient with theories of all sorts as Richard Cobb can speak of Robespierre's "death wish" without feeling the need to explain the term; even G. R. Elton refers blandly to historians' "unconscious" doubts, attitudes, and presuppositions.[15] Certainly Freud was not the first to discover, nor did he have a monopoly on, such psychological categories as the death wish or the dynamic unconscious, but the easy, unapologetic way that historians like Cobb and Elton employ this terminology suggests how secure is their place in the Freudian universe that we all, more or less reluctantly, inhabit today.

This conquest of educated discourse has been a highly problematic gain for psychoanalysis. Freud's position toward the end of the twentieth century is somewhat reminiscent of, though certainly not identical with, Newton's in the middle of the eighteenth. Then, d'Alembert, probably France's most eminent Newtonian, complained about the obtuseness of his predecessors and the ingratitude of his contemporaries toward the greatest scientist who ever lived. When Newton, he said, had first proffered the natural laws of gravitation in his *Principia,* French savants had derided

---

15. Thomas, personal communication, March 31, 1984; Cobb, *Reactions to the French Revolution* (1972), 6; Elton, *Practice of History,* 81, 88, 58. The American historian of the Renaissance, William J. Bouwsma, denying that his sensitive and sweeping paper on "Anxiety and the Formation of Early Modern Culture" (in Barbara C. Malament, ed., *After the Reformation: Essays in Honor of J. H. Hexter* [1980], 215–46), had been directly influenced by psychoanalysis, adds that "Freud is now so generally a part of our common culture . . . that his presence in the background of my thought was important." Personal communication, April 30, 1984.

him for retreating to long-outgrown, medieval, occult qualities; half a century later, when they had integrated Newton's laws into their scientific work, most thought them so
obvious and so long-established that they were now inclined
to dispute Newton's originality. Newton, of course, was
more fortunate than Freud: there was no way of watering
down Newton's stunning discoveries. To accept them meant
to embrace them in their full significance. The reception—
or, rather, the diffusion—of psychoanalysis has been far less
uncompromising. Freud once prophesied that the Americans
would take over psychoanalysis and ruin it. Neither of these
dour predictions has wholly come true. But his point remains as a warning. If Freud has compelled us all, historians and others, to live in his world, to see the mind and
its workings from a new vantage point, to discover things
about ourselves that we would just as soon ignore, the price
he has paid has been in turn, silence, hostility, and mis-
appropriation. It is arguable that the last has been the most
damaging.

2 | ABUSING FREUD

The failure of psychoanalysis to capture the imagination
of historians is evident enough not only from the vast bulk
of historical writing done without the benefit, or against the
grain, of Freud; it is dramatized, a little paradoxically, in
the work of historians, some of them prominent and distinguished practitioners, who appear to know something of the
Freudian dispensation, profess to find some of it relevant,
but have willfully shaped it to their own ends. Consider
Randolph Trumbach's highly regarded, interesting study of
kinship and domestic relations among the eighteenth-
century English aristocracy. Trumbach, intent on decoding
the most intimate materials, felt obliged to canvass the

kind of psychology on which to rely, and decided that "whenever I have felt the need of a psychological theory, I have consciously ignored Freudian and psychoanalytic models." Freud, Trumbach concedes, had produced "some useful information on the history of infancy, but," he adds, "I think it is on the whole a misguided attempt to hitch our wagon to a falling star." Freudian theory strikes Trumbach as "especially inappropriate" in studying child rearing "since it is so profoundly condescending in its attitude toward children." For Freud, he concludes, childhood "is by its nature a disease." Instead, Trumbach prefers John Bowlby's "theory of attachment," which draws on object relations theory and has no use for Freud's notion that intimacy with other human beings arises "as a secondary consequence of the satisfaction of oral, anal, and sexual drives." Even better, Bowlby "never presumes that a disordered adult state is a reflection of a previous one." Finally, Bowlby's ideas enjoy, for the historian, "certain technical advantages." After all, Freud "was interested in instinctive drives that are internal and unobservable," while Bowlby, in contrast, "observes external behavior, which is what the historian will find described in his sources." No question: "For Freud physiology was primary, for Bowlby it is social behavior," and, after all, "the historian is a sociologist and not a biologist."[16]

All this, to put it bluntly, is sheer absurdity. Leaving aside Trumbach's rhetorical flourish about Freud viewing childhood as a disease, which defies sober argument, Freud, far from condescending to the young, discovered and cele-

---

16. Trumbach, *The Rise of the Egalitarian Family: Aristocratic Kinship and Domestic Relations in Eighteenth-Century England* (1978), 9–10.

brated the rich, stirring, often painful diversity of their inner life. More than any other psychologist in history, he provided scientific demonstrations for Wordsworth's over-worked poetic dictum that the Child is father of the Man. This is not all. To treat Freud as a mere physiologist is to overlook his lifelong struggle to find psychological explanations for psychological phenomena; and to argue that Freud was interested in unobservable drives without adding that he spent years discovering ways to make them observable is to make a true statement serve the ends of distortion.

Trumbach's record on Bowlby is no better than that on Freud. He forcibly drags Bowlby out of his natural context within the spectrum of psychoanalytic thought and views him as practically a behaviorist. No one could be more precise than John Bowlby in specifying his agreements and disagreements with orthodox Freudianism: principally, he rejects Freud's psychic energy model and his theory of instincts, but insists over and over in his multivolume study of maternal deprivation that "Throughout this inquiry my frame of reference has been that of psychoanalysis."[17] In fact, his Freudian frame of reference is apparent in every chapter of his work. Besides, Bowlby explicitly presumes that a disordered adult state is a reflection of earlier states.[18] It is bad

---

17. Bowlby, *Attachment* (1969; 2nd ed., 1982), xv.
18. Bowlby says so at length throughout the four-volume series, *Attachment and Loss* (of which *Attachment* is the first), and once again, after twenty years of intensive labor on his life's work: "The key point of my thesis is that there is a strong causal relationship between an individual's experiences with his parents and his later capacity to make affectional bonds." "The Making and Breaking of Affectional Bonds" (1976–77), in *The Making and Breaking of Affectional Bonds* (1979), 135. See also, for this "key point," in the same volume, "Effects on Behaviour of Disruption of an Affectional Bond" (1967–68), and "Separation and Loss Within the Family" (1968–70).

enough to beat Freud with a stick fashioned from misunder-
stood bits of his own writings; it is perhaps worse to fashion
a stick from the writings of those who, whatever their own
"unorthodox" ideas, indefatigably, sincerely, and accurately
proclaim their indebtedness to Sigmund Freud.

These mistakes matter. They may defend the historian
against the disagreeable doctrines of psychoanalysis, but not
against the criticism that inaccuracy invites. Freud and his
ideas have become the property of modern intellectual history; the historian who handles them loosely raises uncomfortable questions about his capacity to get other things
right. When we read, in Donald Lowe's history of bourgeois
perception, that "Freud insisted there was no unconscious
except the id within the person," that flat, self-assured
error—much of the ego and most of the superego, too, are,
according to Freud, unconscious—makes the reader wonder
whether Lowe was really the man to tackle such a demanding topic.[19]

At times, this victimization of Freud is out in the open,
almost deliberate. Among the most telling instances in the
modern literature, Lawrence Stone's monumental study of
English family life from the sixteenth to the nineteenth century may be the most profitable to pursue. The book is particularly pertinent because Stone is a respected and prolific
social historian working in a field in which psychoanalysis

---

19. Donald M. Lowe, *History of Bourgeois Perception* (1982), 25.
Like other historians, Lowe also uses the terms "unconscious" and "subconscious" interchangeably (p. 14). When a historian offers a comment on Freud's ideas of the "subconscious," he generally reveals,
with this apparently casual slip, that he has failed to grasp, or perhaps even glance at, Freud's psychoanalytic writings, in which the
very term appears only early and with extreme rarity. And when
Freud did use it, he did not treat it as synonymous with "unconscious."

could presumably claim a place, if it could claim one any-
where in the historical literature. To make it even more
illuminating, this is a work not on historical method, but of
social and cultural history, squarely in the world of practice
in which historians are most at ease.

Dealing as he does with sexual conduct, paternal authority, and child rearing, Stone finds Freud impossible to evade.
And he borrows psychoanalytic propositions for some of his
arguments. Considering late marriages and low illegitimacy
rates in sixteenth-century England, Stone notes tentatively
that "if one follows Freudian theories," one could argue
that these phenomena "could lead to neuroses that so regularly shattered the calm of Oxford and Cambridge colleges
at this period; it could help to explain the high level of
group aggression, which lay behind the extraordinary ex-
pansionist violence of western nation states at this time."
Here Stone enlists Freud to serve social psychology; in his
pages on James Boswell, he uses Freud to write psychobiography. Gathering the Boswell papers into a pathetic
and malodorous anthology of Boswell's sexual peccadilloes
and counting the number of times Boswell was put out of
action by gonorrhea, Stone makes brave efforts to arrive at a
diagnostic profile. Poor Boswell turns out to have been a
narcissist and a melancholic, burdened by "inherited manic
depression" and by acquired guilt feelings, caught for thir-
teen years, between the ages of sixteen and twenty-nine,
in the toils "of a complex identity crisis," gambling and
drinking.[20]

We might expect that a historian so lavish—if imprecise—
with technical vocabulary might be grateful to Freud. But

---

20. Stone, *The Family, Sex and Marriage in England, 1500–1800*
(1977), 52–53, 572–99.

not at all. Stone treats psychoanalysis with disdain. He cites, in his introduction, four theories borrowed from the social sciences, partly wrong or misapplied, that have "hamstrung" the "serious historical study of the family." Two of these, Parsonian functionalism and extrapolations from biology, are not relevant here. But the other two are distinctly—at least in Stone's mind—psychoanalytic theories. One of these is the "Freudian assumption that the oral, anal and sexual experiences of infancy and very early childhood are decisive in moulding character, which once set can only with the greatest difficulty be modified later on." And this assumption, Stone argues, "blocked the study of personality growth and evolution throughout life in response to the ongoing influences of culture, family and society."[21]

The second Freudian assumption to obstruct serious family history, Stone continues, would appear to be that "sex—the id—is the most powerful of all drives and has not changed over the ages. . . . The eternally repeated Freudian drama of the conflict of the id, the ego and the super-ego stands outside history and is unaffected by it." Stone finds such unhistorical notions easy to explode: "But in fact the sexual drive is itself not uniform," heavily dependent as it is on "an adequate protein diet and the amount of physical exhaustion and psychic stress. It also varies enormously from individual to individual." Moreover, "we know that the super-ego has at times repressed and at times released this drive, according to the dictates of cultural conventions, especially religious conventions."[22]

This is a troubling misreading. It is, of course, a truism that Freud traced adult character and adult neuroses to ear-

21. Ibid., 15.
22. Ibid., 15–16.

lier stages of mental development and to the emotional constellations of childhood. Infantile sexuality is, after all, for all the unsystematic anticipations by other researchers, a decisive discovery of psychoanalytic psychology. But Freud did not intend his emphasis on early experience to devalue biological endowment on the one hand and adult experience on the other. He said so, articulately and often. Endowment and chance, he insisted—and by "chance" he meant the world of the adult little less than the world of the child—"determine man's fate."[23] Freud was steadily engaged in a balancing act: to his mind, prevailing psychological and anthropological theories vastly overrated the shaping power of man's inborn, constitutional inheritance, and against those fashionable views he explored the environmental influences working on the child. For the same reason, he invoked those very early influences to make up for what he rightly regarded as the general infatuation with adolescent or adult traumas. He never surrendered his biological orientation: his stress on the principal drives—sexuality and aggression—sufficiently attests to that. But, in face of doctrinaire theories of unalterable "racial" characteristics or preprogrammed disorders of adolescence, he appealed from nature to nurture.

This, I must repeat, did not mean that he perceived infantile sexual development as a straitjacket from which the grown-up could escape only, if at all, by means of a long, doubtless painful psychoanalysis. As early as 1905, in his epoch-making *Three Essays on Sexuality,* he described

---

23. Freud, "Zur Dynamik der Übertragung" (1912) [*Studienausgabe*] *St.A.,* 11 vols., ed. Alexander Mitscherlich et al. (1969–1975), *Ergänzungsband,* 159n; "The Dynamics of Transference" [*Standard Edition of the Complete Psychological Works of Sigmund Freud*], *S.E.,* tr. and ed. James Strachey et al., 24 vols. (1953–1975), XII, 99n.

the radical novelties that puberty brings to sexual life, noting that while forepleasure in sexual intercourse is an elaboration of infantile sexual urges, "end-pleasure is something new," probably "tied to circumstances that do not arise till puberty." He never doubted, in fact he firmly insisted, that mental activities like rational calculation or the pangs of conscience—the work of the ego and the superego—stand under unremitting pressure from what he flatly calls "the demands of reality." Even the repression of the Oedipus complex, that most private of struggles, works, as he put it, under the "influence of authority, religious teaching, education, reading."[24] The child is, as he grows, open to adaptation. Freud's views, then, far from inhibiting, immensely stimulated "the study of personality growth." They give the adult both the psychological history and the psychological leeway he needs.[25] What is missing from Stone's account is that psychoanalysis is a dynamic developmental psychology.

Stone's reading of Freud's theories of the sexual drives is

---

24. Freud, *Drei Abhandlungen zur Sexualtheorie* (1905), *St.A.*, V, 115, *Three Essays on the Theory of Sexuality*, *S.E.*, VII, 210–11; "Aus der Geschichte einer infantilen Neurose" (1918), *St.A.*, VIII, 188, "From the History of an Infantile Neurosis," *S.E.*, XVII, 72; *Das Ich und das Es* (1923), *St.A.*, III, 302, *The Ego and the Id*, *S.E.*, XIX, 34.

25. See my essay, "Freud and Freedom," in Alan Ryan, ed., *The Idea of Freedom: Essays in Honour of Isaiah Berlin* (1979). In a lecture celebrating the centennial of Freud's birth in 1856, John Bowlby said: "Perhaps no other field of contemporary thought shows the influence of Freud's work more clearly than that of child care. Although there had always been those who had known that the child was father to the man and that mother-love gave something indispensable to the growing infant, before Freud these age-old truths had never been the subjects of scientific inquiry," a verdict with which I agree. "Psychoanalysis and Child Care" (1958), in Bowlby, *Making and Breaking of Affectional Bonds*, 1.

no less inaccurate. To begin with, "sex," in the restricted commonsensical way that Stone employs the term, is not synonymous with the erotic energy, originally highly diffused, that Freud captured with the name of libido. Nor is the libido, in the comprehensive psychoanalytic definition, synonymous with the id, as Stone seems to believe; as the infant's earliest mental organization, the id houses all the drives, whole families of urges which, Stone to the contrary, Freud finds to be as potent as sexuality. Freud was never a pansexualist. Moreover, he saw the frequent unresolvable embroglios between the drives or between drives and defenses, as by no means one-sided; their outcome is in no way predetermined. This is what makes the great Freudian psychodrama that is civilization so tense, so fascinating, and so unpredictable.

Freud, indeed, thought some drives, like hunger, to be far more imperative than the sexual urge, demanding far more rapid, far more direct, satisfaction than erotic needs. It was only, for reasons he thought he could explain, the impulse most neglected by students of the mind. But then, Stone has his troubles with Freud's definition of sex; he can speak, as we have seen, of "oral, anal and sexual experiences," inadvertently equating "phallic" or "genital" with "sexual," as though Freud had not securely built pre-genital sexuality into his developmental scheme. After all, Boswell's narcissism, of which Stone makes so much, is a disorder originating in a very early, markedly pre-genital sexual phase.

I am scoring these points not just to score points. If Stone were right to assert that Freud treated the sexual instinct as unchanged from individual to individual, class to class, age to age, then psychoanalytic theories would have no relevance to the historian; any attempt to specify Freud's possible contribution to the historical profession would be, quite simply, pointless. But Stone is wrong. As a physician who in his psychoanalytic practice treated a wide variety of patients—men and women, Russians and Americans, princesses and housewives—Freud does not need to be told that the sexual drive varies enormously from individual to individual. His classic case histories, written with an eye to rehearsing the repertory of the neuroses, document Freud's recognition, his very celebration, of the diversity of sexual impulsions and behavior.

This sensitive receptiveness to human variety also informs Freud's treatment of the arsenal of psychological defenses that man deploys to ward off overwhelming wishes or intolerable anxieties: defense mechanisms are, in the psychoanalytic scheme, flexible, plastic, anything but unalterable. Freud was not a historian, but he knew that men's minds, even their unconscious minds, change across time and differ across class.[26] Concern for individuality, that mark of the historian, pervades all of Freud's writings, his methodological papers no less than his case histories. "Repression," he tells us, "works in *a highly individual manner.*" So do the other defenses; so do the drives against which they defend. So, too, does ambivalence, which lies at the heart of so much mental activity: "Experience shows that demonstrable ambivalence varies greatly among individuals, groups, or races." The developmental line of each person matches that of all others only as each shares with them the general endowment we call human nature. With all his inescapable family resemblance to his peers, each individual remains, for Freud, just that: individual, unique, unduplicable, and thus, in his particular way, interesting. Freud was intent on

26. See below, Chapter 5.

discovering general psychological determinants; as a scientist of the mind he could do no less. But, as he cautioned in *Civilization and its Discontents,* any generalization puts the researcher "in danger of forgetting the variegated colorfulness—*Buntheit*—of the human world and of its mental life."[27] A historian could not have put it better.

Lawrence Stone's handling of psychoanalytic ideas in his *Family, Sex and Marriage in England* was not some sudden, uncharacteristic eruption of an anti-Freudian animus. In a collection of articles gathered from nearly two decades of reviewing, he returned to the attack: "Nothing in the historical record disproves Freud's theory about how at different stages of infantile development different erogenous zones become the foci of sexual stimulation," nor does that record in any way "belittle the importance of sublimation, or of the unconscious operating with a secret dynamic of its own." This reads like a meaningful, sincere effort at effecting a rapprochement between history and psychoanalysis. But Stone weakens, almost wholly withdraws this concession, immediately. Freud, Stone believes, was unhistorical. After all, he had claimed that four traumas—weaning, toilet training, masturbation, and the adolescent conflict between generations—were decisive for all mankind, and had always been so. He looked for these traumas, found them "among his patients, and therefore assumed [them] to be universal." Yet in actuality, they are "dependent on particular experiences which did not happen to the vast majority of people in most of the recorded ·past, but which were peculiar to

---

27. Freud, "Die Verdrängung" (1915), *St.A.,* III, 111, "Repression," *S.E.,* XIV, 150; "Triebe und Triebschicksale" (1915), *St.A.,* III, 94, "Instincts and their Vicissitudes," *S.E.,* XIV, 94; *Das Unbehagen in der Kultur* (1930), *St.A.,* IX, 197, *Civilization and its Discontents, S.E.,* XXI, 64.

middle-class urban culture of late Victorian Europe." They
are, therefore, these Freudian traumas, "historically inappropriate."[28] The lust to teach Freud what he already knows
seems to be hard to contain.

When Stone's book on the English family appeared in
1977, it quickly became controversial, though no review that
I have seen chose to criticize this particular aspect of its
method. Not even Alan Macfarlane, whose spacious thirty-
page review-essay was a sustained campaign of demolition,
took any of the ample pages at his disposal to comment on
Stone's handling of Freud. A look at Macfarlane's own fascinating, meticulous study of a seventeenth-century English
cleric's outer and inner world, discloses that this rather
striking omission must have been a matter of helplessness
before Freud. In analyzing the "mental world" of his man,
Macfarlane tries to make sense of his dreams, which the
Rev. Ralph Josselin had faithfully noted down in his diary.
Dreams, Macfarlane observes, boldly enough, "point to
the mind's pre-occupations and a discussion of them seems
worthwhile." But which theory of dreams should one adopt?
Macfarlane is agnostic on the subject. "Modern studies on
the subject of dreams suggest that they are not, as Freud
maintained, symptoms of subconscious anxiety states or sub-
limated desires, but more a computer type 'run through' of
the mind's activities in order to discard the superfluous."[29]
It is true enough that in recent years psychologists have put
forward some possible alternatives to Freud's theory of
dreams, but Macfarlane's account of that theory is wrong

28. "Children and the Family" (1966), rev. in Stone, *The Past and
the Present* (1981), 216–17. See below, p. 79.
29. Macfarlane, *The Family Life of Ralph Josselin: A Seventeenth-
Century Clergyman* (1970), 183n. Note again the ubiquitous "subconscious."

on every point. Dreams, according to Freud, are not symptoms, but a mental effort to stay asleep. Nor do they express anxiety states, since even anxiety dreams conform to Freud's fundamental rule that dreams are the disguised and distorted condensations of wishes and recent experiences. Besides, they have nothing to do with sublimation. Evidently, far from having tried Freud and found him wanting, Macfarlane has found Freud trying and has decided to evade him.

All these instances—I could multiply them with ease—add up to a great refusal. It is one thing to reject a methodological instrument one has not had the opportunity to know. It is quite another to reject it after bending it out of shape. These historians have made things easy for themselves; by making nonsense of Freud, they have had no trouble demonstrating that Freud is talking nonsense. I am far from asking all histories to be psychoanalytic histories. The writing of history is a companionable, collective, often quarrelsome yet often cooperative affair. A mere glance at a shelf of historical works discloses an exhaustive menu of themes and treatments. And we all admire some historians—Elie Halévy, Marc Bloch, a handful of others—whom it would seem impertinent, nothing less than preposterous, to imagine as somehow more accomplished in their profession had they had the good fortune to undergo an analysis, or psychoanalytic training.

I am, then, not disputing, or in any way minimizing, the capacity of a competent, unanalyzed historian to grasp the ambiguities and complexities of historical situations or the mysterious mixed motives of historical actors. His work shines in its own light; his writings stand as models to be emulated rather than as efforts to be patronized. But the perceptions of such a historian are, as it were, intransitive;

they depend on the accident of individual talent rather than the ministrations of a dependable psychology. And, often, an accomplished historian shrugs his shoulders in resignation when a psychoanalytic map would have enabled him to go on. Seeking to unriddle the venomous controversies that embroiled Woodrow Wilson, when he was President of Princeton University, with Dean West over the Princeton Graduate School, Arthur Link, probably the most knowledgeable Wilson scholar in the world, admits defeat: "The vagaries of his mind . . . are unfathomable." But Alexander and Juliette George, who quote this observation in their "personality study" of Woodrow Wilson and Colonel House, push forward: "Does not Wilson's fanatical battle with Dean West," they ask, become more fathomable if it is considered in terms of the quest for power and for freedom from domination set in motion in his childhood? It would seem that Wilson construed West's insistence on the validity of his own point of view as a galling challenge to his authority; that at some level West evoked in Wilson the image of his father; that he experienced West's activities as an attempt to dominate him, and resisted with all the violence he had once felt, but never ventured to express, in response to his father's overwhelming domination."[30] These sentences take the reader back to the early chapters of their study, and evoke once again the impotent rage of the oedipal child, laden with guilt for his rage, and forever re-enacting, unconsciously, old battles and unsettled traumas. Here, and in later analytical sections of the Georges' book, the vagaries of Wilson's mind do become fathomable. Psychoanalysis, I cannot stress enough, is not a miracle drug or

---

30. George and George, *Woodrow Wilson and Colonel House: A Personality Study* (1956, ed. 1964), 43. See bibliography, pp. 214–15.

a magic password; it is an informed style of inquiry, supplying answers no one had thought were available before or— even more important—suggesting questions no one had thought to ask.

3 | AN ARENA FOR AMATEURS

It is interesting, though a little disheartening, to see how little some historians have done with Freud. It is equally interesting, though more cheering, to see how much they have done without him. For, I repeat, I am not saying that historians have failed to ask pertinent or profound questions before, or without, psychoanalysis. But their way with motivation, or with psychological causes in general, has often been remarkably casual. Crucial psychological explanations have emerged as a kind of last solution, after all others have proved disappointing. Reflecting on the triumphs of the British navy over Napoleon, Elie Halévy rejects, in succession, a series of explanations that lie readily at hand: better design of British ships, tighter discipline among British sailors, superior numbers in the British fleet. None of these, in fact, had anything to do with Trafalgar and the glorious naval engagements that preceded it. Rather, Halévy concludes after his survey, it was that intangible thing, morale, and morale alone, that gave Britain her victories. Naval officers and their crews enjoyed "universal popularity" in their country. "They protected the safety of all, threatened the liberty of none." For all the incompetence of the officers, brutality of the press gangs, and appalling frequency of mutinies, "in the hour of battle, admirals, officers, and men were reconciled and swooped down upon the hostile ships 'like a falcon on her prey.' Why was this? What was the secret of their strength? It was that they had the country

behind them, and they knew it."[31] Elie Halévy, that consummate French connoisseur of nineteenth-century England,
thus attributes a solid material result—victory at sea—to a
pair of feelings and to their interplay: of trust on the part
of the British population, of pride on the part of its navy.
Halévy does not stop to analyze the origins of these feelings. He notes them, and moves on. But they constitute his
explanation.

Again, speaking of public attitudes toward the poverty
of French peasants at the end of the nineteenth century,
Eugen Weber notes: "Public sensitivity grew as the standard of living climbed. In a world where riches and poverty
had seemed prescribed by a predetermined and unalterable
order, the chief question for most had been to survive, and
economic injustice in the modern sense did not affect the
collective consciousness. Once elementary needs began to be
satisfied, there was time to lay claim to more: better conditions of work, better conditions in general. Time, above all,
to consider possibilities hitherto unsuspected, which towns,
schooling, and, yes, political parties were beginning to suggest."[32] These generalizations seem plausible enough. But
the psychological processes implicit in Weber's account are
in no way self-evident. He seems to assume a certain quantity of energy that a human being can invest in his fantasies
only if circumstances make it available. A life of unrelieved
drudgery rarely leaves room either for realistic radicalism
or for Utopian schemes. Dreams of improving one's lot do
not appear automatically, from nowhere. They require a
ground of optimism, a sense of an open, or at least opening,

---

31. Halévy, *England in 1815* (1913; tr. E. I. Watkin and D. A.
Barker, 1949), 47, 65.
32. Weber, *Peasants into Frenchmen: The Modernization of Rural
France 1870–1914* (1976), 277.

future, and some concrete verbal embodiment—the kind of slogan or program around which wishful fantasies could cluster—before drastic change for the better could even be entertained. I am not suggesting that Weber is wrong; on the contrary, I think he is largely right. The century about which Weber writes saw a marked increase in the public rehearsal of guilt feelings, in what came to be known as social conscience, both religious and secular in formulation, a cultural superego translated into cultural criticism, sociological inquiry, and remedial legislation.[33] The mobilization of hope that Weber describes was part of a wider phenomenon, a mixture of newly felt responsibility and solidly grounded expectations. A psychoanalytically informed view of this phenomenon would probably not have altered Weber's conclusions, but it would have further sharpened his perceptions and suitably complicated his argument. Much of what I have called this mobilization of hope did its work outside the domain of awareness.

To be sure, not all historians are wholly unselfconscious about the motives and feelings of historical actors; at least some of their psychologizing displays a measure of informal analysis. One instructive example is a book by Malcolm I. Thomis on responses to the industrial revolution. Discussing the conviction current among English manufacturers that the problems generated by the industrial system could be solved by paternalistic humaneness, he writes: "This was an idea or ideal that continued to haunt the imagination and suggest a possible way out of the dilemma of the labour-capital dispute. Employers would make friendly ges-

---

33. See Peter Gay, "On the Bourgeoisie: A Psychological Interpretation," in John M. Merriman, ed., *Consciousness and Class Experience in Nineteenth-Century Europe* (1979), 187–203; and *The Bourgeois Experience: Victoria to Freud,* vol. I, *Education of the Senses* (1984).

tures towards their workers and in some way or other successfully establish so harmonious a working relationship
with them that problems would all be solved locally and informally, and the state would never need to interfere. It was
a notion"—here Thomis inserts his analysis—"that relied
heavily for its fulfillment on a highly optimistic view of
human nature and the willingness and altruism of individuals to act generously without the coercion of the law.
Such a view"—and here is Thomis's verdict—"was not justified."[34]

Assuming for the moment that this generalization is
sound, what it displays is commonsense psychology at work
in history; the analysis rests on untested assumptions. The
resolute, unfounded optimism that Thomis discerns, it seems
to me, must have been a composite of partly unconscious
wishes and anxieties: of self-serving notions parading as
complacent expectations, coupled with a solid dash of denial—both defenses against realities daily before the manufacturers' very eyes, defenses mobilized not merely to fatten
their purses but also to assuage their consciences.

Doubtless, psychology is an unsafe instrument, as dangerous to the historian who wields it as to the hapless historical subject on whom he tests it. Its double edge shows in
Donald J. Olsen's account of suburban London in the nineteenth century. "What the Victorians desired was privacy
for the middle classes, publicity for the working classes, and
segregation for both. The ideal environment for individual
and familial privacy was the single-class villa suburb. There
bourgeois respectability could best flourish." It was the
usual kind of respectability: a disheartening spectacle. "The
suburbs that proved most successful were the ones that were

---

34. Thomis, *Responses to Industrialization: The British Experience
1780–1850* (1976), 140.

most suburban, that is to say the most dull, the most uniform, with the fewest cultural or social institutions, since they thereby offered the fewest counterattractions to those of the home and the hearth." Olsen's conclusion is hardly unexpected: "Boredom was the price willingly paid for by a respite from urban tensions. Social segregation simplified problems of behavior, expenditure, and beliefs: one simply did what the neighbors were doing."[35]

This is psychology as satire; witty and, like the rest of Olsen's book, instructive. But the interplay between historical analysis and polemical implications becomes a duel in which polemics shoulder analysis aside. Olsen perceives a contrast between city bustle and suburban quiet, a conflict between cultural demands and domestic relaxation, which generated a willingness to pay the price of conformism to secure the reward of security. Surely, this portrait is telling and at least partially true. But a more penetrating psychology would have blunted, in fact largely obliterated, its satirical features. For it would have compelled Olsen to reckon with the subterranean turmoil of these middling, these mediocre people: he would have felt the heavy toll of their working routine, the pathos, largely hidden from themselves, of seeking safety among the like-minded, the almost fanatical concentration on family pleasures to which public entertainment or engagement of any sort was only a distraction if not a danger—in short, the anxiety lurking behind these presumably free philistine choices. It is a pity about the satire, perhaps. Still: while a psychoanalytic look at these desperately respectable bourgeois would have made Olsen's account less amusing, it would have made it literally more humane.

This does not mean that all historians have been naive or

---

35. Olsen, *The Growth of Victorian London* (1976), 23.

unselfconscious about their psychology. Georges Lefèbvre, one of the most notable autodidacts among historians and a most distinguished student of the French Revolution, patched together his perception of human motives and conduct from sociologists like Emile Durkheim and Maurice Halbwachs, and from a diligent, introspective reading in the masses of testimony that peasants, crowds, leaders of Revolutionary France had left behind, testimony that Lefèbvre knew as intimately as anyone has ever known it. Leftwing in his sympathies, unwilling to denigrate even the most raffish and most eccentric actors on the Revolutionary stage, steeped in the dusty riches hidden in provincial archives, Lefèbvre constructed an invariant sequence of incentives to action, resembling nothing so much as the familiar frustration-rage scheme. It served him well in his analyses of the motives driving Parisians to take the Bastille, peasants to ransack châteaux, nervous provincials to spread rumors about the threatened invasion of brigands. Lefèbvre certainly *saw* these actors more vividly, more in the round, than any of his precursors, whose work had all too often replicated the oversimplifications and the caricatures that the Revolutionary period so easily invites. Although his vision was not wholly uncompromised by his political stance, and the votes he cast in the Third Republic left traces on his manner of dealing with the makers of the First, the gain for historical psychology inherent in his empathetic and informed vision was marked.

But it was limited. That succession of impulses Lefèbvre discovered was a simple, fated progression of mental attitudes. It began with fear, which generated a defensive reaction, which in turn awakened an irresistible need to take revenge on the "others." It was only in a famous paper on revolutionary crowds that Lefèbvre refined this sequence and introduced some sharply observed nuances; here and there, his paper reverberates with faint echoes that might have originated from the Freudian dispensation. In search of "the collective revolutionary mentality," Lefèbvre noted that it was formed, first, by mental acts of generalizing, of abstracting—which is to say, of simplifying experience. The necessary product was the "human type," a bloodless stick figure that, especially in times of emotional effervescence, serves as a substitute for perception itself. Revolutionaries constructed heroes and villains, idealized the ones and endowed them with all the virtues, vilified the others and turned them into shameless exploiters. Psychoanalysts call such drastic and convenient simplification "splitting," and view it as a retreat from more adult modes of perceiving the world. So it was here: the mood that Lefèbvre detected is one of intermingled hope, idealism, and a good deal of anxiety—*inquiétude;* it gives rise to behavior that seems inconsistent but obeys its own iron inner logic. Great expectations are inseparably yoked to the passionate conviction that if these are ever to be translated from wishes into realities, the enemy must be destroyed: "To realize social well-being and to insure the happiness of mankind, one need only suppress the opposing class." Far from sentimentalizing the crowd mentality, Lefèbvre recognized that such heady optimism and high-flying idealism produce "the desire to punish, with which hatred and the thirst for revenge are amalgamated."[36] Groups, however just their cause, are victims of their passions.

These confident propositions hint at a comprehensive psychological explanation. But in the end, Lefèbvre confessed

36. Lefèbvre, "Foules révolutionnaires" (1934), in Lefèbvre, *Etudes sur la Révolution Française* (1954) 278–82. And see Lefèbvre's "Le Meurtre du comte de Dampierre (22 Juin 1791)" (1941), in ibid., 288–97.

himself baffled by the phenomenon of the *mentalité collective*. Is it not, he asked a little helplessly, at least partly a product of "a kind of physiological magnetism?" No wonder that Lefèbvre's readers found themselves baffled also. In the margin of his essay on "Foules révolutionnaires" at the Yale Library, someone has scribbled the plaintive and impatient query, *"Mais, qu'est-ce que c'est la 'mentalité collective révolutionnaire'?"* It seems a valid question, if not altogether generous; for while Lefèbvre did not succeed in tracing revolutionary crowd behavior to its unconscious roots, and while he failed to explain the bond that converts individuals into families of celebration and collective innocence in the midst of murderous aggression, he has at least offered observations to serve as indispensable preliminaries for such an explanation.

As I have already suggested, there is evidence, scattered but heartening—at least to those historians who would welcome psychoanalysis into the fold—that it has now become possible to go beyond these preliminaries. Scholars using Freud have not always produced disasters. And one of them, E. R. Dodds, produced a masterpiece, *The Greeks and the Irrational,* a model of what psychoanalytic history can be; first published in 1951, it has retained its authority through the decades. The emergence of Freud as a possible guide to the past has generated several types of historical inquiry: the highly concentrated psychobiography, the analysis of exceptional situations and exceptional personages—the devastations wrought by riots, plagues, world-historical psychotics. But, as Dodds confidently demonstrated, psychoanalysis can inform the study of dominant moral imperatives, pervasive religious convictions, changing cultural styles, in short, the "normal" past. Thus he invited historians to continue writing history, from a rewarding broader perspective than before.

Dodds's use of Freud, thoroughly well-informed and shrewdly sympathetic, was also, predictably, wholly undoctrinaire. Standing back from his suggestive analysis of how Greek culture moved from shame to guilt, Dodds emphatically declared his independence from psychoanalysis. "I do not expect this particular key, or any key, to open all the doors. The evolution of a culture is too complex a thing to be explained without residue in terms of any simple formula, whether economic or psychological, begotten of Marx or begotten of Freud. We must resist the temptation to simplify what is not simple."[37] Yet this commitment to pluralism in method and explanation alike did not prevent Dodds from adopting, boldly, the ideas of the psychologist whom most other historians have found unpalatable, irrelevant, and frightening. Not long before his death in 1979 I wrote him to ask whether he planned to write anything about Freud's influence on his work, and Dodds replied that he had no intention of doing so, but added: "He did help me to understand myself and other people a little better, but that is a benefit which I share with millions of others." It is a benefit that historians have by and large chosen to reject. At least so far.

---

37. Dodds, *The Greeks and the Irrational* (1951), 49. For a more detailed discussion, see below, pp. 191–96.

2

The Claims of Freud

1 | AN APPEARANCE OF SMUGNESS

Granted that the historian can profit from psychology, why should he accept Freud as a guide? The answer to this inconvenient question is far more problematic than devotees of psychoanalysis have been willing to recognize. The work of E. R. Dodds and a few others carries the conviction of example, but the claim that psychoanalysis can make on the historian deserves theoretical exploration as well as concrete instances. For the psychoanalyst, steeped in his training, his case conferences, his practice, his reading and rereading of the canon, the Freudian dispensation is wholly persuasive. He will find corroborative evidence on all sides, even when and where he is not looking for it: in his children, in the conduct of politicians, but above all in his analysands, with their dreams and associations, their silences and symptomatic acts. Listening to his patients with freefloating attention, that carefully cultivated way of absorbing messages and making combinations, the psychoanalyst gains access to experiences which, one after the other, underscore the prescience and document the genius of the founder. He may amend marginal details in psychoanalytic theory, elaborate findings of his own whose adumbration he is sure to detect in the papers of Freud, or fill in a spot or two on the agenda that the Master proposed but left only in outline. He may address problems, like primitive object relations, at which Freud only hinted. His science, after all, as he likes to say, is still very young. But in its essential contours, his map of the mind remains pretty much as Freud drew and redrew it. The psychoanalyst regards the terms of his trade like regression and repression, projection and denial, ambivalence and transference and the rest of his professional vocabulary, as precise descriptions of very real mental acts. Hence he is tempted to treat skeptics as ignorant or obtuse, certainly as defensive. Their demands for further proofs of what has been proved so often must strike him as perverse, as an obsessive and anxious exercise. Is it not all there in the *Standard Edition of the Complete Psychological Works of Sigmund Freud* as slightly amended here and there by glossators?

The historian, somewhat to psychoanalysts' astonishment and dismay, is rarely prepared to grant these far-reaching claims. He is likely to find the techniques of psychoanalysis esoteric, its language deplorable, and its propositions, to put it generously, remote from his researches into the past. At best, they seem codifications of the obvious; more generally, they will strike him as a bizarre potpourri of farfetched speculations and self-fulfilling prophecies. He reads psychoanalytic literature, if he reads it at all, with the growing suspicion that Freudians are not better than religious fanatics, a tribe of true believers.[1]

The eruption of psychoanalysis into the historian's field of vision has only made his puzzlement before psychology more acute. "The question, 'Yes, but *what* psychology?' " Jacques Barzun has observed, "is important"—important and, he implies, unanswerable.[2] Even if the historian should grant psychology preeminence among his avenues to understanding, he is not prepared to select psychoanalysis as his psychology of choice. Why Freud? Why not Jung, who proposed to explicate collective fantasies and universal myths? Why not the battalion of revisionists—Karen Horney, Erich Fromm, Harry Stack Sullivan—who, with their social psychiatries, stand in convenient, almost reassuring proximity to the world the historian likes to think he inhabits? Why not behaviorists or learning theorists, whose psychologies feed on experimentation and generate the kind of quantifiable information that historians have come to appreciate or at least learned to live with?

These are not neutral or innocent questions. All the disciplines to which modern historians resort—anthropology, sociology, economics—are mired in controversy; they all compel the historian to choose one school in preference to

---

1. The historian Saul Friedländer, sympathetic to the applicability of psychoanalysis to history, has observed that "a great many psychoanalysts—regardless of the 'school' they belong to—consider their interpretation of Freud's thought to be an unimpeachable, monolithic whole, and any attempt to be selective is met with a ferocious opposition more appropriate to the members of a religious sect than to the representatives of a still-evolving scientific discipline." *History and Psychoanalysis: An Inquiry into the Possibilities and Limits of Psychohistory* (1975; tr. Susan Suleiman, 1978), 6.

2. Barzun, *Clio and the Doctors: Psycho-History, Quanto-History & History* (1974), 6.

others. The historian studying industrialization in the nineteenth century commits himself to one type of explanation current in economics and rejects alternatives; his colleague investigating the rise of Protestantism takes a stand on Max Weber's sociology of religion. But the historian's hesitation over psychology is far more tense than the normal indecision of the scholar confronting an unfamiliar discipline; his choice is heavily charged with emotion. He demands of psychology a consensus and precision that no other science of man can command, and requires proofs that psychoanalysts are reluctant to provide.

Their reluctance, however well founded, has markedly reduced the eligibility of psychoanalysis to the historian. They may not be fully aware of it, but psychoanalysts often appear singularly uncooperative with, or at least ambivalent about, the uninitiated venturing to unriddle, perhaps embrace, their enterprise. The historian pressing Freud on his colleagues must concede at the outset that psychoanalytic presentations are anything but ingratiating to even the most benevolent amateur. The empirical and experimental evidence supporting Freudian propositions is impressive, but it has not reached, let alone persuaded, the professional historian, for it has normally appeared in highly specialized technical periodicals, and rarely made concessions to general educated discourse. More troubling still, beginning with Freud himself, psychoanalysts have been anything but hospitable to the kind of public verification that other disciplines take for granted. Writing to the American psychologist Saul Rosenzweig in 1934, Freud politely professed some interest in experimental tests of psychoanalytic assertions, but then brusquely subverted his courtesy by adding that he saw little value in them, since "the wealth of dependable observations on which these assertions rest make them independent of

experimental verification. Still, they can do no harm."[3]
Those untold thousands of hours that Freud had listened to
scores of analysands, those brilliant case histories and illuminating vignettes he had communicated in his papers,
those profuse insights that his followers were contributing
to analytic periodicals, struck him as satisfactory demonstrations of the psychoanalytic verities. For the most part, later
analysts have agreed with him: they have found experimental confirmation at once gratifying and unnecessary. With
the passage of years, the clinical material piled up through
psychoanalytic journals, psychoanalytic monographs, and
psychoanalytic conferences has further enriched the texture
of empirical support. Hence, most analysts have remained
cheerfully content with the analytic encounter as their most
appropriate, and wholly adequate, setting in which to test
the Freudian propositions they apply every day.

Freud had some grounds for his skepticism: many an
experimenter relatively innocent of psychoanalysis would
set up investigations, elicit responses, and offer interpretations that had, whatever he might conclude, only the most
tenuous relevance to psychoanalytic propositions.[4] Yet
Freud's letter to Rosenzweig, which has been much quoted,
has done his cause real harm. But Freud was not consistently
so reserved. In the later editions of his *Traumdeutung*, he
welcomed the "sensitive observations" and "happy examples," in short, the "important contributions" that that mys-

---

3. Freud to Rosenzweig, February 28, 1934, reprinted in the original
in David Shakow and David Rapaport, *The Influence of Freud on
American Psychology* (1964), 129n. And see the detailed comments,
ibid., 130n.
4. Ernest R. Hilgard, "Psychoanalysis: Experimental Studies," *International Encyclopedia of the Social Sciences,* ed. David L. Sills, 17
vols. (1968), XIII, 39.

terious sportsman, balloonist, mystic, the Austrian psychologist Herbert Silberer, had made to the scientific interpretation of dreams. Silberer, impressed by Freud's epoch-making discoveries, schooled himself to systematic self-observation and later subjected others to hypnosis, in order to assess—and assert—the validity of Freud's theory of dreams. This had been before World War I, well before Freud had secured general notice. Somewhat later, in 1919, Freud approvingly cited a now classic paper that Otto Pötzl, a prominent Viennese academic psychologist, had published two years before, observing that Pötzl's "new way of studying the formation of dreams experimentally" differed decisively from "the earlier coarse technique."[5] His distrust of the laboratory was certainly Freud's characteristic stance, but the passages I have just quoted, little noticed yet significant, show him far from unsympathetic to enterprising and well-informed psychological experimenters interested in his findings.

For several decades now, a sizable number of these experimenters, joined by a handful of psychoanalysts, have chosen to follow this Freud, a Freud in a vein relatively expansive, relatively open to the procedures of academic psychology. They have conducted some fascinating experiments and have found it rewarding but very difficult work. The propositions they have ventured to examine deal with mental phenomena so inward, so distant from crude manipulation, quantitative measurement, and even direct observation, that their proofs—and disproofs—have necessarily remained tentative and made their verdicts less than unanimous. The pioneering experiments of Silberer and others were, to be

5. Freud, *Traumdeutung* (1900), *St.A.*, II, 483, 73n, 122n; *The Interpretation of Dreams, S.E.*, V, 503; IV, 49n, 102n. For Silberer and Pötzl, see below, p. 219.

sure, not very esoteric. They fastened on the most spectacular mental manifestation to which Freud had called attention: the appearance of sexual symbols in dreams. In his
Traumdeutung, Freud had assigned symbols a distinctly
secondary place in the work of interpretation, but the early
experimenters found them more accessible to testing than
some of Freud's more intricate theories about the mind.
Hence, they devised hypnotic sessions in which a woman
subject was instructed to dream that her employer had come
to see her and raped her, after which she reported, upon
waking, that she had dreamt about a surprise visit by her
boss who had opened a suitcase he was carrying to take out
a banana—or, in a slightly different version, to let out a
slithering snake. Later experiments would be far less primitive than this, but those exhibiting the dream work making
unacceptable ideas acceptable offered at least anecdotal
demonstrations that there was something to Freud's strange,
subversive ideas after all.

Something, but how much? The Freudian corpus is not a
tightly knit, comprehensive theory in which general laws
can be derived from empirical propositions, and which a
crucial experiment might test conclusively.[6] It is, rather, a
family of closely related, often mutually supporting claims
ranging from empirical statements to limited generalizations
to global theories about the mind. The whole of psychoanalytic theory is something like an imposing, sprawling castle
designed by an architect of such stature that his successors,

---

6. See esp. Paul Kline, *Fact and Fantasy in Freudian Theory* (1972;
2nd ed., 1981), ch. 1, "Freudian Theory and Scientific Method;" and
David Rapaport, *The Structure of Psychoanalytic Theory: A Systematizing Attempt, Psychological Issues,* Monograph 6 (1960), a brave,
suggestive attempt to reduce the multifarious laws and observations
of the Freudian dispensation to system.

adding wings or shoring up insecure walls, have thoughtfully adapted their renovations to his style. This inordinate respect for authority has obscured the fact that some wings and outbuildings enjoy a certain independence from the rest so that a fire damaging one section of this complex might leave the rest unscathed. In a word, the experimental testing of Freudian propositions is never definitive—either way. Still, after literally hundreds of ingenious, increasingly sophisticated experiments employing post-hypnotic suggestion, projective tests, controlled interviews, and precision instruments, we are entitled to draw some far-reaching, though still provisional conclusions. The house that Freud built still stands.

It is likely that some of Freud's most sweeping metapsychological speculations, like his late stark theory of the drives, however suggestive, will always elude experimental scrutiny. And it is certain that broad reaches of psychoanalytic theory require more, and better, attention from experimenters than they have had so far. But the fundaments of his theoretical structure—psychological determinism, the ubiquity of wishes, the dynamic unconscious—have received some impressive experimental support. Similarly, experimental evidence has buttressed the case for Freud's once highly scandalous and still somewhat controversial discovery of infantile sexuality, as well as for the unconscious mechanisms of defense, especially the work of repression. It is in fact in the domain of unconscious defenses that experimental psychologists have launched some elegant investigations known, since Jerome Bruner and Leo Postman christened them in 1947, as studies in perceptual defense. The experimenter (working with a tachistoscope, which can expose words and measure that exposure down to a fraction of a second) shows subjects an array of words chosen, as carefully as possible, for equal length and familiarity. Some of these, like "spoon" or "trees," are likely to be free of emotional connotations while others, like "bitch" or "prick," are laden with affect, possibly enticing or anxiety-provoking, or both. A variant of this procedure takes an ambiguous word like "fairy" and puts it into two markedly different linguistic contexts, one suggesting homosexuality and the other the brothers Grimm. On the theory of repression the subject should be able to read the innocuous words more rapidly, requiring less exposure on the tachistoscope, than those conjuring up erotic or aggressive or guilty feelings. Time after time, these experiments have been, from the psychoanalytic perspective, successful, though given the boldness of the underlying assumptions, their results cannot claim dogmatic status.[7] This would appear to be the nature of reasoning from the experimental testing of psychoanalytic propositions: largely indirect, heavily inferential, and sometimes debatable.

Other aspects of the Freudian corpus—the work of fantasy, transference, and anxiety—have either been the beneficiaries of experimental verification or have enjoyed an access of plausibility as by-products of experiments testing something else. Psychologists have even found telling traces of the much-abused Oedipus complex in some stylish experiments that delineate its contours largely as Freud's theory would predict.[8] It would be a rash and credulous historian who

---

7. In his *The Standing of Psychoanalytic Theory* (1981), the skeptical English philosopher B. A. Farrell has argued, for example, that the studies in perceptual defense are not about repression at all (p. 34); in response see Kline, *Fact and Fantasy,* 210–28.

8. On the Oedipus complex, see below, pp. 93–99. Prediction plays a relatively modest part in psychoanalytic verification since, obeying the principle of overdetermination, a single cluster of causes may have a variety of effects. See below, p. 187.

would claim that all this intensive, still fragmentary activity constitutes secure proof of psychoanalysis as a system. But for the historian to minimize or ignore it would be downright unscientific.

Still, as I have already intimated, psychoanalysts have ignored it as well. Their blithe belief, apparently so smug, that their couch is their laboratory, has irritated observers of psychoanalysis, including many historians. Modesty, they have intimated, would be a far more becoming stance than this self-satisfaction. "In various cults of depth psychology, beginning with Freud," the historian Paul K. Conkin has written, "men have attempted to isolate the general structure of the psyche, importing at least the form of physical concepts into these murky waters. But their terms have been elusive, their affirmed structures too imprecise and too speculative for unambiguous testing, and their concepts too metaphorical, too literary, and too phenomenological for other than loose clinical or suggestive speculative uses." For that one historian, at least, feelings of doubt issue in counsels of despair: regretting what he calls the resort to "metaphorical Freudianisms," he firmly suggests that "rather than offering naïveté advertised as sophistication, the historian might better remain loyal to common-sense wisdom, parochial and ambiguous as it usually is."[9] Conkin seems to find it preferable to explore the caverns of the past by the flickering candlelight of good sense rather than by the dazzling lantern of a professional psychology that lays claim to an illumination it does not really possess. In his impatience with what Marcus Cunliffe has called "Sigmundian arrogance," Conkin has most of his colleagues with him.

---

9. Paul Conkin and Roland N. Stromberg, *The Heritage and Challenge of History* (1971), 165, 170.

2 | REMEMBERING THE FOUNDER

Unbelievers have found the style of psychoanalytic argumentation no less suspect than its substance. Most educated persons who have not been analyzed (and that includes the overwhelming majority of historians) visualize psychoanalysts as guarding arcane mysteries presided over by the authoritarian high priest, the Founder Freud, or by his chosen acolytes speaking in his name. Access to his rites is jealously restricted: psychoanalysts take the self-protective—and outrageous—position that the sole dependable pathway to an understanding of their dispensation is the psychoanalytic experience itself. Throughout his professional career, Freud suggested there was in fact no other way. It is "hard," he wrote in 1932, "to give anyone who is not himself a psychoanalyst an insight into psychoanalysis. You may believe me," he added, almost but not quite apologetically, "we do not enjoy giving the impression of being in a secret society, practicing a secret science." But he remained impenitent. "Nobody has the right to meddle with psychoanalysis who has not acquired certain experiences," and he meant experiences on the couch.[10] If one could not be an analyst, at least one would have to be analyzed to speak with any authority.

It is wholly consonant with this posture of exclusiveness, the stigma of invincible professional snobbery, that psychoanalytic papers and monographs almost invariably invoke the words of the founder—not to embellish an argument or to add a historical dimension, but to serve as potent support,

10. Freud, *Neue Folge der Vorlesungen zur Einführung in die Psychoanalyse* (1933), *St.A.*, I, 507; *New Introductory Lectures on Psycho-Analysis*, *S.E.*, XXII, 69.

if not conclusive proof.[11] As one intellectual historian, Gerhard Masur, once put it, denouncing Freud's intellectual egotism: "When in 1914 he wrote the history of the psychoanalytic movement he stated flatly that he had a better right than anyone else to know what psychoanalysis was. 'La psychoanalyse [sic], c'est moi.' "[12] And did Freud's servile disciples not confirm him in his megalomania?

Masur's allusion to Louis XIV is as inappropriate as his characterization of Freud's presumed ascendancy over his followers is inflammatory. But it remains plausible, in large part because psychoanalysts' public strategies have done little to controvert it. Their apparent certainty that knowledge can be found in the hermetic psychoanalytic situation alone, and that Freud's pronouncements enjoy privileged authority, offend against the most cherished convictions of the historical profession. The first reads like a reminiscence of that unfortunate tendentious maxim "it takes one to know one," which, if applied, would put an end to the historian's enterprise; historians, after all, are committed to entering the world of the other, no matter how distant in time, place, or

---

11. "It is not uncommon even today," the noted psychoanalyst Mark Kanzer observed in 1980, "to find veneration vitiating the true legacy of Freud, which was to explore, innovate and decide for himself without awe of tradition or, for that matter, his own previous opinions." "Conclusion" in Mark Kanzer and Jules Glenn, eds., *Freud and His Patients* (1980), 429. Possibly the most severe self-criticism of this attitude within the psychoanalytic craft that I have come across is by Edward Glover, "Research Methods in Psycho-Analysis" (1952), reprinted in *On the Early Development of Mind* (1956), 390–405, esp. 391–92.

12. Masur did not scruple to call the small group of close followers that Freud gathered around himself "a kind of psychoanalyst's politbureau." His general account of Freud's ideas is on the same level. *Prophets of Yesterday: Studies in European Culture, 1890–1914* (1961), 298–317, esp. 312.

cultural habits, and to treat that other on the individual's own terms, in his or her own way. And while psychoanalysts' slavish dependence on quotations from the Master might be acceptable in scholastic or talmudic disputation, in theological reasoning, it is wholly out of place in a discipline devoted to the scientific pursuit of truth. It may remind historians of Alfred North Whitehead's celebrated aphorism, "A science that hesitates to forget its founders is lost," inviting the conclusion that psychoanalysis has been lost to science almost from its inception, ever since Freud's first disciples established the habit of clinching arguments by reciting a relevant passage from his papers.

In actuality, the psychoanalytic dispensation has been neither quite so inaccessible, nor so authoritarian, as these pronouncements and these forensic habits might imply. There is, after all, a massive literature of psychoanalytic popularization, to which Freud himself contributed diligently all his life. He delivered accessible lectures, alive with vivid pictures and telling instances, sensitive to the questions and doubts his listeners might raise; they are invitations to think out the problems and propositions of psychoanalysis in the genial, in no way condescending, company of their discoverer. A benign seducer, he would begin his expositions with ordinary experiences like slips of the tongue or forgetting of names to establish that the mind is governed by laws and that the unconscious exercises great influence on mental activity, before launching into his more difficult theory of the neuroses. It is not an accident that he cast some of his popular presentations in dialogue form. He knew better than anyone, for he had experienced all these doubts himself, what was offensive, improbable, even incredible, about his ideas. Mobilizing all his extensive literary resources to illustrate the workings of the mind without betraying its complexity, and to present the unpalatable side of human nature without losing his audience, Freud took time out from his crowded days to write lucid articles for encyclopedias, short textbooks, and comprehensive presentations for a wider public. His last book, which he did not live to finish, was an outline of psychoanalysis—a fitting coda to the labors of a lifetime. He would not have devoted so much effort to such expositions if he had thought the scientific authority of the psychoanalytic situation as exclusive, and conclusive, as he sometimes claimed it to be.

Moreover, it is striking how often, and how earnestly, Freud punctuated his metapsychological and his clinical papers with disclaimers, calling attention to areas of uncertainty and sheer ignorance. Freud was a masterly debater; his strategies of persuasion would have done credit to the most accomplished trial lawyer. He was, no doubt, an advocate of genius, and he could hardly help noticing that his highly personal mixture of wit, forcefulness, and scientific prudence was an appealing stance that could not hurt his cause, no matter how disagreeable or implausible his ideas might at first seem. Yet, while Freud's public hesitations and appeals for patience had their uses in propagating his message, they were something better than manipulative tactical devices; they faithfully record in each instance the state of the discipline he would spend decades refining and transforming.

Psychoanalysis has been subjected to the most severe reproaches, among which dogmatism and incoherence are the most enduring. But the first of these is unjust and the second overstated. Freud's life work, read chronologically, discloses psychoanalysis as a young science in flux, as the charting and recharting of little-known terrain. Both for the educated public, to men and women who, he knew, would remain strangers to the analytic couch, and to his fellow psychoanalysts, Freud dramatized the spectacle of a search, of a continuing inquiry thirsty for new findings and receptive to drastic revision. The didactic psychoanalytic literature, which Freud initiated in commanding fashion, could never serve as a full substitute for the intimate, distinctive experience of undergoing a psychoanalysis, but it could bring the historian within the range of recognition of how Freud and his followers perceived the human mind to be working. H. Stuart Hughes's engaging suggestion that at least some young historians undergo analysis or do some work in a psychoanalytic institute has, as one might expect, found practically no resonance in the profession. But, though imaginative and very demanding, calling as it does for an investment of time, money, and energy that few historians can be expected to venture, it is a perfectly rational idea.[13]

Even the historian, though, who only learns about psychoanalysis through reading in the literature cannot help discovering the astonishing range of Freud's perception, his unparalleled gift for reading evidence, making combina-

---

13. Hughes, "History and Psychoanalysis: The Explanation of Motive," *History As Art and As Science: Twin Vistas on the Past* (1964), 42–67. Hughes's proposal, in fact, once we think through its implications, is in line with the professional historian's way of mastering his auxiliary sciences and, for that matter, his material in general; it is an invitation to secure the kind of competence that he would find wholly unobjectionable if other disciplines were at issue. To experience the psychoanalytic situation, with its charged relationship between analyst and analysand and its pressure for regression, is akin to the historian of Columbus's voyages traversing Columbus's routes under Columbus's conditions—akin, though even more difficult. For a different, less exacting perspective, see Fred Weinstein and Gerald M. Platt, *Psychoanalytic Sociology: An Essay on the Interpretation of Historical Data and the Phenomena of Collective Behavior* (1973), 1n.

tions, and anticipating objections. He is bound to recognize, therefore, that Freud's position in the discipline he founded is as exceptional as are the techniques his discipline employs. The conditions under which Freud came to his epoch-making discoveries were highly unusual and quite unpromising: an ambitious neurologist who had failed more than once to secure fame, a reputable physician who had commendable cures to his credit, he traveled, reluctantly, indeed painfully, far from his medical starting points. Freud could have tested the stratagem of resistance, of which he would later make so much in his clinical papers, in himself. Much against his will, he discarded the prevailing physiological interpretations of mental events, and respectable hypotheses about mental illness, in favor of his scandalous propositions. There is good evidence that he was far from easy about the sexual etiology of the neuroses and the sexual alertness of children. He found his way by intently observing his patients who taught him much.[14] And he penetrated the smoke screen of good reasons to glimpse the features of real reasons by an unprecedented self-analysis. He had no model for this courageous exploration of his inner states, his dreams, associations, wishes, and fears, but had to invent it as he went along, and assimilate its results as he made terrifying discovery after terrifying discovery.

It is hard for the coolest of historians to confront these heroic years of Freud's life without falling into hyperbole. He took much from others, from poets, novelists, even from psychologists. But the architecture of his theory, and most of the materials from which he constructed it, were largely,

---

14. For this point, see Peter Gay, "Sigmund Freud: A German and his Discontents," in *Freud, Jews and Other Germans: Masters and Victims in Modernist Culture* (1978), 29–92, esp. 82–88.

astonishingly, his own. Historians, trained to recognize and to respect the distinctiveness of each individual, come to see that Freud's stature differs from that of other scientific geniuses. Freud once told Marie Bonaparte, not without envy, that Einstein was fortunate: Einstein had after all done his work in the company of scientific giants all the way back to Newton while he had been compelled to labor in the dark, alone.[15] Sigmund Freud, we now know, somewhat overstated his isolation, both from his fellow psychologists and from his precursors; the unconscious, repression, and even infantile sexuality had been glimpsed, if in rudimentary form, by a handful of contemporaries, philosophers and psychologists alike. Ancestor-hunters might attend to Dr. Adolf Patze, an obscure *Wundarzt* "first class," in Grabow near Stettin, who, in 1845, in a pamphlet on bordellos, observed in a footnote that "the sexual drive already manifests itself among little six-, four-, even three-year-old children."[16] Moreover, the debt Freud owed such medical luminaries as Ernst Brücke and Jean-Martin Charcot was always obvious— and always acknowledged. But the medical and psychological atmosphere of his time, most charitably described perhaps as not unhospitable to the germination of psychoanalysis, in no way shakes Freud's position as the lonely founder of an eminently subversive science.

Biographers anxious to debunk the claims for Freud have documented his dependence on the sexologists of his time, and on his friend Fliess, but they have been unable to erase, or even compromise, the "myth" of Freud the Founder.[17]

---

15. Freud to Bonaparte, January 11, 1927, Ernest Jones, *The Life and Work of Sigmund Freud, 1919–1939: The Last Phase* (1957), 131.
16. Patze, *Ueber Bordelle und die Sittenverderbniss unserer Zeit* (1845), 48n.
17. The most recent canvass of Freud's debts is Frank J. Sulloway,

Indeed Freud, even if he indulged himself in some polemical exaggerations, anticipated them. He was an unsurpassed reader in the scientific literature: the opening chapter of *The Interpretation of Dreams* is a comprehensive, in every way generous, bibliographical review of available monographs, recent or ancient; his *Three Essays on Sexuality* lists, on the first page, no fewer than nine contemporary students of sex from whose writings he had profited; his book on jokes singles out four writers on humor whose publications had been important to his own, particularly the philosopher Theodor Lipps whose recent study of jokes had, he handsomely acknowledged, given him "the courage and the possibility to undertake this essay."[18] In his retrospective papers, in the very names he gave his children, Freud gratefully immortalized these debts.[19] He was, in fact, prepared to qualify his claim to the title Founder of Psychoanalysis; the credit for bringing it into being, he wrote more than once, should go to Josef Breuer. Freud was a giant standing on the shoulders of tall men. His originality was, like all originality, a composite: it included recognizing the implications of his predecessors' work and following them through to the end—he had the courage of their discoveries. He put

Freud, Biologist of the Mind: Beyond the Psychoanalytic Legend (1979), which, despite its high-pressure insistence on Freud's dependence on Fliess (perhaps because of it) I find less than wholly persuasive.

18. Freud, *Der Witz und seine Beziehungen zum Unbewussten,* (1905), *St.A.,* IV, 13n; *Jokes and their Relation to the Unconscious, S.E.,* VIII, 9n.

19. Freud named one of his sons Ernst after Ernst Brücke, and another Martin after Jean-Martin Charcot, two of the senior colleagues whom he most admired. See Peter Gay, "Six Names in Search of an Interpretation: A Contribution to the Debate over Sigmund Freud's Jewishness," *Hebrew Union College Annual,* LIII (1982), 295–307.

together, in fertile juxtaposition, ideas that earlier explorers had glimpsed only fitfully and separately. And he made seminal discoveries of his own.

Nor was his attitude that of a religious prophet or a charismatic leader, whatever some of his epigones have tried to make of him. As he listened to his patients, so he listened to his experience and his followers: the history of psychoanalysis is, for its first four decades, largely the history of Freud changing his views on the structure of the mind, on therapeutic action, on the nature of the instincts, on female sexuality, and on anxiety—a very catalogue of his responsiveness to new material and new ways of seeing familiar material. The larger, immensely important theme of object relations, those early experiences before the advent of the Oedipal phase, has come to flourish, without objections from the "orthodox," since Freud's death in 1939. Some psychoanalysts have revised Freud's views on female sexuality, others have questioned the utility of treating aggression as a fundamental drive, yet they have not been read out of the club.[20] It is largely from the outside, and through the

---

20. The eminent psychoanalyst Leo Stone has disputed the category of "aggression" as a unitary idea ("Reflections on the Psychoanalytic Concept of Aggression," *The Psychoanalytic Quarterly*, XL [April 1971], 195–244); earlier, Otto Fenichel, whose authority among the psychoanalytic establishment remains unimpaired, raised serious questions about Freud's dualistic instinct theory ("A Critique of the Death Instinct" [1935], in *The Collected Papers of Otto Fenichel, First Series* [1953], 363–72); while a group of respected psychoanalysts and analytically oriented psychologists have urged the elimination of metapsychology from the corpus of Freud's accepted work. (I note especially some of the papers of George S. Klein, such as "Two Theories or One?" [1970], in Klein, *Psychoanalytic Theory: An Exploration of Essentials* [1975], 41–71, and those collected by Merton M. Gill and Philip S. Holzman in memory of Klein, *Psychology versus Metapsychology* [1976].)

defensive tone that some psychoanalysts adopt—a defensiveness that matches the attitude of their most stubborn adversaries—that psychoanalysis has gained the undeserved reputation of a monolithic cult.

At the same time, to be sure, it displays much sturdy continuity. It is not only that Freud persisted in holding to the cardinal ideas of psychoanalysis all his life; in the corpus of his writings he foresaw difficulties and suggested solutions that continue to interest thoughtful psychoanalysts today. I instance only the amazing papers on technique dating from before World War I. To return to, and reexplore, Freud's work is a memorable experience. This does not justify the psychoanalysts' habit of citing Freud as the decisive authority. But it puts that habit into its context. What were they to do with such a father, the genius who seemed to have invented everything? It was as impossible to forget or deny him as it was to kill him. Any of these acts, though psychologically understandable, would have been signal ingratitude and sheer scientific stupidity. The only possible solution was to come to terms with him and acknowledge his stature. The historian watching this poignant spectacle and rethinking Freud's position must candidly acknowledge that in the history of the modern mind, improbable though this may seem, it is virtually unique.

3 | A CONTROVERTED THEORY

Freud's monumental stature is no guarantee for the validity of his system. Critics' charges of arrogance against the founder and servility against the disciples (two sides, they will say, of the same clipped coin) are grave enough. And other, potentially far more damaging, criticisms hover in the wings. For more than half a century, Freud's system of ideas has been denied the status of a science altogether. Psychoanalytic theory, its detractors have insisted, is merely a cozy club of mutually reinforcing notions, as corrupt and self-serving as a political machine riddled with nepotism; it amounts to self-validating propositions immune to testing, and proclaims its "discoveries" in language so loose, so imprecise and cloudy, that it fits all human experience whatever. And to account for everything with ease is to account for nothing at all. It is in this disparaging sense of that term, then, that psychoanalysis has been called a religion, a compendium of grandiose, poetic myths.

To judge from pronouncements of the 1970s and 1980s, this argument, though far from new, has lost none of its appeal. David Stannard, for one, assessed "major parts" of psychoanalytic theory to be "quasi-mystical." Significantly but not surprisingly, when these critics dispose of Freud, they draw their lethal metaphors from religion. "The history of Freudian psychoanalysis," Jacques Barzun writes, with suave but misplaced specificity, "has gone through at least three phases in eighty years, finally branching out into as many sects as there are theorists and practitioners."[21] These rebukes and dismissals go back to the days just after World War I, when the youthful Austrian philosopher Karl Popper—he was then all of seventeen—ranked psychoanalysis among the "pseudosciences" clamoring for attention in revolutionary Vienna. The collapse of the Austro-Hungarian Empire, and the upheavals that convulsed its capital, had generated a heady atmosphere of intellectual innovation. "The air," Popper would later recall, "was full of revolutionary slogans, ideas, and new and often wild theories;" in

---

21. Stannard, *Shrinking History: On Freud and the Failure of Psychohistory* (1980), 87; Barzun, *Clio and the Doctors,* 33.

that swirling effervescence, a cool, critical mind pressing for acceptable evidence—a mind like Popper's—was as necessary as it was rare. The most impressive intellectual construct under heated discussion was Einstein's theory of relativity, but three other theories, all in the human sciences, also stirred intense excitement: Marxism, Adler's "individual psychology," and psychoanalysis. Now these three, Popper noticed, were in no way short of proofs. On the contrary, for the initiate, they had remarkable *"explanatory power"*; psychoanalysis, with the others, appeared "to be able to explain practically everything that happened." Once one was a convert, one "saw confirming instances everywhere: the world was full of *verifications* of the theory." But this happy condition decisively disqualified its scientific pretensions. "Confirmations should count only if they are the result of *risky predictions*. A theory which is not refutable by any conceivable event is non-scientific. Irrefutability is not a virtue of a theory (as people often think) but a vice." Psychoanalysis, in short, violated the fundamental scientific principle of falsifiability. Popper was glad to concede—some of his admirers have not shown themselves quite so generous—that Freud had seen some important matters correctly; moreover, he thought, true sciences originate in precisely such myths as Freud's. But he nevertheless insisted, severely enough, that "the 'clinical observations' which analysts naively believe to confirm their theory cannot do this any more than the daily confirmations which astrologers find in their practice." In the very year, 1919, that Popper reached this fatal conclusion, Sidney Hook read Freud and formulated his own principle of falsifiability. He went about asking psychoanalysts on what evidence they would acquit a child from having an Oedipus complex. The evasive and indignant replies he collected convinced him that psychoanalysis is a "monistic dogma," and Freud among the "poetic mythologists."[22]

Considering the skepticism that Popper's criterion for dependable knowledge has increasingly aroused among philosophers of science, any consideration of them might rank as a work of supererogation. His test of falsifiability, at least in the stringent form that Popper gave it, has come to appear both logically dubious and psychologically unconvincing.[23] The sciences, and scientists, do not work quite like

---

22. Karl R. Popper, "Philosophy of Science: A Personal Report," in C. A. Mace, ed., *British Philosophy in Mid-Century* (1957), 156–58, a lecture of 1953 and also reprinted in *Conjectures and Refutations: The Growth of Scientific Knowledge* (1963; 2nd ed., 1965), 33–65; Sidney Hook, "Science and Mythology in Psychoanalysis," in Hook, ed., *Psychoanalysis, Scientific Method and Philosophy: A Symposium* (1959), 214–15, 223. Popper never changed his mind. "No description whatsoever," he wrote more recently, "of any logically possible human behavior can be given which would turn out to be incompatible with the psychoanalytic theories of Freud, or of Adler, or of Jung." *Objective Knowledge: An Evolutionary Approach* (1972), 38n. The most emphatic follower of Popper on this point (apart from David Stannard) is Sir Peter Medawar, who has had much fun with Freudian assertions; see his *The Art of the Soluble* (1967), 14–15, 62–64, and *Induction and Intuition in Scientific Thought* (1969), 6–7, 49–50.

23. The issue is a tricky one; witness this authoritative comment by Ernest Nagel, the philosopher of science, scarcely a devotee of psychoanalysis: "Dr. Medawar apparently endorses Popper's claim that while no scientific theory can be conclusively established, theories are definitively refutable. Now there undoubtedly is a formal asymmetry between verifying and disproving universal statements. But it is an overstatement to maintain that theories are therefore conclusively falsifiable. For while a single instance that contradicts a theory does refute it, whether an apparently recalcitrant fact really is incompatible with the theory can often be decided only in the light of various assumptions which are accepted (in the context of a given investigation at any rate) as sound." "What is True and False in Science," *Encounter*, XXIX (September 1967), 70. For telling refuta-

that. Solid positive evidence, whether gathered through responsible observation or in controlled experiments, remains the most eligible support that scientific claims can muster. If I touch on Popper at all in the following pages, in company with other charges against psychoanalysts' claims that they are engaged in doing a human science, I do so because historians in search of arguments against Freud continue to set great store by Popper's supposedly devastating argumentation. Stannard resorted to it in *Shrinking History,* with gusto and without hesitation. And in 1984, reviewing a psychoanalytic study of Ronald Reagan by the American historian Robert Dallek, the political journalist Robert Sherrill used it again: "What is wrong with Dallek's theory that Reagan's childhood has shaped the present Administration? Perhaps nothing. In any event, it's not the kind of theory that can be proved wrong."[24] By themselves, some of the other reproaches addressed to psychoanalytic procedures—taking advantage of the patient's suggestibility, refusing to submit analytic conclusions to independent audit—are serious enough. In combination with Popper's strictures, they have satisfied many critics of Freud as conclusive.

To be sure, psychoanalysts' assertions—laws of the mind, deep readings of novels or paintings, interpretations offered during the analytic session—must be open to rational criti-

tions of Popper's view in the context of psychoanalytic argumentation, see Clark Glymour, "Freud, Kepler, and the Clinical Evidence" (1974), in Richard Wollheim and James Hopkins, eds., *Philosophical Essays on Freud* (1982), 12–31, and B. R. Cosin, C. F. Freeman and N. H. Freeman, "Critical Empiricism Criticized: The Case of Freud," in ibid., 32–59.

24. Sherrill, "How Reagan Got That Way," a review of Dallek's *Ronald Reagan: The Politics of Symbolism* (1984), *The Atlantic,* CCLIII, 3 (March 1984), 130.

cism, to ratification and revision through further experimental inquiry, clinical experience, and logical reflection. Otherwise, if they smoothly fitted all conceivable situations and explained all conceivable conduct, they would elevate—or debase—the psychoanalyst into an inspired prophet. Popper would then be right: the analyst would be no better than the astrologer who finds welcome, wholly expected, reinforcement for his pseudoscientific beliefs with every horoscope he casts. The royal road to psychoanalytic knowledge would turn out to be a treacherous path to self-serving superstition. Fortunately, we need not decide between these conflicting views by mere guessing. The corpus of Freud's papers, the record of later analytic practice, and the experiments of the last decades, offer unmatched opportunities to assess the characterization of psychoanalysis as Popery in psychology.

The experimental evidence I have cited before serves to throw doubt on these dismissive appraisals. Beyond that, the psychoanalytic hour, as preserved in case histories and shorter vignettes, offers additional material to refute them. Indeed, Freud's reception of his analysands' communications, far from exemplifying, or evading, the logical problem of verification in psychoanalysis, exposes it explicitly and offers rich suggestions for its resolution. In the eyes of Popper or Stannard, a patient's responses can do nothing but confirm his analyst's conjectures. His Yes, it appears to them, means Yes, but so does his No—a convenient way with testimony that Freud once summed up, in his usual alertness to objections, with that pungent English saying, "Heads I win, tails you lose." The manner in which "our patients bring forward their ideas during the analytical work," so Freud describes this suspect procedure, "gives us occasion for some interesting observations. 'Now you will think I want to say something insulting, but I really have no such intention.' We recognize that this is the rejection, by means of projection, of an idea that has just swum to the surface. Or: 'You ask who this person in the dream can be. My mother it's *not*.' We correct: 'So it is his mother.' In interpretation we take the liberty of disregarding the negation and of selecting the pure content of the idea itself."[25]

This cavalier insensitivity to negative responses, Freud's critics have insisted, extends to all of the psychoanalyst's interpretative activity, securing his pronouncements the enviable stature of absolute irrefutability. If the analysand assents to his analyst's interpretation, this guarantees its accuracy; but if he rejects it, this guarantees its accuracy all the more. Freud confronted this charge squarely. "If the patient agrees with us," he wrote about interpretations in a late paper, paraphrasing some unnamed skeptic, "then it is right; but if he contradicts us, then that is only a sign of his resistance, which again puts us in the right. In this way we are always in the right against the helpless poor individual whom we are analyzing, no matter what attitude he may take to our imputations."[26] This states Popper's case with Freud's customary lucidity. Thoroughly schooled in the methods and the presuppositions of positivist science, Freud scarcely needed to be told that analysands' utterances offer logical as much as empirical obstacles to verification.

They were obstacles, however, that Freud was confident psychoanalysts could surmount. His rebuttal to the objections he himself stated is quite as striking for its calm man-

25. Freud, "Konstruktionen in der Analyse" (1937), *St.A., Ergänzungsband*, 395, "Constructions in Analysis," *S.E.,* XXIII, 257; "Die Verneinung" (1925), *St.A.,* III, 373, "Negation," *S.E.,* XIX, 235.
26. Freud, "Verneinung," *St.A., Ergänzungsband,* 395; "Negation," *S.E.,* XIX, 235.

ner as for its acute grasp of his critics' concerns. Freud's refusal to yield to prolix counterarguments, or to downright irritation, is a measure of his self-assurance. His position is, quite simply, that all these plausible disparagements drastically distort psychoanalytic procedure. Analysts, he notes, are as skeptical of affirmations as they are of negations; a patient's dissent from an interpretation is not always material that indirectly confirms the analyst's conjecture, but may be a perfectly valid and convincing disproof of that conjecture. In fact, as psychoanalysts writing on technique have repeatedly pointed out, the so-called "good patient" may actually be the most intractable of analysands. The patient who never misses a session, always arrives on time, offers free associations without stopping, floods the hour with meaningful dreams and, above all, unhesitatingly accepts all of his analyst's interpretations may be defending his neurosis far more tenaciously, because far more subtly, than an analysand whose resistance is out in the open.[27]

What the psychoanalyst, after all, is listening for is not ingratiating docility but the messages, whatever form they may take, that manage to evade his patient's unconscious censorship to rise to the level of utterance and, he hopes, ultimate intelligibility. They may take the form of a slip, an association, a gesture, a dream, a habitual lateness, a mistake in filling out the monthly check—or the manner of accepting, or rejecting, the analyst's interpretations. From fragmentary, normally involuntary revelations, the psycho-

---

27. The classic paper on this type, still worth reading, is Karl Abraham, "Über eine besondere Form des neurotischen Widerstandes gegen die psychoanalytische Methodik" (1919), Abraham, *Gesammelte Schriften in zwei Bänden,* ed. Johannes Cremerius (1971; ed. 1982), I, 276–83.

analyst gradually builds up his comprehension of his patient's neurosis and unriddles the dynamics of his character. Psychoanalysis, we know, is the science of suspicion; it lives by the conviction that things are not what they appear to be. But it recognizes that often, confusingly, things are also indeed what they appear to be. Like the historian, the psychoanalyst must grant that the life of the mind is exceedingly complicated.[28]

All this means, of course, that the psychoanalyst, precisely like the historian, must not rush to judgment. The psychoanalytic situation is at once a forum for candor and an arena of resistance. What with the analyst's rare interventions and his even tone, the analysand's supine posture and his confidential disclosures thrown into the void, it is designed to foster the confessional mode. At the same time, the patient's unwillingness to yield up his secrets and give up his malady interferes with his professed, most sincerely held intention to reveal, without hesitation and without editing, all that comes to his mind. The process of psychoanalytic detection, then, is a joint venture, but always very difficult and very devious. Both the analyst and, once he has been initiated into the mysteries, the patient, must read elusive clues, and must, for long months, remain tentative about their meaning. That is why, in his papers on technique, as in his case histories, Freud properly insisted that the psychoanalyst is anything but exempt from error, and, much of the time, far from certain. "At times," Freud wrote in a short paper directed against what he called "wild" psychoanalysis, "we

---

28. See especially, Marshall Edelson, "Is Testing Psychoanalytic Hypotheses in the Psychoanalytic Situation Really Impossible?" *PSC*, XXXVIII (1983), 61–109.

guess wrong, and we are never in a position to find out everything."[29] An analysand's inner life is so rich, and his capacity for disguise so highly developed, that the most incontrovertible diagnosis is bound to be incomplete and may turn out to be wrong in the end. The patient's assent to an interpretation may show that bedrock has been reached, or that he is withholding troubling information; his negation, that the psychoanalyst's trained surmise has touched a sensitive spot or that it is actually wide of the mark. An interpretation is a small experiment, offered in all good faith—teasing is not part of the psychoanalytic armamentarium—but not wasted, often suggestive, even when it fails. "Everything," to quote the psychoanalyst's favorite cliché, "is grist for the mill."

Among all the analyst's skills, that of listening is the most prized, and here, as so often, Freud has long stood as the model for his profession. Those very early case histories he published, with Breuer, in 1895—the finger exercises for psychoanalysis—already document his productive passivity. Frau Emma von N. and Fräulein Elisabeth von R., among others, taught him the art of listening. They instructed Freud in attending to the most long-winded, least coherent of his patients' tales, rationing his interventions, and, above all, gaining sufficient inner freedom to be astonished at what they were telling him.[30] Keeping this sense of astonishment alive is among the most prized technical acquisitions

---

29. "Über 'wilde' Psychoanalyse" (1910), *St.A., Ergänzungsband,* 140; " 'Wild' Psycho-Analysis," *S.E.,* XI, 226. This short paper is eminently worth reading as a prescription against irresponsible and hasty diagnoses. And see Freud, "Konstruktionen," *St.A., Ergänzungsband,* 400; "Constructions," *S.E.,* XXIII, 262.
30. The most revealing passages are in Freud and Breuer, *Studies on Hysteria* (1895), *S.E.,* II, 61, 63, 129, 138, 172, and Freud, "The Neuro-Psychoses of Defense" (1894) *S.E.,* III, 52–53.

of the psychoanalyst; it serves as an antidote to attacks of infallibility. After all, the psychoanalytic situation is not a sporting contest intended to win points, but a cooperative exploration devised to make discoveries. Negative utterance occupies an exposed, insecure place in psychoanalysis, but, his reputation to the contrary, the psychoanalyst can take No for an answer.

He can do so because, whatever the travesties may hold, psychoanalytic thought aspires, within the limits of a depth psychology, to the demanding conditions of dependable substantiation. This is true in the teeth of all the appearances. Consider Freud's important short paper on "Character and Anal Erotism" of 1908, in which he reported that he had found a number of his patients to be at once orderly, parsimonious, and obstinate. While this conjunction of traits varied in intensity and relative proportions, Freud thought it "incontestable that somehow all three belong together." He perceived this constellation to be evidence of a common childhood experience: an inordinately delayed capacity for anal continence coupled with an unusually keen pleasure in anal retention. "The constancy of this triad of properties in their character," Freud was led to suspect, "may be brought in relation with the wasting away of their anal eroticism": the adult's character was, then, the heir of certain infantile fixations, incompletely overcome. He concluded that the "permanent character traits" of these patients were "unchanged continuations of the original drives, sublimations, or reaction formations against them."[31]

This, I submit, is a stunning assertion, a red rag to the partisans of falsifiability. Freud's diagnosis of anal eroticism

---

31. Freud, "Charakter und Analerotik" (1908), *St.A.*, VII, 25, 26, 30; "Character and Anal Erotism," *S.E.*, IX, 169, 170, 175.

applies to patients exhibiting a triad of observable traits, to patients exhibiting the very opposites of these traits, *and* to patients exhibiting their imaginative transformation. Freud seems to be asserting nothing less than if the analysand is neat, stingy, and stubborn, this indicates an anal fixation; if he is slovenly, generous, and pliable, the same diagnosis holds; and if he is fortunate enough to enlist his character pattern in more dignified spheres of activity to become a deviser of railroad timetables, the president of a savings bank, or a persistent runner in the Boston Marathon, these adult adaptations only serve to document his inability to surmount remnants of his infantile resistances to toilet training and of his inordinate pleasure in withholding his feces. On this showing, the diagnosis of anal eroticism can never go wrong. And if it can never go wrong, it is meaningless.

In fact, even though the diagnosis covers much ground and is receptive to a cluster of symptoms, it makes claims neither to universality nor to infallibility. Freud did not propose the anal character to be everyone's lot; unlike some of his more enthusiastic disciples, mainly outside the psychoanalytic camp, he did not even accord it the dubious honor of being the organizing trait of modern capitalism. The constellation is, for him, one of several possible character structures. Many individuals sufficiently overcome their anal eroticism in the course of their more or less healthy development; others display only traces of it, which recede before the demands of other, more prominent traits. Character is a result, a many-layered thing, with a history of its own, far more various and less obvious than a definable disease like tuberculosis or hypertension. One may enter the career of banking, or become a fanatical runner, for numerous reasons. The logic of Freud's characterology, then, envisions many occasions when a diagnosis of anal eroticism would be overly simple or mistaken. "We are accustomed," he wrote in his famous case history of the "Wolf Man," "to trace back interest in money, *in so far as it is libidinous and not rational in its nature,* to excremental pleasure," and, he added, with that sturdy common sense that has so often been denied him, "We expect normal people to keep their relations to money wholly free from libidinal influences and to regulate them in accord with realistic considerations."[32] Freud was never one to deny the pressures of external realities.

Besides, for all its unsettling capacity to embrace contradictory manifestations, the diagnosis of "anal eroticism" is falsifiable. A conjecture early in the course of an analysis, a kind of covert prediction that this is the pattern the analysis will reveal, may turn out to be simply untenable in the light of further clinical exposure. The touchstone of this diagnosis, as of others, is the measure of emotions invested in the patient's motives, thoughts, and actions. "A normal train of thought," as Freud once put it, "however intense, can be managed in the end." It acquires diagnostic interest only if someone is unable "despite every conscious and willed effort of thought," to "dissolve or dispose of it." If Little Hans (to exploit one of Freud's best known cases) is affectionate with his father, this alone is not enough to awaken the psychoanalyst's suspicion that the little boy's demonstrative love conceals disavowed hatred. It is only "the excessive measure and compulsive character of the tenderness" which "reveals to us" that love and hate clamor

---

32. Freud, "Aus der Geschichte einer infantilen Neurose ("Der Wolfsmann")" (1918), *St.A.,* VIII, 188; "From the History of an Infantile Neurosis," *S.E.,* XVII, 72. Italics mine.

for preeminence in Hans's unconscious.[33] Where there is smoke, there is not always fire; there is room for passionate indignation or passionate admiration. The psychological clues that the whiff of smoke may in fact betoken a banked fire are unmeasured agitation, inappropriate irritability, fanaticism that the surrounding culture does not license. A vivid instance of what Freud called "the excessive measure and compulsive character" of an emotion is the defensive maneuver of reaction formation, in which an impermissible aggressive or erotic wish has been covered over by exaggerated conduct pointing in the opposite direction. It is harmless enough to feel compassion for animals, but the furious antivivisectionist arouses the suspicion that he once harbored the most cruel infantile sadism. The bellicose pacifist displays, with his single-mindedness, the traces of a very similar early past. Such stratagems are, for Freud, not a matter for reproach: without them, cleanliness or modesty, valuable cultural habits both, could hardly arise. But whether, or how strongly, such unconscious stratagems are at work depends on the vehemence and obsessiveness with which beliefs are held and convictions defended. Goethe earnestly forcing himself to ascend the spire of the cathedral at Strasbourg undertook that climb not to obtain a pleasurable glorious view of the town and the surrounding countryside, but, rather, to cure himself of vertigo, an aversion that weighed on him like a reproach to his manliness and lowered his self-esteem. Thus his overt act concealed what

---

33. Freud, "Bruchstück einer Hysterie-Analyse" (1905), *St.A.,* VI, 128, "Fragment of an Analysis of a Case of Hysteria," *S.E.,* VII, 54; "Hemmung, Symptom und Angst" (1926), *St.A.,* VI, 247, "Inhibitions, Symptoms, and Anxiety," *S.E.,* XX, 102. On the question of multiple causation in history and its analysis, see Peter Gay, *Art and Act: On Causation in History—Manet, Gropius, Mondrian* (1976).

the psychoanalyst Otto Fenichel has called the counter-phobic attitude, a hidden neurotic agenda that would pique a psychoanalyst's, or a psychoanalytically trained historian's, attention precisely because Goethe engaged in this piece of bravado with a passionate intensity incompatible with the uncomplicated search for enjoyment. The key to these matters, open to verification—and falsification—like more ordinary observations, is the presence or absence of irrational excitement, the quality and extent of emotional engagement, the size of the gap between the actual and the rationally necessary expenditure of energy. These are not very exact measures, and judgments will differ. But they are as precise and as telling as anything can be in a psychology working with mental materials that really matter.

The findings of psychoanalysis speak directly to the historian's passion for complexity. This is how people are: buffeted by conflicts, ambivalent in their emotions, intent on reducing tensions by defensive stratagems, and for the most part dimly, or perhaps not at all, aware why they feel and act as they do—why they sabotage their own careers, repeat disastrous affairs, love and hate with a passion that in their sober moments they find incomprehensible. Human feelings and actions are highly overdetermined, bound to have several causes and contain several meanings.[34] As discoverers and documentors of overdetermination, psychoanalysts and historians, each in their own manner, are allies in the struggle against reductionism, against naive and

---

34. Some of these causes and meanings are social: I am not arguing that the motives and acts of individuals alone determine the course of history, or that the conflicts the historian is principally interested in are precisely the conflicts with which the psychoanalyst deals every day. For the social bearing of Freudian propositions, see below, Chapter 5.

crude monocausal explanations. My analysis of the logic of psychoanalytic inquiry and my exploration of psychoanalytic styles of thinking aim at more, therefore, than the need to correct caricatures of Freudian theories and procedures. Nothing less is at stake than the psychoanalytic view of human experience and, with that, its relevance to the historian's work. It is precisely the apparent illogic of psychoanalytic observations, the prominence they assign to unresolved tensions, that have made Freud into the supreme geographer of the mind. Man, for Freud, is a creature of contradictions and concealments. Love and hate, the urge to destroy and the need to caress, coexist in everyone. The firmest postures and most doctrinaire convictions mask doubts and anxieties. Don Juan is afraid of impotence, perhaps of being a repressed homosexual. "Antitheses," as Freud put it, "are always closely connected with each other, and often paired off in such a manner that the *one thought is conscious too strongly; its counterpart, however, is repressed and unconscious.*"[35] It is this jostling of contrary, irreconcilable emotions that makes the Oedipus complex a paradigm of human existence. The little boy loves and hates his father at the same time; the little girl warmly embraces, in the evening, the mother she had wanted to see dead in the afternoon.

All these tributes to complexity, which defy neatness and seem to offend the principle of parsimony, are, I repeat, singularly appropriate to historians, who must deal with people—individuals and groups—in action every day of their working lives. It is inconvenient that persons should harbor conflicts, and it makes verification a strenuous and risky

---

35. Freud, "Bruchstück einer Hysterie-Analyse," *St.A.*, VI, 129; "Fragment of an Analysis of Hysteria," *S.E.*, VII, 55.

business, especially since the psychoanalyst insists that the most interesting battles occur in the unconscious and leave only fragmentary traces. Freud, the messenger of the bad news, has been treated as such messengers often are, as though he had invented it. But this is only to defend against having to cope with the subtle interweaving of motives and constraints, conscious wishes and unconscious obstructions, objective realities and mental representations that constitute the mental life of those whom it is the historian's business to understand.

Many historians have heard the music of the past but have transcribed it for penny whistle. To be sure, as I have said before, the most accomplished and most sensitive historical craftsmen have appreciated, and tried to capture, the overwhelming diversity of human conduct, man's encounters with power, technology, nature—and himself. At their best they have been elegant, moving, penetrating. But history calls for more searching explorations even than theirs. What psychoanalysis can bring to the assessment of past experience is a set of discoveries and a method—fallible, incompletely tested, difficult to apply yet, I am persuaded, the best we now have—to register the broken surfaces and sound the unplumbed depths of human nature.

3

Human Nature in History

1 | AGAINST THE HISTORICISTS

Discovering Sigmund Freud toward the end of his life, William James thought him "a man obsessed," with "fixed ideas," an incomprehensible dream theory, dangerous notions about symbolism, and bigoted incomprehension of religion. But, in his characteristic open-minded way, James wished him well. "I hope that Freud and his pupils will push their ideas to their utmost limits," he wrote late in 1909, "so that we may learn what they are. They can't fail to throw light on human nature."[1]

Historians have been, by and large, less generous. They would agree that Freud was a man obsessed, but they have doubted that psychoanalysis could throw much light on human nature. To the degree that they see any plausibility in

---

1. William James to Theodore Flournoy, September 28, 1909, Henry James, ed., *The Letters of William James,* 2 vols. (1920), II, 327–28.

it at all, historians have assigned the Freudian dispensation a confined, carefully fenced-off domain of validity. Psychoanalysis, born and raised in Vienna, has seemed to them quintessentially Viennese, quite irrelevant outside its defined and highly constricted sphere, its theories valid (if they are valid at all) for the archetypal psychoneurotic patient, the bored, affluent, repressed Jewish Viennese *Hausfrau,* and for her alone—except perhaps for her American sister. "Freud," as Henri Ellenberger, the historian of depth psychology, has flatly put it, "was Viennese to his fingertips." Other historians have spun out the implications of this perception. The "time-bound quality" of Freud's "world of ideas," the German social historian Hans-Ulrich Wehler has complained, has often been "underestimated." Freud's "scientific discourse," Wehler believes, drew, after all, on "highly specific problems of the Austrian *fin-de-siècle* bourgeoisie." And for David Hackett Fischer, the first of "five substantial failings" in Freud's theory is that "it is in its aboriginal condition narrowly culture-bound." Lawrence Stone is only apparently less severe; he broadens Freud's grasp beyond Vienna to middle-class, nineteenth-century Europe only to qualify his grudging concession almost out of existence: "Nothing could be more false," he argues, "than that the sexual experiences and responses of middle-class Europeans in the late nineteenth century were typical of those of all mankind in the past, or even of Europeans in the previous three centuries, or even of all classes in late Victorian society."[2] For these historians—and they

---

2. Henri F. Ellenberger, *The Discovery of the Unconscious: The History and Evolution of Dynamic Psychiatry* (1970), 464–65; Hans-Ulrich Wehler, "Geschichtswissenschaft und 'Psychohistorie,'" *Innsbrucker Historische Studien,* I (1978), 201–13; David Hackett Fischer, *Historians' Fallacies: Toward a Logic of Historical Thought* (1970),

speak for a consensus—Freud presides over a shrunken territory.

There is no reason to connive in the liquidation of the Freudian empire. Avidly as historians have embraced and propagated the legend of the Viennese Jewess as the characteristic analysand, formidable though its tenacity, its relation to the true state of affairs remains tenuous. Necessarily Freud, especially in the first years of his practice, fed his thinking and theorizing with the disclosures of the patients who came to consult him. He could enlarge his evidential base only as his reputation spread and he acquired followers, collecting case material they would contribute to the pool of psychoanalytic knowledge. But from

189; Lawrence Stone, *The Family, Sex and Marriage in England 1500–1800* (1977), 15–16. In the polemical history of his movement, in a sarcastic passage, Freud himself confronted this charge: "We have all heard about the interesting attempt to explain the emergence of psychoanalysis out of the Viennese milieu. Janet, as late as 1913, did not scruple to use it, though he is surely proud of being a Parisian, and Paris can scarcely claim to be a city more severe in its morals than Vienna. According to his *aperçu*, psychoanalysis, notably its assertion that neuroses are to be traced back to disturbances in sexual life, could only have originated in a city like Vienna, in an atmosphere of sensuality and immorality foreign to other cities, and simply represents the reflection, so to speak the projection into theory, of these special Viennese conditions. Now, I am really no local patriot, but this theory has always seemed quite exceptionally nonsensical to me, so nonsensical that I have sometimes been inclined to assume that the reproach of being Viennese is only a euphemistic substitute for another, which one does not like to put forward publicly. If the premises were the opposite, then one might give it a hearing. . . . The Viennese are neither more abstinent nor more nervous than others living in large cities. Sexual relations are a little less embarrassed, prudery is less marked than in the cities of the West and North so proud of their chastity." "Zur Geschichte der psychoanalytischen Bewegung" (1914), *Gesammelte Werke*, X, 80–81; "On the History of the Psycho-Analytic Movement," *S.E.*, XIV, 39–40.

the outset, as I have noted, Freud had analysands more diverse than the legend allows for. Later, the patients he treated, or learned about, came to represent a fair cross section of the middle and upper strata of Western civilization: the mature no less than the young, men as well as women, gentiles as much as Jews, English laymen and American physicians. Unfortunately, we have nothing like an exhaustive catalogue of Freud's analytical patients, but his most-quoted cases stake out wide horizons of mental distress: little Hans was a five-year-old boy, the Wolf Man a Russian aristocrat, Schreber a German judge, H.D. an American poet, Marie Bonaparte a French princess, Dora the sister of a friend, and Sigmund Freud—possibly his most instructive patient—not bored, not affluent, not a woman, and not very Jewish. After World War I, as Hanns Sachs has reported, Freud conducted more analyses in English than in German.[3]

Fragmentary as our information about Freud's practice may be, we know enough to say that he could draw on a sizable repertory for his ideas. This alone, of course, does not safely, or by itself, guarantee the applicability of the psychoanalytic dispensation across cultures and ages. But Freud was confident that he could reasonably make inferences from his clinical experience about human beings remote in time and place, and that for two reasons: neurotics, as he came to see, are like normal people in most respects—

---

3. Peter Gay, "Sigmund Freud: A German and his Discontents," *Freud, Jews and Other Germans: Masters and Victims in Modernist Culture* (1978), 29. Even if Freud's evidence had been drawn from as narrow a sample as his detractors like to assert, the truth of his claims would remain unaffected, though it would certainly be less plausible. In fact, as it happens, the variety of his cases was impressive. The impossibility of establishing a full census of Freud's cases is, of course, due to the archival restrictions facing researchers.

so much like them, indeed, that the very notion of normality must be put in doubt. They exaggerate, distort, and tendentiously select traits that every human possesses, thus conveniently dramatizing their operations. Moreover, these traits, to Freud's mind, are special cases, or derivatives, of fairly stable universal dispositions that could be gathered up under that much used, much abused rubric, human nature.

Obviously, a psychology valid just for some Viennese around the turn of this century would be meaningful only for the few specialists who happen to be writing histories of their city around 1900. A psychology claiming to shed light on human nature would have relevance to the entire historical profession. But the idea of human nature is, for historians, by no means a comfortable one. They have long found it necessary to ponder the question of how they may define it; whether, in fact, there is such a thing at all. The issue may seem abstract, but it has been thoroughly domesticated in the historical profession. I said at the beginning that historians operate with a theory of human nature, but much of the operation is secret—even to them. Indeed, the question whether human nature exists was one that the historicist school, Ranke and his followers, asked throughout the nineteenth century, less as an innocent interrogation than as an act of polemical aggression against the philosophes, its eighteenth-century predecessors. In their historical writings, so the Rankeans argued, the philosophes had retailed that supreme fiction they called human nature, a fixed set of passions and motives they professed to have observed at work across all ages and all civilizations. This invention, the historicists darkly intimated, had done the writing of history a signal disservice by frustrating any truly *historical* perception of the past. Those once famous volumes by Gibbon and Voltaire and Hume struck them as two-dimensional, lacking at once the necessary distance from, and the equally necessary identification with, their human materials. *The Decline and Fall of the Roman Empire,* or *Le siècle de Louis XIV,* or the *History of England* were to their mind not histories at all but (as we might say today) exercises in retrospective sociology.

This denunciation of Enlightenment historians proved to be more than just a nineteenth-century platform for a new departure in an old discipline. It was a necessary act of intellectual parricide, but it has survived, as critique and postulate, into our century. R. G. Collingwood in England, Benedetto Croce in Italy, Ortega y Gasset in Spain, Lucien Febvre in France have all spread the same good news: Man (to recall Ortega) has no nature; what he has is history. "I know that man's essential nature is unchanging through time and space," wrote Lucien Febvre sarcastically in 1925, with that vehemence so characteristic of him, "I know that old tune. But that is an assumption, and I might add, a worthless assumption for a historian. For him, as for the geographer . . . man does not exist, only men."[4] The classic history of this posture, Friedrich Meinecke's *Entstehung des Historismus,* published in 1936, was anything but a detached, neutral account; it was a categorical repudiation of the very idea of human nature which, Meinecke was certain, had long obstructed historical thinking.

The two dynamic principles that Meinecke celebrated in the historicist vision and thought fatally absent from all histories operating with a theory of human nature, were individuality and development. Meinecke granted "a kernel

---

4. Lucien Febvre, *Life in Renaissance France,* ed. and tr. Marian Rothstein (1977), 2.

of truth" to what he called the philosophes' "generalizing view of historical-human forces." But he insisted that this view "failed to comprehend the deep transformations and the multiplicity of forms which the mental and spiritual life of individuals and communities undergo for all the persistence of basic human qualities." To exhibit the Enlightenment's anti-historical bias in all its dismal flatness, Meinecke reached for two exhibits from David Hume: "Mankind are so much the same, in all times and places, that history informs us of nothing new or strange in this particular." And again: "The Rhine flows north, the Rhone south; yet both spring from the *same* mountain, and are also actuated, in their opposite directions, by the *same* principle of gravity. The different inclinations of the ground, on which they run, cause all the difference of their courses." This mentality had to be overcome before the discipline of history could really establish itself. And it *was* overcome, naturally by German thinkers, to reach "the highest stage in the understanding of human affairs that has yet been reached."[5]

In essence, the historicist dispensation is a commentary on Ranke's celebrated dictum: Every epoch is immediate to God.[6] What Ranke meant to say was that the historian must treat each event and each age as induplicable and must allow each its own value, judging it not from the superior vantage point of hindsight, but as it would have judged itself. Ironically, Meinecke himself, in his pride, turned his back on this large-minded injunction at critical moments. He looks down on the philosophes, almost literally, from the "highest stage of understanding" which he rather com-

---

5. Friedrich Meinecke, *Die Entstehung des Historismus*, 2 vols. continuously paginated (1936), 2–3, 203–3,4.
6. Peter Gay, *Style in History* (1974), ch. 2.

placently confesses to have reached: *their* epoch was not so close to God, after all, as his own. Certainly Meinecke's plea for historicism unwittingly documents some of its unfulfilled promises, for, curiously enough, while the historicists elevated the junction of detachment and empathy into their supreme principle, they freely offended against it. In contrast, the philosophes, though men with a mission, sometimes realized just that principle. Voltaire urged that "We must be on guard against the habit of judging everything by our customs." Gibbon thought that the "philosophic spirit," by which he meant the historical spirit, could be cultivated by the "habit of becoming in turn Greek, Roman, the disciple of Zeno or Epicurus." And David Hume, the very philosopher who had insisted on linking Rhine and Rhone, asked, "Would you try a Greek or Roman by the common law of England?" and replied, "Hear him defend himself by his own maxims; and then pronounce."[7] A reading of the philosophes' historical writings will show that such proclamations were not merely pious talk or easy good intentions.

It cannot be my purpose to promote the reputation of historians working in the eighteenth century at the expense of those working in the nineteenth. The historicists, for all their ingratitude, all their self-satisfaction, made substantial professional advances in historical method and historical practice over the method and the practice of the Enlightenment. Their passion for the archives was one that the philosophes did not share. The men of the Enlightenment reveled in the classical and instructive drama that, for them, constituted the past, and hence failed to do justice to the full

---

7. See Peter Gay, *The Enlightenment: An Interpretation,* vol. II, *The Science of Freedom* (1969), 380–85.

variety of the human experience. Voltaire, said Stendhal, "lacked *the comprehensive soul,* a quality necessary in any poet. This is why all his characters resemble one another."[8] He was speaking of Voltaire's tragedies; he could have voiced the same reproach against Voltaire's histories. But the historian's professional commitment to change need not blind him to the pervasiveness of structure—which is, in any event, motion at a deliberate pace—any more than his cult of individuality can eliminate the need to draw comparisons or to make generalizations. The historian who equates his craft with story-telling is as one-sided a practitioner as the historian impatient with what he calls *l'histoire événementielle.* It sounds almost banal to say it, but it needs saying once again: the agitated currents of change cover, sometimes to invisibility, the slow-moving depths of persistent human wishes, gratifications, and frustrations. "The historical sense," as T. S. Eliot once aptly put it, is "a sense of the timeless as well as the temporal."[9] Even Meinecke, the historicists' high priest of development and uniqueness, felt after all compelled to acknowledge something of the sort in his rather left-handed concessions to "a kernel of truth" in the Enlightenment's view of the past, and to a certain "persistence" in "basic human qualities." There is poetic justice in the fact that Goethe, whom the historicists took as their patron saint, at times lent eloquent support to the antihistoricist posture. In the Classical Walpurgis-night in *Faust,* he has Mephistopheles complain that he had come to the nocturnal revels thinking to find strangers only to encounter, alas, close relatives. It was, he said, an old

---

8. Geoffrey Strickland, *Stendhal: The Education of a Novelist* (1974), 28.
9. Eliot, "Tradition and the Individual Talent" (1919), *Selected Essays* (1932), 14.

story from the Harz Mountains in Germany to distant Greece—nothing but cousins:

> *Hier dacht ich lauter Unbekannte*
> *Und finde leider Nahverwandte;*
> *Es ist ein altes Buch zu blättern:*
> *Von Harz bis Hellas immer Vettern!*

Goethe's spokesman here, to be sure, is a devil, jaded, world-weary, sarcastic.[10] But his observation, prompted by a seductive parade of erotic vampires and female demons, suggests a general truth of which students of humanity from Goethe to Freud have been very much aware: the exigent, insatiable manifestations of sexual fantasies, for all their individual forms, make a family of desire. Historicists were inclined to make light of such fundamental resemblances.

The most emphatic among sociological historians will certainly not deny the reality of movement; nor will the most devout of Ranke's disciples deny the reality of persistence: the tired cliché, "continuity and change," usually pressed into service as a catch-all title for a collection of miscellaneous essays, attests to that. There is room in the historical profession both for those who, like Namier or Braudel, analyze structures and for the majority, who narrate sequences. Most historians cannot help doing both. Clearly, the issue is a matter of emphasis. But emphases make a difference. After all, the historian who openly admits to be working with the idea of human nature conjures up among most of his colleagues the unpalatable vision of anemic classifications, and of static, monotonous reiterations that violate man's experience of the past as diversified,

---

10. Goethe, *Faust, Der Tragödie Zweiter Teil*, Act II, lines 7740–43.

unfolding and unfinished. But in fact human nature has its own history; change is a set of subtle variations that the world plays on persistent, often elusive themes.

If it is change, then, that makes history possible, it is persistence that is the foundation of historical understanding. Like the game of chess, human nature constructs dramatic and inexhaustible variety from a few elements and a handful of rules. Yet discriminations must be made and are possible. David Hume's assertion that "history informs us of nothing new or strange" in human passions and conduct seems unduly pessimistic: for the experienced practitioner—as for the seasoned psychoanalyst—life histories retain their capacity to generate the new and the strange. But they move along familiar paths, occur at more or less anticipated moments. That is why history—like psychoanalysis—is partly predictable yet invariably fascinating. Human nature make much of little.

2 | DRIVES AND THEIR VICISSITUDES

The historian's and the psychoanalyst's experiences with their human materials converge and overlap; yet the psychoanalyst's perception of human nature does not appear obviously useful to the historian's concerns. Its relevance must, as it were, be teased out. The ground to which psychoanalytic theory appeals to establish the continuity of experience is the claim that all humans share some inescapable universal preconditions. Man enters life the most unfinished of animals, pathetically in need of nourishment and protection by others; he is born with few instinctual drives and those plastic and, for all their tenacity, educable for good or ill. The unconscious, wrote Freud in his great paper of 1915 on the subject, "is alive, capable of development." Learning does the work of the precisely programmed instincts that are the lot of other sentient beings—that is why man is preeminently the cultural animal. Much of the information that other animals carry in their genes, the human child absorbs from its environment. As we all know, ways of feeding and of training differ drastically from culture to culture, region to region, class to class and even, though less markedly, from family to family. But the need for years of care and tuition is common to all humans. What Freud called man's "long childlike helplessness and dependence"[11] is an inescapable biological reality with variable, though foreseeable, psychological consequences. It makes the modern historian, the ancient Egyptian, the Kwakiutl Indian, to return to Goethe's word, into cousins.

But, though far freer than other animals in the adaptations he may construct and defenses he may develop, man is not wholly without instinctual drives and these, malleable as they are, underscore the family resemblances that his prolonged tutelage had imposed on him in the first place. Among these drives, sexuality and aggression occupy center stage for the psychoanalyst. And these two drives, matured, combined, disguised, serve as the fuel for human action. They make history.

It would be idle to claim that Freud's instinct theory is wholly free from obscurity. Freud himself was never satisfied with it, and attributed some of its difficulties to the precarious position that instinctual drives occupied in contemporary biology and psychology. The region of the instincts, he wrote in 1932, is one "in which we are labo-

---

11. Freud, "Das Unbewusste" (1915), *St.A.*, III, 149, "The Unconscious," *S.E.*, XIV, 190; *Das Ich und das Es* (1923), *St.A.*, III, 302, *The Ego and the Id*, *S.E.*, XIX, 35. For more on development, see below, pp. 156–62.

riously struggling for insights and for our bearings"; for him the theory of the instincts was "our mythology." Drives, he wrote, "are mythical entities, splendid in their indefiniteness."[12] He wrote this a decade after he had unveiled his structural theory, in which he significantly revised his view of the drives and gave his final dualism so fateful a form that many psychoanalysts would refuse to follow him all the way. In the pioneering years, Freud had postulated two sets of instincts—sexual and egoistic—the one serving the perpetuation of the human race, the other that of the individual. Then, in the early 1920s, he confronted the mighty constructive energies of Eros with the equally mighty energies of destruction, the death instinct. But by no means all the confusion has been of his own making. I have already quoted Lawrence Stone noting, in scathing criticism of Freud's presumed rigidity, that "the sexual drive is not uniform," but "varies enormously from individual to individual." Actually Freud himself said it better.

He said it, in fact, often and clearly.[13] Freud recognized that biological endowment varies from infant to infant: its inborn portions of drive strength or sensitivity to stimulation, or its predisposition to anxiety, are particular to each. It is not a problem for psychoanalytic theory that there are

---

12. Freud, *Neue Folge der Vorlesungen zur Einführung in die Psychoanalyse* (1933), *St.A.,* I, 529; *New Introductory Lectures on Psycho-Analysis, S.E.,* XXII, 95.

13. "We must make clear to ourselves that every human being has acquired a certain specific way of his own [*eine bestimmte Eigenart*] of conducting his erotic life through the combined working of innate disposition and influences working on him during his years of childhood." "Zur Dynamik der Übertragung" (1912), *St.A., Ergänzungsband,* 159 (and see the long footnote to the same page); "The Dynamics of Transference," *S.E.,* XII, 99 (and 99n).

placid babies and active babies: child analysts have made much of that. Moreover, psychoanalysts consider the drives to be not simple, single urges manifesting a simple, single need, but clusters, made up of frequently discordant wishes striving for satisfaction. Situated on the border line "between the mental and the somatic," the instinctual drives differ in their source, their pressure, their aim and, most of all, their objects. In fact, the object, Freud emphatically argues, "is the most variable thing about a drive; it is not in its origin annexed to it, but only assigned to it as it proves suited to make satisfaction possible." In the course of its life history, "it may be changed at will, frequently."[14] Thus the assignment of erotic objects, like their vicissitudes—the love of one's self or one's mother, one's classmate or one's wife— is in large measure the work of culture translated into mental representations in the individual. What I said earlier about human nature in general applies to the drives in particular, and for the same reason: they have their history.

At this point the psychoanalyst's theory, and the historian's experience, of human nature can profitably meet. The psychoanalytic view of the drives accounts for both uniformity and variety; the proposition that drives are a varied cluster united in a family of impulsions toward satisfaction offers good reasons why the historian may recognize and analyze human motives among remote individuals and societies without reducing them to pale copies of his own cultural traits. The group of drives known collectively as aggression—the rather less portentous term into which most psychoanalysts have translated Freud's death instinct—dis-

14. Freud, "Triebe und Triebschicksale" (1915), *St.A.*, III, 86; "Instincts and their Vicissitudes," *S.E.*, XIV, 122.

plays an even wider repertory of possible fields for action than the sexual drive without wholly concealing its common origin.

The same mixture of plasticity and similarity character-izes the mechanisms of defense. It is a constant of human life—another common experience articulated in an astonish-ing but not unlimited variety of ways—that the child will see some at least of its wishes as threats to its good opinion of itself, to its supplies of love and approbation from others, and, in the most radical instances, to its very survival. The psychoanalyst reflecting on the mind in action sees conflicts evaded, appeased, never wholly mastered, and is bound to treat life as a tragicomedy of unslaked desire and perilous consummations, anxious warnings and troubling defensive restraints. Human nature at work seems to invite, in fact impose, unstable compromises that repeatedly establish and almost as frequently escape fragile accommodations among the warring factions of the mind. "If there were no such thing as human nature (a doctrine which the late Professor Collingwood came very near to holding)," the English his-torian Richard Pares once wrote in a thoughtful essay on the historian's business, "no general laws could safely be laid down, nothing could be predicted, nothing even could be detected, in history. Yet human nature itself varies in time, as a result of the historical process, and failure to treat it as doing so renders history unlifelike."[15] Variety from uni-formity, uniformity behind variety—there is nothing in Pares's statement to which a psychoanalyst could take ex-ception.

---

15. Pares, "The Historian's Business" (1953), in *The Historian's Business and Other Essays,* ed. R. A. and Elizabeth Humphreys (1961), 7.

The most telling (and most problematic) instance of human nature in action is probably the Oedipus complex.[16] With pardonable satisfaction, Freud claimed pride of discovery, for it exhibits with exceptional force the vicissitudes of the drives, the purposeful activity of the defenses, and the drama of development. Later psychoanalysts have cherished this triangle no less. That incredulity Sidney Hook encountered when he asked psychoanalysts to imagine a child without it, and which so irritated him, is highly instructive: the Oedipus complex stands, in their minds, as *the* critical developmental experience, one that makes man human. Yet historians have done little but ridicule it. To A. J. P. Taylor, for one, wondering out loud, "How did anyone ever manage to take Freud seriously?" the Oedipus complex was just one of Sigmund Freud's "bright," by which he meant ridiculous, ideas.[17]

Yet, while it was a bright idea, it was anything but ridiculous. It was only very complicated. Freud saw no single dominant version of the complex even among his contemporaries or his fellow-Austrians; and he thought, as we know,

16. In a persuasive paper, "The Waning of the Oedipus Complex" (1979), the eminent psychoanalyst Hans W. Loewald has argued that while there has been a certain "decline of psychoanalytic interest in the oedipal phase and oedipal conflicts" in favor of "early stages of self-object differentiation, on separation-individuation, on the primitive origins of object relations," an "increased understanding of pre-oedipal issues, far from devaluating oedipal ones, may in the end help to gain deeper insight into them. "Loewald, *Papers on Psychoanalysis* (1980), 384–404. The quoted passage is on 386–87. This cautious formulation is congruent with my own view (see above, p. x) that the object relations school remains firmly within the Freudian ambiance.

17. Review of William Bullitt and Sigmund Freud, *Thomas Woodrow Wilson: A Psychological Study* (1967), in *The New Statesman and Nation,* May 12, 1967, 653–54.

that the way it was resolved or repressed depended heavily on "the influence of authority, religious teaching, education, reading." Extended across times and cultures, its twists and turns become almost dizzying in their ingenuity. In short, the oedipal triangle that Diderot bluntly described in *Le neveu de Rameau* (a description Freud quoted with delight more than once) may be the most familiar, but is also its most primitive form: "If the little savage"—this is Diderot's picturesque way of referring to the son of Rameau's nephew—"were left to himself, preserving all his foolishness and adding to the small sense of a child in the cradle the violent passions of a man of thirty, he would strangle his father and lie with his mother."[18] This is the Oedipus complex people have heard of: in the course of his psychosexual development, the little boy discovers passionate desires for his mother and an equally passionate sense of rivalry with his father. The consequences of this eruption in his young life are momentous, both at the time and for the years ahead. The boy's superego—his conscience and the panoply of his guilt feelings—is the heir of the Oedipus complex; frightened by the vehemence of his desires and threatened by fantasies (and perhaps the reality) of adult retaliation, he retreats from his quest for his mother, internalizes his father's anger and prohibitions, and, as he grows up—if he is lucky—seeks out more suitable, which is to say, nonincestuous, objects to gratify his erotic needs.

Most nonanalysts defining the Oedipus complex, whether they accept it as a sober fact or reject it as an extravagant fiction, stop here. For the professional Freudian, though,

---

18. See, for the passage from Diderot, Freud, *Introductory Lectures on Psycho-Analysis* (1916–17), *S.E.,* XVI, 338; "The Expert Opinion in the Halsmann Case" (1931), *S.E.,* XXI, 251; *An Outline of Psycho-Analysis* (1940), *S.E.,* XXIII, 192.

this version of the complex is only the beginning. In pursuing and clarifying this portentous domestic encounter, Freud expanded and complicated its operations in all directions. He did not reserve it for boys: girls, too, traverse the oedipal phase, adoring their fathers and disliking their mothers. Nor did he doubt that different classes and cultures experienced it differently. He explicitly noted that the "simple Oedipus complex" is "by no means the most frequent."[19] For him, the complex is a powerful illustration of man's fundamental and ineradicable ambivalence—the often unresolvable coexistence of love and hatred. The child does not just hate its sexual rival, but loves that rival at the same time; this is the struggle, so hard for a youngster to manage, that lends the oedipal phase its poignancy. The Oedipus complex has been finely called a school for love;[20] it may be called, with equal pertinence, a school for hatred. Both formulations appropriately stress its pedagogic function: the Oedipus complex is at best a *school,* a developmental phase that serves not merely to generate neurosis, but also to tame emotions and channel them in legitimate forms. It at once exposes the child to its passions and teaches it to cope with them. And it ramifies through the range of mental life from the childhood years on, leaving its traces in ambition and resignation, and in culture's most energetically defended taboos.

It is no easy thing to feel the presence of ill-assorted, vehement erotic and destructive wishes. Their energy, as well as their targets, expose the child to the difficulties of the human lot at a very early point in its young life, when it

---

19. Freud, *Das Ich und das Es, St.A.,* III, 300; *The Ego and the Id, S.E.,* XIX, 33.
20. I owe this felicitous formulation to Dr. George Mahl (personal communication, 1977).

is ill-prepared for such onslaughts. All it senses, in a torrent of urgent and conflicting feelings, is the probability—the very desirability—of defeat. For it is bound to be dimly aware that if its wishes were gratified, the consequences would be catastrophic; if they were detected, the punishment would be fearful; if they were frustrated—the most likely outcome—the disappointment would be acute. To be sure, the child for the most part only rehearses its violent crimes of passion in its mind or in occasional pathetic verbal or physical gestures; too small and too weak, it cannot translate inchoate emotions into overt action. But that does not lessen the risks; for the child, wishing and doing are the same, and committing murder or incest in thought is as unforgivable as committing them in the parental bed. The oedipal phase may be a school, but it is a hard school, and its lessons may never be wholly or felicitously absorbed.

One of the most prominent yet least regarded aspects of the Oedipus complex is its continuous traffic with culture: from the years of his first discoveries onward, Freud underscored its variability with his pregnant comparison of its operation in *Oedipus Rex* and *Hamlet:* "the changed treatment of the same material" in these two plays, he noted before 1900, "reveals the whole difference in the mental life of these two widely separated cultural epochs: the secular advance of repression in the emotional life of mankind." While in *Oedipus Rex* "the child's fundamental wish-fantasy is brought out into daylight and realized as in a dream," in "*Hamlet* it remains repressed; and we learn of its existence only—much as we would with a neurosis—from the inhibiting operations that stem from it."[21] Freud's read-

21. Freud, *Die Traumdeutung* (1900), *St.A.,* II, 268–69; *The Interpretation of Dreams, S.E.,* IV, 264.

ing of Sophocles and Shakespeare remains in dispute.[22] But the point at issue here is that Freud, though insisting on the persistence and preeminence of the Oedipus complex throughout human experience, never slighted its possible range of expression or its social dimensions. Thus this very complex, belying its reputations as a fixed point on a rigid, unvarying itinerary that all humans in all ages must traverse, testifies to Freud's essentially historical orientation.

This rapid sketch of one among Freud's most controversial insights should correct familiar misreadings. It should dispose once and for all of the popular myth that it is late nineteenth-century Vienna incarnate. But the record of historians' responses offers little reason for optimism. Considering the prominence that Freud assigned to the Oedipus complex, it is surely not astonishing that it has generated vehement debate in addition to some sophisticated research. Nor is it really so astonishing that the public controversy has normally been conducted with sovereign disregard of the technical literature. I have already quoted A. J. P. Taylor. Again, the popular American historian Page Smith has instanced precisely the Oedipus complex as "one important reason that psychoanalytic theory is basically antithetical to history." His objection, as I understand it, appears to be not that the "father-son conflict" has been disproved but that it is depressing. "If taken seriously," he writes, the Oedipus complex "would destroy history," for "written history is, in essence, the effort to pass on to the sons the wisdom of the fathers, and thus to preserve, rather than destroy, the continuity between generations." Hence Freud

---

22. See E. R. Dodds, "The Misunderstanding of 'Oedipus Rex'" (1966), in *The Ancient Concept of Progress and Other Essays on Greek Literature and Belief* (1973), 64–77.

offers nothing more than "an endless, agonizing process of rejection." Actually the oedipal experience does exactly what Smith seems to desire: it generates the incest taboo and the pangs of conscience in the child and thus passes on to the sons the wisdom of the fathers. David Hackett Fischer has a somewhat more creditable objection; in his raids on the fallacies of other historians, he finds fault with the English anthropologist Geoffrey Gorer for seeing "the historical relationship between Anglo-America and Europe in terms of a national Oedipus complex," and he rejects as exceedingly odd the political family tensions that Gorer had unearthed.[23] He has a point, but such reductionism violates the spirit, not merely of history but of psycho-analysis.

Reductionism is, without doubt, one of the besetting temptations of psychohistory, and I shall take the opportunity to comment on it later.[24] Here I only want to note that the predominating evidence from experimental psychology, sociology, and anthropology strongly suggests, though it does not conclusively prove, a good fit between Freud's theory and human experience—everywhere. The oedipal triangle has made its appearance in all recorded cultures, even in the Trobriand Islands, that splendid anthropologists' laboratory in the South Pacific that has generated so much controversy among social scientists, including the reach of the ambivalent domestic drama that Freud first discovered within himself.[25] The Oedipus complex appears to be the

---

23. Smith, *The Historian and History* (1964), 130–31; Fischer, *Historians' Fallacies*, 192.

24. See below, pp. 184–86.

25. David Stannard has made much of papers that seem to throw doubt on, and skeptically treats one that supports, the Oedipus complex. He does not omit (and is pleased to cite) Bronislaw Malinow-

lot of humans everywhere, and it has left its deposits both in expected and in exotic places: in politics and religion, education and literature, even in the market place. The impact of illicit love and intimate hate on the incest taboo has been a prominent theme in ancient myths and modern novels, and testifies to the vitality of the child's half-buried passions for its parents in later life and in a wider world. The familial metaphors writers have been employing for centuries to characterize the nature of governmental authority, the relations of God to man, the responsibility of factory owners for "their" employees, and a host of other entanglements of power, love, and cruelty, are more than literary tropes. The debate over the ubiquity and centrality of the Oedipus complex is thus, for the historian, anything but academic. Metaphors may become debased linguistic tokens, worn smooth with the passage of time and cheapened by frequent devaluations of the rhetorical currency. But even then, perhaps especially then, they are splendid clues to a pervasive aspect of human nature at work.

3 | ANATOMY OF SELF-INTEREST

One powerful reason, I am convinced, why historians have resisted the lure of the psychoanalytic version of human na-

---

ski's much debated critique of this nuclear Freudian complex among the Trobriand islanders. *Shrinking History: On Freud and the Failure of Psychohistory* (1980), 85–93. But note the brilliant essay by Melford E. Spiro, *Oedipus in the Trobriands* (1982), which demonstrates conclusively that Malinowski badly misread his materials, and that these very materials offer strong grounds for attributing an Oedipus complex to the Trobriand islanders. The debate continues, but Freud's discovery retains its authority—and its suggestiveness for the historian.

ture is their commitment to the dominance of self-interest in human affairs. Self-interest conjures up none of the heavy artillery of the Oedipus complex, unconscious desires, concealed conflicts, and the rest of the Freudian arsenal; none of it seems necessary to explain why manufacturers clamor for high tariffs, chemical companies sabotage health inspectors, real estate speculators bulldoze historic neighborhoods, magazine editors favor low postage rates, or admirals lobby for increased naval budgets. Self-interest explains, at least to most historians' satisfaction, the performance of diplomats during negotiations, the movement of troops across frontiers, the maneuvering of policy makers among fiercely competing blocs known, significantly enough, as "interest groups." It explains princes protecting Luther and Bismarck tampering with despatches, workers calling strikes and rural laborers establishing seasonal patterns of migration: survival is also an interest. Historians know, and they can muster impressive instances at a moment's notice, that politicians want to have power, business executives want to earn money, generals want to make war. If, for psychoanalysis, man is the wishing animal, he is, for the historian, the selfish animal. The two are not identical: the first struggles to reduce his tensions under the unremitting impress of his unconscious; the second lives under the sway of conscious egotism.

Historians, to be sure, have long had sufficient cause to know that man does not live by self-centered planning alone. They have encountered, and sought to make sense of, the authority of custom and of loyalty, the suicidal fervor of the fanatic and the tenacious hatred of the partisan. They have puzzled over the pull of religious and nationalist sentiments. Georges Lefèbvre, with his cycles of panic, resentment, and revenge, has not been a solitary outsider in his profession.[26] A sophisticated economic historian like Thomas Cochran has recognized that precisely *as* an economic historian he must leap the traditional boundaries of his discipline: "Each culture has its own forms of economic irrationality or inconsistency. In some, it is excessive responsibility for the entrepreneur's family. In others, such as in the United States, one form may have been persistent over-optimism." It follows, for Cochran, that "Economic or 'market-oriented' decisions depend not on an automatic reaction but on the entrepreneur's interpretation of market forces and trends." The need for psychology is implicit in these assertions. It becomes explicit in the seminal essays of Richard Hofstadter, who specialized in the passionate side of American politics, but was never, at the same time, disposed to see politics simply as theatre: "We have at all times," he wrote, "two kinds of processes going on in inextricable connection with each other: *interest politics,* the clash of material aims and needs among various groups and blocs; and *status politics,* the clash of various projective rationalizations arising from status aspirations and other personal motives."[27]

Some historians are now taking such discriminating psychology for granted. In an illuminating essay on economic development during the July Monarchy, Christopher Johnson speaks, in passing, of the "complacent gentry" which, averse from speculation, "mainly sought stable income and

---

26. See, as another instance, B. H. Liddell Hart epitomizing the "fundamental causes" of World War I "in three words—fear, hunger, pride." *History of the First World War* (1930; ed. 1972), 1. I shall take up this point below, Chapter 4.

27. Cochran, "Economic History, Old and New," *American Historical Review,* LXXIV (June 1969), 1567; Hofstadter, "The Pseudo-Conservative Revolt" (1954), in *The Paranoid Style in American Politics and Other Essays* (1963), 53.

social prestige from their landed holdings." The way that the gentry defined its self-interest was far from crude; it decided to take no chances but, rather, to reduce uncertainty— his adjective "complacent" conceals a variety of defensive maneuvers from which anxiety was not absent. Again, Johnson describes another powerful social force, *"la haute banque* of Paris,"* as being "torn between defense of vested interests (above all the rights of the Bank of France) and the profits to be reaped in transport and industrial investment." I am not proposing that we feel sorry for these troubled financial magnates, but it is striking how, facing unclear and contradictory signals, they fell prey to conflict; their strategies of investment were not simply rational decisions about maximum advantage—though they were that, too. They were also the product of private debates in which the willingness to gamble was pitted against the fear of failure. We can read Johnson's essay as a psychodrama, in which risk-taking triumphs over timorousness in the end: "More important than all the policy making and legislation was the *image* of a bourgeois monarchy." In short, perceptions counted more than facts, though obviously enough, facts forcefully imposed themselves on perceptions. Late in the 1840s, "in canton after canton throughout France," most "employers as well as employees, rural as well as urban, had been won to the idea of economic progress. A kind of mania for improvement seemed to have captured the nation." No wonder that Johnson should have chosen as his epigraph a remark by the tonesetting banker Emile Péreire, *"Le crédit, c'est la confiance"*; it links feelings to finance.[28]

---

28. Christopher H. Johnson, "The Revolution of 1830 in French Economic History," in John M. Merriman, ed., *1830 in France* (1975), 139–89 passim.

Again and again, Johnson's essay invokes the language of self-interest, and it is, of course, true that confidence is, at least in part, the child of calculation. But it is an effect that becomes a cause. To say, as Johnson does, that during the 1840s French financiers, investors, manufacturers, and merchants redefined what they perceived to be their interest is to invite an analysis of motivation and conduct that goes beyond coarse self-interest itself.

A number of historians, then, have thoroughly amended their simplistic ideas about the primacy of self-centered motivation in history. But many even among them, to say nothing of the others, have found self-interest irresistible. What has reinforced their rationalism is doubtless that they have found the sway of self-interest most imperative in those spheres that loom largest in their work: in politics and economics and, above all, in that broad border province where politics and economics mingle and merge. The worlds of commerce and industry, of diplomacy and war are, in most history books, Hobbesian jungles, where gladiators clash openly and persistently. The higher the stakes of profit and power, the less concealed, it seems, the self-interest in play. And stakes grow very high indeed, largely because the resources for which competing interests struggle are nearly always scarce. Self-interest, the historian is compelled to note, changes things, even when it proves, in his judgment, ill-conceived, vicious, possibly self-defeating.[29]

---

29. This confidence in self-interest as the most potent of sources for action does not flag even among the Marxists, for whom the self-interest of individuals or groups are, as we know, yoked to their relations to the means of production and to their place in time. As Marxist historians see it, the most exalted agents of the overriding historical process have the interests they must have, but it *is* interests they have, or, more accurately perhaps, that have them.

Whatever the historian's politics, his analysis of self-interest usually has something derisive, something debunking, about it: over and over, interests lurk as unacknowledged low motives posing as lofty concerns. Manifest moral or patriotic sentiments cannot divert—on the contrary, they only stimulate—the critical historian's curiosity about their latent content: the passion for gain. Thus, in his celebrated dissection of the interests driving the Founding Fathers, Charles Beard argued that the high-level debate over an instrument like the Constitution of the United States was a cover for the protection of investments. "Different degrees and kinds of property inevitably exist in modern society," Beard laid it down; "party doctrines and 'principles' "—and Beard put "principles" into quotation marks to underscore his ironic distance from America's folk heroes—"originate in the sentiments and views which the possession of various kinds of property creates in the minds of the possessors; class and group divisions based on property lie at the basis of modern government; and politics and constitutional law are inevitably a reflex of these contending interests."[30]

Much in the same way, the maverick radical German historian Eckart Kehr discovered more than half a century ago the machinations of domestic interests behind the energetic campaign, launched in the 1890s, to finance the expansion of the Imperial navy. This ambitious construction program was dressed up in the language of patriotism, of pride in Germany's place on the strategic map and worry over England's efforts to isolate the German Reich. But, Kehr charged, it was actually a series of sordid maneuvers de-

---

30. Beard, *An Economic Interpretation of the Constitution of the United States* (1913), 15–16; see Richard Hofstadter, *The Progressive Historians: Turner, Beard, Parrington* (1968), 207–45.

signed to gather money and influence. Franz Neumann, following Kehr, summed up the case in *Behemoth*, his influential study of Nazi Germany and its antecedents: the German Empire founded in 1871 was an imperialistic enterprise that mobilized its forces by driving liberals from the bureaucracy, turning the army into a "tool of reaction," and, finally, reconciling the conflicting interests of "agrarian and industrial capital." Landowners demanded tariffs to improve their precarious position; industrialists demanded free trade to keep imported materials cheap and wages low. "A historic deal," Neumann concludes, "put an end to the conflict. The industrial groups were pushing a big navy program and the agrarians, who had been either hostile or indifferent before, agreed through their main agency, the Prussian Conservative party, to vote for the navy bill in return for the industrialists' support for the protective tariff."[31]

This critical stance is by no means new among historians: two centuries ago, Edward Gibbon took undisguised pleasure in unmasking the hidden motives of Roman statesmen, the ugly political reality behind the constitutional rhetoric.[32] This slightly prurient, almost voyeuristic gratification in uncovering the hidden continues to enjoy considerable prosperity among historians. It is no accident that they like to visualize self-interest, once they have exposed it, as naked.[33] Yet, for all the fascination with self-interest, historians have

---

31. Neumann, *Behemoth: The Structure and Practice of National Socialism, 1933–1944* (1942; 2nd. ed., 1944), 3–6. Kehr's volume is *Schlachtflottenbau und Parteipolitik, 1894–1901* (1930).

32. See Peter Gay, *Style in History*, ch. 1.

33. Thus Richard Cobb: "People are not prone to own up to the pull of naked self-interest." *Reactions to the French Revolution* (1972), 177.

rarely troubled to analyze its psychological status or to trace its actual incidence in human life.

I must add that, in this crucial issue, psychoanalysts have been of little assistance. In one of Heinz Hartmann's papers on ego psychology, he numbers the "strivings for what is 'useful', egoism, self-assertion," among the "functions of the ego," and suggests in passing that they are important activities, especially relevant to social scientists. He is speaking about the pursuit of self-interest. But while he recognizes that "the importance of these tendencies has been somewhat neglected," he does nothing, whether in this paper or in any other, to repair that neglect.[34] "Interest" or "self-interest" or even "ego interest" do not appear in the index of Hartmann's collected papers; nor does the psychoanalytic literature yield more than some perfunctory glances at what the man in the street, the moralist, the political scientist—and the historian—have treated as the most potent of human impulsions. In some of his metapsychological papers, Freud refers to interest casually and links, almost identifies, it with libido or with charged mental energies, but he never followed up this fertile suggestion.[35] Self-interest has not been, as Hartmann put it, somewhat neglected; it has been almost totally neglected.

---

34. Hartmann, "Comments on the Psychoanalytic Theory of the Ego" (1950), in *Essays on Ego Psychology: Selected Problems in Psychoanalytic Theory* (1964), 135.

35. See Freud, "On Narcissism: An Introduction" (1914), *S.E.*, XIV, 82; "Instincts and their Vicissitudes," ibid., 134–35; "Repression" (1915), ibid., 150. That unfortunate "English" word "cathexis," which has been used to translate Freud's perfectly ordinary term *Besetzung*—charge, investment—could (as the psychiatrist Dr. Ernst Prelinger has suggested to me) be straightforwardly rendered "interest." The loss would be minimal and the gain significant. And see below, pp. 109–11.

An exploration just how historians may legitimately employ the idea of self-interest and how psychoanalysts may bring their studies of unconscious urges and conflicts to bear is therefore long overdue. As a general explanatory device, after all, self-interest is bedeviled by a dilemma.[36] Defined narrowly, as the purely rational adaptation of means to material ends, its range is severely constricted, for there are few such adaptations in unadulterated form. In any event, the cool calculations that shape actions are less interesting (and often in the long run less important) than the passions that produced the calculations in the first place. On the other hand, defined broadly, self-interest is little more than a tautology: it is, in this definition, whatever individuals or groups proclaim it to be, or unwittingly reveal it to be by their actions. Altruism or masochism, though they would seem to run counter to self-interest, are actually devious instances of it. The bigot instigating pogroms, the merchant maximizing profits, the saint seeking martyrdom are all following their self-interest. Thus, to enlarge self-interest into a universal motive is to render it diagnostically useless to the historian, who, like any other analytical student of human affairs, must discriminate if he wishes to explain.

To begin with the very surfaces of awareness, it is notorious that not everyone perceives his true self-interest clearly; many suffer from what Lenin argued the working class, left without guidance from a trained elite, must al-

---

36. For a fascinating exploration of the confusions inherent in the idea, see Macaulay's devastating review, "James Mill's essay on Government: Utilitarian Logic and Politics," *Edinburgh Review,* No. xcvii (March 1829), conveniently reprinted in Jack Lively and John Rees, eds., *Utilitarian Logic and Politics* (1978), which also includes Mill's original essay, the subsequent polemics, and an illuminating introduction.

ways suffer: false consciousness. Men—and women—may be blind to their authentic advantage because they have long been habituated to submissiveness and are being kept from grasping and pursuing that avantage by "interests" only too eager to keep them uninformed and passive. Those interests, of course, have everything to gain from the creation, and perpetuation, of false consciousness: whether they are men intent on persuading women to remain domestic and ador- ing or masters insinuating that slavery is a benign institu- tion. The advertising industry is essentially built around the intention of awakening, or manufacturing, wishes that will eventually be integrated into the social structure of collec- tive desire. In the company of sociologists and political sci- entists, modern historians have ventured to analyze this sort of political, social, and commercial manipulation. What the psychoanalyst has to contribute to this exploration of self- interest, genuine and artificial, is how individuals and groups internalize these deceptions and take them to be their own idea.

False consciousness or true consciousness, to be sure, are equal before the historian's critical and, one hopes, impar- tial eye; he is concerned to resist the temptation of con- descending to his subjects. He may wish the working class to be rebellious, lament the "damned wantlessness of the poor." But what men have *thought* to be their interests, wisely or foolishly, is historical information that he cannot afford to ignore. Charles Tilly, a student of collective action in modern European history, has suggested that the histo- rian must "treat the relations of production as predictors of the interests people will pursue on the average and in the long run," but, at the same time, "rely, as much as possible, on people's own articulation of their interests as an explanation of their behavior in the short run."[37] I would add that the historian must do still more: he must trace the perception of interest to their multifarious, often conflicting sources.

At this point, of course, the historian crosses over into the domain that psychoanalyst has made his own. To the extent that historians explore wishes which, rationally translated into plans of action, add up to individual or collective self-interest, they deal with conscious manifestations. But such organized programs of desire are an outcome, the vector of many forces, both palpable and obscure. They are obviously strong enough, and remote enough from their primitive origins, to have defeated the censorship. Still, close enough to their unconscious progenitors, they permit the psychoanalytically oriented historian to discover their family tree. Inevitably, the ego plays a dominant role in the formation and formulations of interests: it disguises, particularizes, orchestrates inchoate feelings of need until they ripen, clarifies what they really amount to, and devises means for gaining the ends they envision. All the historical illustrations I have offered included purposeful rational action that involved making plans, mobilizing resources, anticipating resistances. To realize an interest is, in more than one respect, an *economic* activity; it seeks to pour out the smallest expenditure of energy that will obtain the most favorable possible results.

---

37. Tilly, *From Mobilization to Revolution* (1978), 61. Tilly defines "interest" tersely, without reference to psychological dimensions, as "the shared advantages or disadvantages likely to accrue to the population in question as a consequence of various possible interactions with other populations." (54). See Fred Weinstein, "The Problem of Subjectivity in Sociology" (unpublished paper, 1980), 2–5.

But even the lust for gold is far from simple. It may be absolute, an obsession like the one haunting Balzac's Old Grandet; it may be functional, a means to facilitate the acquisition of power, or art, or lovers. It may be a derivative of anal-retentive fixations, an emblem of sexual potency, a delayed oedipal triumph. It may manifest itself indirectly: the passion for power (as historians have often, and rightly, argued) may be instrumental in the acquisition of money which, in turn, may gratify a wide variety of needs including the assuaging of anxiety. Once analyzed, self-interest becomes very complicated indeed, and one reason for its complexity is the very special ways in which the ego functions as the adversary of the instinctual drives. The ego works against their intemperate demands for the instantaneous discharge of tension, against their inability to tolerate delay. But it, too, schemes for securing gratification, if possible on a level of satisfaction higher than that available to the undiluted primitive wish. Self-interest, to put it into psychoanalytic language, is a product of the reality principle serving, while it affronts, the pleasure principle.

The psychoanalyst can say still more. The wishes that eventuate in self-interest may be instinctual or defensive in origin. They may stem from the erotic or aggressive drives in search of amorous targets or hapless victims, they may constitute an attempt to keep anxiety at bay—or they may, in elusive proportions, stem from a mixture of both. "Certain ego attitudes, which appear to be instinctual," Otto Fenichel has observed, "nevertheless serve a defensive function. The expressions 'instinct' and 'defense' are relative."[38] A defense, in a word, is also a wish. The pursuit of self-

---

38. Fenichel, *The Psychoanalytic Theory of Neurosis* (1945), 475. For more on defenses, see below, pp. 163–68.

interest includes both the getting and the keeping of gratifications.

This view of self-interest visibly implies a continuous interplay between need and control. Much like a neurotic symptom, self-interest is a compromise formation; and much like the ego, an interest must cope with three generally hostile forces: the outside world (the depository of competing interests), the superego (which pours out distressing reminders that others too have valid claims and that one's own claims are at best suspect), and the id (which incessantly generates wishes). That is why the idea of a self-interest wholly rational, clearly perceived, and consistently pursued, is largely an abstraction. Yet it is not a fiction. Servants of an organization, as Reinhold Niebuhr showed many years ago, find the ruthless realization of its advantage far less troubling than the realization of their own: institutions like corporations, literally soul-less, are machines of self-interest—though even these machines, all too human at least in this, misread the information they receive, suffer attacks of panic, and at times break down altogether.

All of this points to the domains the historian must learn to know better—the scope of self-interest, the recognition and possible reconciliation of conflicting interests. The two are related but not the same. It is only too obvious that interests may be narrow or wide, shallow or deep, short-range or long-range. To shift from one of these modes to the other, to expand one's perception of one's "true" self-interest may be the response to a moral demand, but it is a matter of calculation: a shift from what the psychoanalyst calls primary to secondary process thinking. At the turn of the nineteenth century, Jeremy Bentham even attempted to devise a measuring stick, his much-maligned felicific calculus, to enable individuals, groups, and governments to increase the general yield of pleasure by discovering the mixtures of benefits and injuries that each course of conduct would entail—to serve, in short, the interests of all by understanding the interests of each. Bentham may have been naive. His scheme, in fact, has been called harsher names than this. It certainly substantiates the admixture of rationalist Utopianism that dogged his hopes for a science of society. According to Bentham, a person could calculate the value of a pleasure (or pain) by attending to its intensity, its duration, its certainty, its propinquity, its fecundity and its purity, and, finally, its social dimension: its extent.[39] The calculus criticizes itself; there is no dependable way of quantifying individual elements of pleasure, no rational way of comparing them. And hidden impulses may derail, or spoil, the most carefully calculated plans. But Bentham's general idea was, I think, sound enough. The indulgence in heedless pleasure entails later pain, which rational reflection can predict and possibly avoid. Bentham saw man as an animal under the governance of the pleasure principle who could be educated to obey the sober injunctions of the reality principle. This was not—certainly not in Bentham's hands—an invitation to asceticism; rather, it was a call to dose pleasure for the sake of greater pleasure, and to accept some unpleasure for the sake of avoiding greater unpleasure.

Bentham's felicific calculus suggests that what should most concern the psychoanalytically oriented historian is the quality of reality testing both in situations of quiescence and of ferment, and the mechanisms, conscious and unconscious

---

39. See Jeremy Bentham, *Introduction to the Principles of Morals and Legislation* (1789), and Elie Halévy, *The Growth of Philosophic Radicalism* (1901–4; tr. Mary Morris, 1928), esp. 26–30.

alike, that regulate the relation of impulse to action. He should look, in short, to the analytical, integrative, and synthetic work of the ego, for these capacities are strained to the utmost by the demands that raw self-interest imposes on them. They are strained in large measure because interests do not simply expand or contract. Often, and decisively, they conflict with one another.

An illustration from common practice may sketch the dimensions of the problem. A conflict of interests is a familiar experience for a government official who must pass on contractors' bids or on the quality of their performance. His principal loyalty is to his employer, the state, but his private wish may be for a post with one of the suppliers he is evaluating. As a public servant, his assignment is to be disinterested, to judge without fear or favor; as a private citizen, his desire may be quite simply to amass riches. The situation is unambiguous and his duty clear, but his appetite or his anxiety may throw weight onto the other side of the scale.

On the surface, this dilemma seems wholly in the domain of moral awareness. But its roots are lodged in the largely hidden battle between desires and inhibitions. What makes a dereliction of duty imperative, or attractive, or even conceivable? The need for money is, after all, not a fixed quantity; the sense of insecurity is a highly subjective feeling. This particular conflict of interests is a subterranean battle between the official's cultural superego, the values of probity and objectivity to which he is pledged, and his rational ego sniffing the prospective profits which, in the end, may supersede his professional commitments. All these, it is necessary to remember, have components that are largely unconscious. The official's cultural superego rides piggy-back, so to speak, on the superego he acquired as a boy; his ego is a compound of desires and judgments, fantasies and reflections, in which his past continues to play its devious part. Whatever decision he eventually makes, one would expect him to pay his unconscious conflict the tribute of headaches, and, at least occasionally, a sleepless night.

This vignette may serve, with allowances for individual idiosyncrasies, as a model for the clashing interests that all humans find they must reconcile partly below the threshold of conscious reasoning. Surely the very range of human interests is a source of continuing hesitations and uncertainties. A human being is, after all, an anthology of attachments, and their hierarchy of importance is not always evident. Several loyalties may lie cheerfully side by side, though they, too, can become causes of disagreeable decisions; one *can* be a good husband, a devout Catholic, a passionate stamp collector, an adept bridge player, and a skillful welder all at the same time without being forced to choose among these interests—though I would suspect that such a happy integration represents the resolution of earlier struggles, the adjustment of the conflicting demands for time and attention of varied passions, a decision to moderate the demands of some pleasures for the sake of tasting them all.

One striking demonstration of such endemic conflicts of interest is the incompatible claims of love. Like the appetite for money, the energy of love is not a predetermined quantity. But this much is clear: it is impossible to love everything and everybody with equal fervor. The narcissist loves himself at the expense of others; the uxorious husband loves his wife at the expense of his children; the chauvinist loves his country at the expense of other countries. But in these instances, the conflicts have already been resolved, or shoved aside: the husband who loves his wife so much that he neglects his children has made a choice—by no means consciously—among the objects he invests with his libido. Such choices may generate no more than occasional twinges of manageable jealousy or of mild regret, or they may produce severe strains, within the mind or within the family. Psychoanalysis, in sum, has far more to contribute to the anatomy of self-interest than psychoanalysts have so far acknowledged. Here is one good instance where the historian may demand more explanatory help from analysts than they have so far given—though no more than they could give.

4

Reason, Reality, Psychoanalysis and the Historian

1 | TWO WORLDS IN TENSION

For all his obeisances to the forces of unreason loose in the past, the historian can hardly escape the impression that his discipline inhabits a territory strictly separate from that of psychoanalysis. The points where they touch, it would seem, are points of tension. Psychoanalysis broods on landscapes of fancied rapes and mental murders, of uncontrolled fantasies and florid symptoms, of dreams, distortions, and delusions. It seems appropriate that the most heroic moment in Freud's career should symbolically illustrate this view of the mind as a maker of fictions. For some years, in the early 1890s, Freud had been inching his way toward a comprehensive psychology of the neuroses. He was relying, in large part, on the scandalous confessions of his female patients; one after the other reported that she had been seduced in childhood by her father. But in the fall of 1897, Freud told his friend and sole confidant, Wilhelm Fliess, that these stories had become incredible to him, and he acknowledged that he no longer knew where he stood in his venturesome and lonely exploration. "The ground of reality," he recalled later, "had been lost."[1] What had been gained in its place was the ground of fantasy. Freud's patients had largely imagined these parental assaults, and his understanding of their imaginative activity would give his psychology far more solid, far more extensive theoretical foundations than the most sensational revelations had ever offered. It was on the ground of fantasy that the house of psychoanalysis was built.

It follows naturally that reason, the companion of reality, seems to be quite as unwelcome in the psychoanalytic situation. The patient on the couch is enjoined to follow the single cardinal precept that Freud laid down for treatment:

---

1. "Zur Geschichte der psychoanalytischen Bewegung," *Gesammelte Werke,* ed. Anna Freud et al., 18 vols. (1940–68), X, 55; "On the History of the Psycho-Analytic Movement," *S.E.,* XIV, 17. See also Freud to Fliess, September 21, 1897, *The Origins of Psycho-Analysis: Letters to Wilhelm Fliess, Drafts and Notes: 1887–1902,* ed. Marie Bonaparte et al. (1950; tr. Eric Mosbacher and James Strachey, 1954), 215–18. Freud, of course, never abandoned the idea of parental seduction: in the *Three Essays on Sexuality,* to note only one place of several in his writings, he emphatically notes that while he had exaggerated its importance in the evolution of the sexual constitution of individuals, it remained a very real threat, especially to young girls (*S.E.,* VII, 190–91). I had drafted this chapter long before Jeffrey Moussaieff Masson, early in 1984, created a certain stir with his sensational polemic, *The Assault on Truth: Freud's Suppression of the Seduction Theory,* in which he denounced Freud for a cowardly retreat from his correct theory that neuroses are caused by parental sexual assaults on children, to the safer, less offensive theory that these reports were fantasies. I was not the only reviewer to point out that this reading of psychoanalytic history is a tissue of absurdities. (See Peter Gay, *The Philadelphia Inquirer,* February 5, 1984.) *The Complete Leters of Sigmund Freud to Wilhelm Fliess, 1887–1904,* ed. 2nd tr. Masson (1985) arrived as I was reading page proofs.

to permit all associations free access to his awareness and to impart them with as little editing, as few corrections, as humanly possible. The fundamental rule reads like a deliberate and provocative insult to civility. The patient is supposed to report not merely all the trivialities and obscenities that sober human beings normally screen out from their speech, and often from their thoughts, but also the most absurd, the least consequential, of his mental meanderings. What is more, the transferences, the patient's feelings of love and hatred for the analyst that the psychoanalytic situation elicits, are in all their guises displacements of time, person, and feeling. It is as though psychoanalysis is bent on undoing the highest achievement of the ego: the capacity to organize and govern the unruly mass of impulses and ideas that lies beneath the surface of human consciousness. This is not the mental landscape in which the historian is most at home.

The incompatibility between the psychoanalyst's and the historian's worlds appears to be so blatant that any call for reconciliation must sound Utopian. Unlike the psychoanalyst, the historian handles hard realities: food scarcities, urban agglomerations, technical innovations, strategic territories, religious institutions. When he studies conflicts in which mind has a share—class antagonisms or clashing interests—he finds them so palpable, so materialistic, as to be almost tangible. The Marxist historian, too, lives in a daylight, hard-edged world. True, his scheme, in which classes or individuals attempting to serve only themselves unconsciously serve the cunning of history, assigns conspicuous room for the operation of forces behind the backs of the actors. But he is confident that he can unriddle these forces as he specifies the concrete historical situation in which these actors must perform. I have made the point that historians have not been unmindful of potent irrationalities in the past. But when they have been compelled to deal with the murky underworld of the concealed and contradictory emotions that are the psychoanalyst's chosen playground, they have done so with visible aversion, and have turned away after feeding their readers with a few observations borrowed from commonsense psychology. It is significant that the influential school of French historians grouped around their celebrated professional journal, the *Annales,* have been on the whole satisfied with citing as their favorite psychologist Lucien Febvre, who was not a psychologist at all, and have catalogued collective states of mind under the resounding name, *mentalités,* without troubling to trace back these states to their roots in the unconscious mind.[2] The worlds of the historian and of the psychoanalyst remain worlds apart.

There is a way of bringing them together with a stroke of the philosophic pen: by pointing out that a fantasy or delusion is a reality to those who experience them—individuals certainly act on them. As the sociologist W. I. Thomas once observed in a much-quoted aphorism: "If men define situations as real, they are real in their consequences." This expansive redefinition of reality may sound glib, but it is not trivial. It underscores the share of the mysterious and unex-

---

2. The perfunctory chapter by Georges Duby on "Histoire des mentalités" in the bulky *L'Histoire et ses méthodes,* a volume in the *Encyclopédie de la Pléiade,* ed. Charles Samaran (1961), 937–66, is a telling instance. Among recent French historians, those who have turned to Freud at all, Emmanuel Le Roy Ladurie (see his classic *Les Paysans de Languedoc,* 2 vols. [1966], esp. I, 394–99) and Alain Besançon (esp. in his essays in *Histoire et expérience du moi* [1971]) are quite exceptional. But see now also the few—but promising—pages on dreams in Jacques Le Goff, *Time, Work, and Culture in the Middle Ages* (tr. Arthur Goldhammer, 1980), 201–4.

pected in human affairs; it tempts the historian to paraphrase the inevitable tag from *Hamlet* and say that there
are more things in heaven and earth than are dreamt of in
our histories. Freud, who, of course, knew his Shakespeare
well, liked that line, though he chose to express the senti-
ment in the words of Leonardo da Vinci: nature, he wrote,
"is full of countless causes which have never entered experience."[3] Conversion hysteria, in which blocked affects and
denied desires find outlets in physical symptoms, is only the
most vivid demonstration that feelings and wishes are real
enough.

We have ample opportunity, in psychoanalysis and out,
to catch these countless causes at work. The analysand,
bringing to bear his self-observing ego to assist and at times
anticipate his analyst in offering interpretations, and the
historian attempting to set aside his prejudices and tran-
scend his parochial perspectives, both seek to make sense
of elusive psychological activities.[4] But while such a promo-
tion of obscure mental events into comprehensible inner
realities is impressive, it is not by itself enough, for it fails
to touch the vast array of objective facts and rational conduct that, together, are the historian's principal business.
Freud's evolving views of unconscious processes seem at
first glance quite intransigent, intent on frustrating all ecu-
menical efforts. In its depths, the unconscious domain, as he
describes it, is a stranger to morals and logic, secretive and
defensive, with an unholy passion for privacy. Freud was

---

3. "Eine Kindheitserinnerung des Leonardo da Vinci" (1910), *St.A.*,
X, 159; "Leonardo da Vinci and a Memory of his Childhood," *S.E.*,
XI, 137.
4. For the observing ego, see the justly famous paper by Richard
Sterba, "The Fate of the Ego in Analytic Therapy," *Int. J. Psycho-
Anal.*, XV (1934), 117–26.

fully aware that his theory of the unconscious had aroused a certain scandal in the scientific and philosophical communities, for throughout his lifelong, energetic advocacy of psychoanalysis he never ceased to defend it against these obstinate, obtuse philosophers and psychologists who persisted in making consciousness coextensive with mind. His defense was something more than defensiveness. To Freud, as he put it in a distinctly odd metaphor, the unconscious is "the only lantern in the darkness of depth psychology."[5] Certainly by 1915, when he published his metapsychological paper, "The Unconscious," he took the view that the inaccessible regions of the mind are more sizable, and doubtless more important, than those with which we are on easy, intimate terms.[6] It was not the unconscious, but consciousness, that needed explaining.

The historian is bound to agree that consciousness needs explaining, but not in the way that Freud had in mind. If Freud came to find the very existence of conscious activity a little astonishing, the historian is likely to be quite as astonished, and no less frustrated, by the privileged position that psychoanalytic theory assigns to the most esoteric and uncommunicative of mental processes—frustrated, and ready to consult other, more forthcoming schools of psychology. But psychoanalysis is not the study, let alone the glorification, of the unconscious alone. Freud, it is true, saw the core of the unconscious not merely as enormously powerful, but also as closed off from the world; only its representatives, or derivatives, come to public notice. He was certain that one can approach the id (as in the 1920s he came

---

5. Freud, *Das Ich und das Es* (1923), *St.A.*, III, 287; *The Ego and the Id, S.E.*, XIX, 18.
6. Freud, "The Unconscious," *S.E.*, XIV, 159–215, esp. 167.

to call the "dark, inaccessible part of our personality") only "with analogies"; he, and his fellow analysts, thought of the id as "a chaos, a cauldron full of bubbling excitations."[7] But it did not follow for Freud that all mental events beyond the watchful eye of consciousness are equally distant from it, or equally reluctant to come forward. There is much mental activity, he thought, that lies barely outside its field of vision, much that is capable of being "called to mind." What is more, even those obscure energies bubbling in that chaotic cauldron must by their nature force themselves on awareness somehow. It would be sheer anthropomorphism to portray them as clamoring for expression. Man's somatic needs—hunger, fatigue, lust—are dumb, deaf, and exigent; it is their psychological spokesmen who compel attention by making demands, normally highly specific, for gratification. Thus Freud recognized the irresistible pressure toward the world that issues from the most secret recesses of the psyche. Men delude themselves and seek comfort in dreams. But it is largely in reality that satisfaction will be sought and may sometimes be found.

2 | IN SEARCH OF REPRESENTATIONS

Freud also saw a reciprocal movement, from reality to the mind. Physical stimuli intruding on the psyche, emotional injuries wrought by beloved figures, unresolved problems

---

7. Freud, *Neue Folge der Vorlesungen zur Einführung in die Psychoanalyse* (1933), *St.A.*, I, 511; *New Introductory Lectures on Psycho-Analysis, S.E.,* XXII, 73. Two distinguished psychoanalysts, Max Schur, in *The Id and the Regulatory Principles of Mental Functioning* (1966), and Roy Schafer, in *Aspects of Internalization* (1968), esp. 148–49, have noted a certain crude and fluid structure in the id. But for them, too, its elusiveness and mystery remain.

posed by society, all present themselves and must be mastered, compromised with, adapted to—or denied. These outside forces, in cooperation and conflict with inner urges, shape the individual's fundamental erotic and aggressive styles, his critical choices, his strategies and evasions in love, business, and war. Even the Oedipus complex, as I have already shown, owes its history as much to the opportunities offered and the prohibitions issued by others as it does to instinctual drives and to anxieties. In general, what current generations of psychoanalysts have come to call "object relations" are not merely sources of danger, misinformation, and confusion, but also, and significantly, teachers of true worldliness. Just as the mind pursues reality, reality invades the mind.

This psychoanalytic sketch of mental activity, though it firmly places mind in the world, is scarcely attractive. The human mind appears in it much like a modern military dictatorship: inordinately suspicious, addicted to secrecy, insatiable in its demands, armed to the teeth, and not very intelligent. It employs battalions of censors to prevent domestic news from leaking out, and of border patrols to prevent hostile ideas from reaching, and possibly subverting, its people. Yet often neither the censors nor the patrols have the wit, or the agility, to carry their assignments through. At night especially, but also at unguarded moments during the day, messages, disguised as dreams, slips of the tongue, or neurotic symptoms get out; and perceptions, dressed in innocuous garb, get in. Both, however, pay a price for their intrepid penetration of the energetically defended frontiers: they are gravely distorted, treacherously translated, sometimes crippled beyond cure. At the least they are heavily masked, much like revelers at a Venetian carnival recognizable only (if they are recognizable at all) to the schooled and sensitive interpreter. Indeed it was not until Freud discovered these messages to *be* messages that we have begun to decipher them systematically, not until he understood the mauling that perceptions take at the hands of mental defenses that we have confidently established their deviant and oblique relationship to reality.

Worse than being merely unattractive, this reality is a Walpurgisnacht, gloomy, obscene, and mendacious, where nothing is what it appears to be. It can only repel the historian whose characters, however villainous, generally live by the legible code of selfish motives or the perspicuous pressures of mundane necessity. The mental activities by which Freud sets such store sound uncomfortably enough like the ravings of psychotics or the babbling of toddlers.

Psychoanalytic literature daily enriches this bleak account. The unconscious of Freud's theory, which his successors have not questioned, is a storage bin in grave disarray holding volatile childish materials that never penetrated into consciousness, and much other stuff, of remote or recent vintage. It includes such explosives as erotic wishes and moral prescriptions, the wildest sexual fantasies and the harshest self-reproaches. Since the unconscious has no sense of order, it casually stores contradictory thoughts side by side; since it has no sense of time, infantile deposits are as fresh as yesterday's additions. And many deposits are very infantile indeed.[8] Freud's theories of neuroses and of dreams read like explications of this assertion. Adult neuroses are belated, heavily distorted reenactments of unfinished emotional business, and dreams are productions whose ultimate origins can be traced to childhood wishes. But if the great

---

8. *"The unconscious in mental life is the infantile."* Freud, *Vorlesungen zur Einführung in die Psycho-Analyse* (1916–17), *St.A.*, I, 214; *Introductory Lectures on Psycho-Analysis, S.E.*, XV, 210.

lover is merely seducing his mother over and over again, if the muscular bully is forever testing his little prepubertal manhood, if the rational scientist finds himself bedeviled by superstitions he has preserved intact from primitive stages of his mental organization—still more to the point: if politicians are only gratifying their own boyhood fantasies while they arouse those of others, then history is nothing more than an infinite regress, cruelly, interminably extended, in which superannuated little boys and girls solemnly replay the games of their tender years.[9] Reality and reason, in this Freudian nightmare, seem continuously filtered through almost impenetrable layers of unreliable memories and, more insidiously, of repressed material. These, once again, are surely not the realities, certainly not the principal realities, that the historian encounters and wants to recount and explain.

Psychoanalysts have a favorite rejoinder for the skeptic who tries to discredit their reductionism by instancing the glories of art or the subtleties of philosophy: the fruit, they will say, does not resemble its roots; fond gardeners cherish their lovely flowers no less because they were grown in manure. It is, to be sure, a Freudian axiom that the artist, the statesman—any adult—forever carries his childish needs and terrors around with him, and that character is little more than an organized grouping of fixations. But this in no way implies that the psychoanalyst takes the discovery of remote

---

9. "No underestimation of the influence of later experiences is suggested by [psychoanalysts'] emphasis on the earliest; but the later impressions of life speak in analysis loudly enough through the mouth of the patient; thus for the claims of childhood the physician must raise his voice." Freud, " 'Ein Kind wird geschlagen' (Beitrag zur Kenntnis der Entstehung sexueller Perversionen)" (1919), *St.A.*, VII, 235; " 'A Child is Being Beaten.' A Contribution to the Study of the Origin of Sexual Perversions," *S.E.*, XVII, 183–84.

origins as equivalent to an exhaustive explanation in psychoanalysis or, for that matter, in history. For he is aware
that external reality, more and more of it, lies along the
path of maturation.[10]

Even in dreams and in psychoses, where the powers of
reason and reality are feeble, their faces veiled, the two
command surprising authority. In fact, it was precisely in
the nightlife of the psyche, whether in a peaceful bed or a
mental hospital, that Freud and his fellow analysts discovered unsuspected touches of both. In the exhaustive, authoritative survey of the scientific literature with which he
inaugurates his magisterial work on the interpretation of
dreams, Freud notes that many earlier investigators had seen
but little, if any, objective content in the dream; they had,
rather, considered it a mental production of an inferior
kind, bearing little relation to external events and receiving
no assistance from man's higher intellectual powers. Dream
interpreters who had, in contrast, professed to find dreams
meaningful, invariably invoked what the scientist must regard as the peculiar "reality" of superstition, in which the
dream becomes a supernatural messenger and a mysterious
agent of prophecy. Freud's own theory of dreams was, of
course, decisively different. It shared the conviction of the
most unlettered servant girl that dreams indeed have meanings, but found those meanings in the natural world and, in
particular, in the encounter of the dreamer with his own
passions and his immediate environment.[11]

---

10. George Devereux, *Dreams in Greek Tragedy* (1976), xix, and
Sandor Ferenczi, "Stages in the Development of the Sense of Reality"
(1913), *First Contributions to Psychoanalysis* (1952) 213–39. And
see below, p. 190.
11. Freud, *The Interpretation of Dreams,* ch. I (1900), *S.E.,* IV. On
primitive projection in dreams, see esp. E. R. Dodds, *The Greeks and
the Irrational* (1951), a book I discuss in some detail below, pp. 191–96.

The psychoanalytic theory of dreams is too well known to require extended discussion: the manifest dream—the dream the dreamer dreams and partially recalls on awakening—dramatizes, in heavily distorted guise, a hidden wish that has been drastically edited to slip past the censorship. This, the heart of Freud's theory, is not my concern here. I want to stress, instead, his thesis that the latent dream thoughts find a place in the manifest dream only by utilizing recent, usually quite insignificant materials borrowed from the dreamer's ordinary life, almost invariably from the previous day. These are the "day's residues," which link up the most distant desires to the most immediate, most "actual" past.[12]

The tactical utility of the day's residues is patent: they are the means by which forbidden thoughts and repressed wishes evade the censor; their employment of apparently indifferent recent memories is a politic device to secure publicity for ideas that are anything but indifferent. But the day's residues have even larger significance: they are evidence of what has aptly been called the mind's search for representational material.[13] Man's mind is neither an athlete nor a mystic: it cannot vault great distances or dispense with realistic modes of expression. Its most dazzling reversals and most acrobatic leaps prove, on analysis, a solemn, pedestrian progression along a tightly welded associative chain—a chain largely invisible only because so many of its links are repressed. Its most bizarre inventions are not wholly drawn from the imagination; they are versions, and pieces, of experience. The sudden and dramatic self-disclosures of the unconscious are illusions; the unconscious advances

---

12. See Freud, *Interpretation of Dreams, S.E.,* IV, 165–88.
13. I owe this perception, and phrase, to Dr. Ernst Prelinger.

methodically from the depths toward the daylight of consciousness, and uses, with a pedantic eye for detail, the
common mental materials it picks up along the way. More
than once, Freud defined neurotics as those who, finding the
world intolerable, turn away from reality.[14] But they are far
from disdaining reality on their very retreat from it; however disfigured, however unrecognizable, the world is always with them.

The world is even with psychotics, whose flight from reality is far more precipitous. Daniel Paul Schreber, the
classic textbook paranoiac, eloquently attests to this oblique
commerce. In his exhaustive memorandum, a plea to be released from the mental institution where he was confined,
Schreber developed an intricate theory of the universe, complete with a full-blown theology, a messianic mission calling
on him to undergo a radical sexual transformation, and ingenious torturing devices whose ministrations he had been
compelled to endure. Only the agglutinative German language can do justice to his Kafkaesque inventions; witness
that miraculous machine designed to tie Schreber's head together, the *Kopfzusammenschnürungsmaschine*. Nothing
could seem more remote from real life than this. Yet the
psychoanalytic investigation of Schreber's appeal discloses
that his religious system and those terrifying machines echo
Schreber's childhood experiences.[15] His father, an ortho-
pedist and something of a celebrity in his time, has been

---

14. "In neurosis, a piece of reality is avoided by a kind of flight, in
psychosis it is reconstructed." Freud, "Der Realitätsverlust bei Neurose und Psychose" (1924), *St.A.*, III, 359; "The Loss of Reality in
Neurosis and Psychosis," *S.E.*, XIX, 185.
15. See Freud, "Psychoanalytic Notes on an Autobiographical Account of a Case of Paranoia" (1910), *S.E.*, XII, 3–83.

called a "social, medical, and educational reformer";[16] in other words, he was an educated crank and neurotic pedagogue who regularly put his son, Daniel Paul, and his other children, into a mechanical contrivance he had devised to improve their posture. As one compares Schreber's astonishingly moving, superbly logical, and utterly mad brief for freedom with his father's graphically illustrated treatises, one is impressed less by Schreber's inventiveness than by the ingenuity with which his mind managed to incorporate, and reconstruct, his all-too-real tribulations into a coherent, if irrational *Weltanschauung*. Schreber imagined relatively little; instead, he distorted almost everything, often only slightly.

Schreber's mode of proceeding is far from unusual among inhabitants of mental hospitals. The tributes that psychotics levy on reality, and for which Freud supplied important theoretical as well as clinical explanations, are adequately documented in the psychiatric literature. Thus, "shortly after World War II," August Hollingshead and Frederick Redlich reported, "some Japanese patients changed their paranoid delusions of being Emperor Hirohito to being General MacArthur."[17] Such pathetic relevance, it appears, is common. That Japanese megalomaniacs should choose, for their deluded impersonations, an American conquistador who really had bested their own divine emperor impressively testifies to the uncommon realism, downright reasonableness, with which the mad can "choose" the forms that their symptoms will take.

---

16. William Niederland, *The Schreber Case* (1974). Han Israëls' revisionist thesis, *Schreber, Father and Son* (1981) supplies fascinating new material and corrects numerous misconceptions.

17. August B. Hollingshead and Frederick C. Redlich, *Social Class and Mental Illness* (1958), 359.

To be sure, the weight that the neurotic lends the slights offered him, or the status that the psychotic assigns to the voices he hears, cannot soberly be called realistic. Still, it should be clear by now that the mental lives of neurotics and psychotics are tapestries that, though twisted, discolored, patched up with awkward stitches and depicting fantastic scenes, have woven into them significant strands taken from life, from real slights and real voices. Whether deranged, neurotic, or only dreaming, the human mind needs, and greedily seeks out, realistic representations for the sake of visibility, precision and pictorial sharpness, as embodiments of its urges and anxieties—and it finds what it seeks in its immediate neighborhood. People become neurotic, or go mad, in a specific setting. They are never beset by some general neurosis or some indefinite phobia, but weave their symptoms from stories they have heard, incidents they have seen, anxieties they have felt, all expressed with a pictorial and verbal vocabulary they share with their more fortunate contemporaries. And both the setting and the vocabulary are the historian's ticket of entrance to the world of psychoanalysis.

What holds true of neurotics and psychotics necessarily holds true even more for those whose intercourse with their human environment is less disturbed, which is to say, less distorted. As its motor skills and mental capacities develop, the child steps, in Freud's terse formulation, from the pleasure principle to the reality principle. In the beginning, he postulated, the infant seeks satisfaction by hallucinating the realization of its imperious wishes. At first ignorant and later uncertain of the boundaries dividing it from the world, and for a long time unable to differentiate between thoughts and acts, it is compelled to discover, through painful and repeated disappointments, that wishes are not automatically translated into actuality and that mental self-sufficiency is an illusion. So, gradually and with repeated back-sliding, the child's psychological apparatus decides at last to see what the external world is really like and, with that, make attempts to realize its desires by changing that world.[18] Here, and elsewhere, Freud subscribed to the Baconian maxim that knowledge is power. In the long run it is better to face disagreeable truths than bask in agreeable illusions. That is the lesson of the reality principle the child so reluctantly learns. No wonder many adults flee into self-delusion.

The human animal does not mature with a smoothly co-ordinated unfolding of its potentialities. Quite the contrary, its emotional and intellectual developmental lines are out of phase in the most problematic fashion; the sexual drives especially resist relinquishing the pleasure principle.[19] Yet eventually it may assimilate the external world with its full mental and physical resources, an adaptation comprised only by the constraints that its neuroses impose. Its sexual wishes, which are at first unabashedly auto-erotic and then organize themselves around narcissistic self-love, divert their amorous intentions from the self and seek satisfaction with, and through, others; its burgeoning powers of attention, judgment, remembering, thinking—which is a practical rehearsal for action—all display its growing engagement with the rational appraisal of reality. Perhaps most impressively: deploying all these capacities, the reality principle teaches the child to postpone gratifications. Education supports this quest for the real by positing goals and setting limits, by

---

18. Freud, "Formulierungen über die zwei Prinzipien des psychischen Geschehens" (1911), *St.A.*, III, 18; "Formulations on the Two Principles of Mental Functioning," *S.E.*, XII, 219.
19. See Anna Freud, *The Ego and the Mechanisms of Defence* (1936, tr. Cecil Baines, 1937), ch. 11.

enforcing a compulsory recognition of others; it is "an incitement," as Freud baldly put it, to overcoming the pleasure principle. Even art, that talented refugee from reality, returns to offer it a new vision of itself. The artist will "shape his fantasies into new kinds of truths," Freud writes, "which are given house room by men as valuable reflections of reality."[20]

The historian has no reason to be sentimental, any more than Freud, about these little triumphs. They are never unalloyed but inevitably compromised by partial failures. Historians experience these inescapable imperfections most poignantly in their own work; they set themselves the commendable ideals of objectivity, even-handedness and empathy, but know that they can never quite attain them, any more than psychoanalysis ever fully realizes *its* ideal, the completely analyzed person. Moreover, the realities the individual makes his own may be grim, as may be the reasons for propelling him to undertake their assimilation in the first place. The resolution of the Oedipus complex is, as we know, tied to threats (or at least fears) of castration. Worse, an accurate appraisal of external reality can generate troubling tactical and ethical problems. Pleasures, as Heinz Hartmann has argued, are "in store for the child who conforms to the demands of reality and of socialization; but they are equally available if this conforming means the acceptance by the child of erroneous and biased views which the parents hold of reality."[21] The child in its domestic set-

---

20. Freud, "Formulierungen über die zwei Prinzipien," *St.A.*, III, 23; "Formulations on the Two Principles," *S.E.*, XII, 224.
21. Hartmann, "Notes on the Reality Principle" (1956), in *Essays on Ego Psychology: Selected Problems in Psychoanalytic Theory* (1964), 256.

ting will normally trade the pleasures of independent action and accurate knowledge for those of parental praise and social acceptance: the child of bigots finds it rewarding to grow up a bigot; the child of authoritarians, to grow up a conformist. No wonder Freud was a pessimist. He would have endorsed T. S. Eliot's observation that mankind can stand very little reality.

Sobering up little dreamers to the tainted joys of worldly knowledge is largely the work of the ego. The procedure that children develop as they circle, ever more closely, around the reality principle is what Freud called "reality testing," the making of impartial judgments that distinguish fantasies from actualities by comparing ideas with perceptions—to separate what one wishes from what one sees, to be able to *see* what one sees, in a word, to accept the universe. It was in his last major phase, during the 1920s, that Freud turned his attention to the institution that performs this testing. The ego is responsive to the external world, its agent and representative in the mind and, at times, its master. It is the seat of reason. But reality and reason are intimate friends without being inseparable companions: mathematical thinking or logical excogitation, which stand at the apex of rational activity, often take little if any notice of experience at all; they weave patterns remote from the world. But for the most part, rationality has the task of confronting actualities in ways that irrational thinking does not: to obey empirical evidence, extend hospitality to objective clues, make convictions corrigible. It is in its mediating, controlling, calculating, often reasonable and always embattled activity, that the ego provides its menu of materials for the historian. When I said that historians are at home with hard realities, this is what I meant: when they deal with mind, they principally deal with ego functions—with man's recognition of ineluctable necessity, his purposeful efforts at bending the environment to his desires, his making things in obedience to the possibilities that the world presses on him.

It is therefore important to be clear about what psychoanalytic ego psychology implies and does not imply. Its name is in some ways unfortunate. Ego psychology did not desert Freud's somber realism; it is by no means psychoanalysis without psychoanalysis. Though it takes the workings of reason for its province, ego psychology in no way confines itself to reason. Defensive stratagems—projection, repression, reaction formation, and others—are ego functions almost wholly unconscious and almost wholly nonrational. Just as Freud never equated "mental" with "conscious," he never equated "normal" with "rational."[22] This only underscores the point that the researches of ego psychologists mesh with the rest of psychoanalytic inquiry to work toward a comprehensive theory of the mind. I cannot reiterate often enough (and it matters to the historian) that Freud, healer and, even more, scientist, aimed from the beginning at a general psychology. That his theories originated in his clinical encounters with a colorful variety of neurotics was a historical accident that, he was confident, would not obstruct his access to the laws governing normal functioning.

---

22. "Jealousy is among the affective states that one may describe, much like mourning, as normal." But, "though we call it normal . . . jealousy is by no means wholly rational, that is, born of actual conditions." Freud, "Über einige neurotische Mechanismen bei Eifersucht, Paranoia und Homosexualität" (1922), *St.A.*, VII, 219; "Some Neurotic Mechanisms in Jealousy, Paranoia and Homosexuality," *S.E.*, XVIII, 223.

3 | A LADDER OF PERTINENCE

Freud's governing ambition, coupled with his conflict model of development and his insistence on detecting hidden neurotic admixtures in the coolest of calculations, throws serious doubts on the conventional perception of how his ideas might serve historical investigation. Common sense would appear to dictate a ladder of pertinence: in the sphere of rationality, psychoanalysis would remain mute; with nonrational sentiments and conduct, that vast region of social and cultural habits we call custom or tradition, it would have illuminating ideas to contribute, sharing honors as an auxiliary discipline with anthropology and sociology. Freud would come into his own, then, principally with irrationality, enforcing a virtual monopoly of explanatory competence.

But here, as so often, common sense misses the mark. Psychoanalysts firmly assert their competence in the explication of rationality, not only because they see it persistently entangled with nonrational and, beyond that, with irrational springs of action, but also because of their interest in the work of the ego that aims to make humanity master of nature and itself. True, in 1914 Freud offered an engaging disclaimer, significantly enough when he was talking about that psychoanalytically so interesting passion, the lust for lucre: "We expect from normal people," he wrote, "that they will keep their relation to money wholly free from libidinal influences and regulate them by realistic considerations."[23] This is a refreshing and strategic moment of mod-

---

23. Freud, "Aus der Geschichte einer infantilen Neurose" (1914, publ. 1918), *St.A.*, VIII, 188; "From the History of an Infantile Neurosis," *S.E.*, XVII, 72. Discussing the analyst's fee, Freud offers an unembarrassed and terse summary of the mixed realms of rational

esty, but, as psychoanalytic theory could have told Freud, the most sensible ideas and behavior of "normal people," whoever they may be, are much like manifest dreams or neurotic symptoms: compromise formations compounded of archaic desires and day's residues, impulsive gestures and pondered stratagems. What measure of rationality historians assign to certain historic acts—Napoleon invading Russia in 1812 or Britain abandoning the gold standard in 1931—must depend on the vantage point from which their judgment is made: from that of the actor's perceived immediate advantage or of his implicit long-range goals, that of the impact his act will leave on his intimate circle or on such larger fields of implication as society or posterity.

Among the many examples illustrating the problematic place of rationality in human action I shall adduce only Max Weber's driven tradesman. This very embodiment of the Protestant ethic thinks only of his business and of making money; he cannot bring himself to relax, let alone retire.[24] In the twentieth-century version, this much abused type has earned a prominent niche in the folklore of capitalist masochism. We encounter him in the literature of bourgeois self-castigation as the obsessive manager whose conduct in the office or in the factory is impeccably controlled, if single-minded and ruthless, but whose long, intense hours of work are punctuated with anxiety and whose

---

and nonrational thought as exemplified in men's dealing with money: "The analyst does not deny that money is most prominently a means for self-preservation and the securing of power, but he maintains that powerful sexual factors participate in the valuation of money." "Zur Einleitung der Behandlung" (1913), *St.A., Ergänzungsband,* 191; "On Beginning the Treatment," *S.E.,* XII, 131.

24. The *locus classicus* is Max Weber, *The Protestant Ethic and the Spirit of Capitalism* (1904–5; tr. Talcott Parsons, 1930).

private life is probably nothing short of disastrous. Ridden with ulcers, isolated for all his compulsive sociability, friendless the moment he suffers reverses, affluent and miserable, he is often served up as proof for the inhumanity of capitalism, even toward its profiteers.

Although such tendentious moralizing does not really advance the analysis of the emotional backdrop before which presumably rational actions play themselves out, it points to their complex nature. Certainly "rationality" is too indistinct a general name to discriminate among the divergent mental operations it is meant to describe; Weber's classic distinction between *Zweckrationalität* and *Wertrationalität* at least makes a beginning at salutary discriminations. The first, *purpose rationality,* concentrates exclusively on the adaptation of means to ends, the application of whatever knowledge and intelligence are at hand to resolve a problem or realize a wish. A bank robber carrying the most advanced available set of tools and observing the most alert precautions is exercising purpose rationality in its purest form. So is a diplomat astutely deceiving his counterpart in negotiations by offering impressive-sounding but empty concessions. Activities like these invite an internal, technical appraisal exclusively concerned with the standards governing the craft—burglary, diplomacy—in question. Such an appraisal offers no purchase to psychoanalytic explanations, but it is also, and equally, indifferent to all other kinds of external scrutiny, whether from sociology, economics, political science, or ethics. The sole judgments relevant to the weighing of purpose rationality are whether the actor's intentions had a reasonable chance of succeeding, and whether they were matched by their execution.

It is when the historian begins to engage with intentions themselves, thus entering the terrain of *value rationality,*

that psychoanalysis acquires a more visible explanatory function. For the values that intentions embody may in themselves be less than rational. It is only too obvious that the
conduct of Weber's businessman is rational, nonrational,
and irrational all at once. It is rational in its methods: he
pursues, clearheadedly, with all the resources at his command, ends he does not find it necessary to question. It is
nonrational in its aims: he fails to examine his ends largely
because they reenact the habits and imitate the choices of
others he admires. It is irrational in its origins: the fanatical
single-mindedness of his planning, which blinds him to its
consequences even to himself, can only spring from needs
and anxieties that elude whatever self-awareness he can
muster. His critical failure of reason, concealed behind an
ostentatious display of schedules observed and targets met,
is not rescued, it is only masked, by the applause of his peers.
Their approval is a cultural symptom. What has happened
(and, according to Max Weber, had to happen in the days
of mature capitalism) is that by isolating his chase of profits
and power from the rest of his mental economy, he has
contaminated his perceptions and corrupted his ideals.
What parades as rationality can be profoundly irrational. The
psychoanalyst can dissolve this apparent paradox: each fundamental institution of the mind—id, ego, superego—has
aims of its own that often, all too often, conflict with the
aims of the others. That old psychoanalytic commonplace,
the ego is the enemy of the id, oversimplifies a complex
scene of combat in which alliances shift, confrontations wax
and wane.[25] Much personal history is the sum of such conflicts.

---

25. I am indebted, in this paragraph and this section as a whole, to a
stimulating short article by Donald Davidson, "Paradoxes of Irra-

The nonrational sphere for its part presents the historian with far fewer intellectual conundrums and the psychoanalyst with far more urgent calls for his employment. Men most of their lives act on familiar cues and orient themselves by familiar signposts. They do not make and rarely revise their world, and occupy structures—morals, religion, the law—that enshrine and preserve what has been. Such cultural "automatisms," to borrow a term from Heinz Hartmann, save much strenuous thinking. In ways that will not surprise the psychoanalyst, these social solutions for individual problems make life easier. The drives, after all, as Freud consistently maintained, are conservative by nature; change, even change for the better, is bound to arouse anxiety. Custom and tradition, these organized repetitions, with their soothing monotony, their principled refusal to examine their origins and question their operations, assuage and bind anxieties.

In themselves, institutionalized habits offer the historian endlessly interesting materials; challenged by unrest and innovation, they become more interesting still. Much like rational behavior, custom-ridden behavior asks to be judged within a specific context, by concrete experiences. What is adaptive for one person, one class, one epoch, may be maladaptive for other persons, other classes, other epochs. In times of upheaval, the refusal to reform styles of thought and patterns of authority can foster panic or rage, and can generate, rather than control or resolve, conflicts. During these exhilarating and frightening moments, which historians have long found so absorbing, moments when the cake of custom begins to crumble, the nonrational shades into,

---

tionality," in Richard Wollheim and James Hopkins, eds., *Philosophical Essays on Freud* (1982), 289–305.

and is often overpowered by, the irrational. It is there that the opportunities for psychoanalysts to perform as unrivaled expert witnesses have been acknowledged (at least by some historians) to be virtually unlimited. It was on collective irrationality, after all—on men's uncontrolled responses to devastating epidemics, charismatic leaders, or economic catastrophes—that William Langer in his famous presidential address built his call to the historical profession to find uses for psychoanalysis in its work. Even historians inclined to be skeptical of Freud's ideas have reluctantly granted them a certain efficacy in the realm of "social psychopathology."[26]

For once, appearances are less than wholly deceptive. Impulsive conduct, self-deluded enthusiasms, endemic anxieties do seem to be the proper province for the psychoanalyst's specialized competence. Heady insights beckon. But, precisely at this promising juncture, wielders of the Freudian scalpel have too often succumbed to misplaced confidence and rash diagnoses: the temptations are as thick on the ground as the looming rewards. It is true that Freud emphatically cautioned against the enlistment of his discipline in such acts of aggression. "In my opinion," he wrote in 1922 to an American correspondent, "psychoanalysis should never be used as a weapon in literary or political polemics."[27] Yet, once sufficiently infuriated, even Freud could fall short of his stringent professional ideals. In the notorious posthumous psychological study of Woodrow Wilson, largely written by William Bullitt but approved by the aged Freud, he permitted his aversion to the self-appointed, intrusive

---

26. David S. Landes and Charles Tilly, eds., *History as Social Science* (1971), 70.
27. Freud to William Bayard Hale, January 2, 1922. Typescript copy of an unpublished letter in William Harlan Hale Papers, Yale University Library.

Messiah from the West to override his carefully cultivated analytic neutrality. Since then, in his shadow, the psychoanalysis of detested politicians, living or dead, has become a minor and irritating cottage industry.[28]

Analysts have on occasion indulged in this destructive game. So have historians. In his brilliant, extremely influential *Making of the English Working Class,* E. P. Thompson has vindictively mobilized against a religious community he loathes the very psychoanalytic vocabulary he deplores when others have used it against radicals he admires. "What we must not do," he notes, reasonably enough, "is confuse pure 'freaks' and fanatical aberrations with the imagery—of Babylon and the Egyptian exile and the Celestial City and the contest with Satan—in which minority groups have articulated their experience and projected their aspirations for hundreds of years." Indeed, "because the luxuriating imagery points sometimes to goals that are clearly illusory, this does not mean that we can lightly conclude that it indicates a 'chronically impaired sense of reality.'" After all, "abject 'adjustment' to suffering and want at times may indicate a sense of reality as impaired as that of the chiliast." But this sensible caution against reducing real social grievances to psychological disorders turns out to be politically self-serving, for Thompson fails to carry it over to the Methodists, whose anti-revolutionary impact on the English working classes has aroused his ire. The Methodists' luxuriant fantasies, he writes, show "undertones of hysteria and of impaired or frustrated sexuality," a "morbid preoccupa-

---

28. The most penetrating (and sympathetic) reviews of a production that has been held against Freud, not wholly without justice, are a pair of essays by Erik H. Erikson and Richard Hofstadter, "The Strange Case of Freud, Bullitt, and Woodrow Wilson: I, II," *The New York Review of Books,* VIII, 2 (February 9, 1967), 3–8.

tion with sin and with the sinner's confessional," a "cult of 'Love' which feared love's effective expression, either as sexual love or in any social form which might irritate relations with Authority," and an obsessive "concern with sexuality" that "reveals itself in the perverted eroticism of Methodist imagery."[29] There is good reason to suppose that both Thompson's warning against reductionism and his analysis of the underlying erotic origins of Methodist imagery are correct enough. But an even-handed employment of psychoanalytic concepts and of historical methods would have revealed that the chiliasm of the radicals had erotic roots no less concealed, no less "perverted," than that informing the Methodists, and that the Methodists, no less than the radicals, deserve to be studied sympathetically rather than be subjected to an intense search for psychopathology. Psychoanalysis rightly applied does not foster such double standards; its contribution to the historian in search of objectivity is to help him detect and disarm his prejudices, not to serve them.

There is no denying that to wrench psychoanalysis out of its accustomed sphere, the analytic situation, is a risky business. But the profit the historian may reap from applying psychoanalytic explorations of reason and its enemies make these risks worth taking. I have shown how Georges Lefèbvre struggled to make sense of the psychological side of the French Revolution, with its subtle interweaving of fanatical idealism, conservative resistance, thoughtful planning that characterized the participants' perceptions and policies. The Freudian dispensation would have eased his perplexities, for it disposes over dynamic, many-layered explanations of men-

---

29. Thompson, *The Making of the English Working Class* (1963), 49–50, 40, 370.

tal products that are far more adequate to their composite and puzzling nature than the grand simplicities that most historians have felt compelled to accept as satisfactory.

The pertinence to the historian of the psychoanalyst's way with external reality is rather less clear-cut. For the analyst, we know, this reality is distinctly secondary to the psychological reality of fantasies and mental representations. The worlds of psychoanalysis and history, I said at the beginning of this chapter, are worlds apart. They will, and should, remain so. But just as historians can, under the impress of psychoanalysis, enlarge and enrich their sense of historical reality, so psychoanalysts, attentive to what historians have discovered about past events, can enlarge and enrich their sense of psychological reality. Even the isolated individual whom the psychoanalyst encounters in his clinical setting is, after all, a social animal who crowds his unconscious, constructs his dreams, feeds his anxieties with experiences he has taken in from the world that is his habitat. But that deserves a chapter of its own.

5

From Couch to Culture

In 1913, surveying the contributions to the study of culture that his discipline had already accomplished, Freud speculated about the ways his individualistic psychology could serve the exploration of collective experience. "Psychoanalysis," he wrote, "establishes an intimate connection" between the "psychological achievements of individuals and of societies by postulating the same dynamic source for both. It starts with the fundamental idea that it is the principal function of the mental mechanism to relieve the person from the tensions which his needs create in him. Part of this task can be fulfilled by extracting satisfaction from the external world; for this purpose it is essential to have mastery over the real world." But since, he adds, "reality regularly frustrates the satisfaction of another part of these needs, among them, significantly, certain affective impulses," the human animal confronts a "second task, that of finding some other way of disposing of the unsatisfied impulses." Persuaded

144

that psychoanalysis has already thrown shafts of dazzling light on the origins of religion and morality, justice and philosophy, Freud concludes that "the whole history of culture only demonstrates which methods mankind has adopted to bind its unsatisfied wishes under changing conditions, further modified by technological progress, wishes sometimes granted and sometimes frustrated by reality." This passage, I think, is nothing less than an ambitious agenda for historians, an invitation whose implications neither psychoanalysts nor historians have even begun to explore.[1]

Others abound in Freud's writings. Quite concretely, he thought of the conscience as a social legacy that the individual internalizes and thus makes his own. "The guardian" of the ego ideal, it was first transmitted by the "critical influence" of the parents, to which were added in time, "educators, teachers," to say nothing of an interminable "swarm" of cultural influences that includes "fellow-men, public opinion." In one of his late, probably most cited essays on culture, *Civilization and its Discontents,* he developed the idea of a cultural superego at some length. Even more generally, in *Totem and Taboo,* he had already argued that the full explication of a problem "should be historical and psychological in one." His proposal, though here specifically restricted to totemism, claims validity for the whole range of human experience in need of explanation. Again, opening his monograph on crowd psychology, Freud flatly maintains that the contrast "between individual and social or mass psychology," apparently so unbridgeable, "loses a great deal of its sharpness upon close examination." After

---

1. "Das Interesse an der Psychoanalyse" (1913), *Gesammelte Werke,* 18 vols. (1940–68), VIII, 415; "The Claims of Psycho-Analysis to Scientific Interest," *S.E., XIII,* 185–86. Peter Gay, *The Bourgeois Experience: Victoria to Freud,* vol. I, *Education of the Senses* (1984), 14.

all, "in the mental life of the individual, the Other is quite regularly involved, as model, as object, as helper, and as adversary. Hence individual psychology is, in this extended but thoroughly justified sense, from the start social psychology at the same time."[2] For Freud, sociology and the other social sciences are parasitical on psychology.

These are bold propositions, but the reader of these pages will not find them particularly unexpected. By rights, in fact, this chapter should be short; it only draws out the implications of what I have already said about the psychoanalytic view of human nature, the social dimensions of the Oedipus complex, and about man the cultural animal in general. But the historian's doubt whether, at best, psychoanalysis can ever apply to more than the life of the individual justifies more extensive exploration of my theme. "Psychoanalytic history," Donald B. Meyer has argued, "must be biographical in its orientation."[3] It is true enough that any Freudian ambition to supply wider illumination raises some difficult questions. After all, the last traces of Freud's notions about the "racial" mind or inherited collective psychological dispositions that haunted his work have been weeded out by his successors as redundant, almost embarrassing reminders of nineteenth-century scientific supersti-

---

2. Freud, *Zur Einführung des Narzissmus* (1914), *St.A.*, III, 62, *Narcissism: An Introduction, S.E.*, XIV, 96; *Das Unbehagen in der Kultur* (1930), *St.A.*, IX, 266–69, *Civilization and its Discontents, S.E.*, XXI, 141–44; *Totem und Tabu* (1912–13), *St.A.*, IX, 394, *Totem and Taboo, S.E.*, XIII, 108; *Massenpsychologie und Ich-Analyse* (1921), *St.A.*, IX, 65, *Group Psychology and the Analysis of the Ego, S.E.*, XVIII, 69.

3. Meyer, in a most appreciative review of Erikson, *History and Theory*, I, 3 (1961), 291–97. David Hackett Fischer has quoted this view, but has adapted it into a stern warning, *Historians' Fallacies: Toward A Logic of Historical Thought* (1970), 193.

tions about a "group soul." The psychoanalyst's double doors guarding his consulting room, his resistance to experiments in group healing, his passionate devotion to confidentiality compromised only by the occasional publication of clinical materials in scientific papers, impenetrably disguised—all focus unremitting attention on the isolated patient, alone with himself, his unconscious, and his analyst. In any event, the dialogue between analyst and analysand is a kind of conversation with oneself, in which one partner has the floor nearly all the time. In the hands of the psychoanalyst, sweeping generalizations about "the" experience of a whole class or a whole culture are likely to dissolve into prudently discriminating assertions about experiences in the plural.

It is not an accident, then, that when at its Fall meetings in 1977, the American Psychoanalytic Association offered a panel on "psychoanalytic knowledge of group processes," this was a signal rarity; its chairman, Burness E. Moore, concluded with the wan hope that analysts would henceforth "discuss group processes more often than every 21 years."[4] Nor is it an accident that when historians experimenting with Freud have analyzed collective conduct, they have almost invariably expanded metaphors borrowed from psychoanalytic terminology originally designed for narrower and far less elastic purposes. This is what Richard Hofstadter did in his essay on the paranoid style in American politics; this is what some other historians have done in their efforts to read revolutions as straightforward, slightly disguised oedipal combats, or to encompass an era by labeling it an age of narcissism. Freud's central idea that every human is continuously, inextricably, involved with

4. Moore, *J. Amer. Psychoanal. Assn.*, **XXVII** (1979), 156.

others and that individual and social psychology are at bottom the same is a sophisticated modern version of the old idea—as old as Plato—that the individual is culture writ small, culture the individual writ large. Used incautiously, this imaginative assimilation of two very different entities can lead to pathetic oversimplifications. Freud was not a simplistic thinker. But his propositions touching on the psychoanalysis of culture require more painstaking analysis, more solid demonstration, than they have so far received—even in Freud.

1 | BEYOND BIOGRAPHY

Sigmund Freud was by no means the first to note that collective bodies—a mob in action, an army in battle, a nation at war—yield to impulses that their members would normally control, probably disclaim, when they are not enjoying the embracing presence of likeminded believers around them. For highly visible political reasons, the unpredictable and worrisome conduct of the human "herd" came to be studied with anxious intensity from the middle of the nineteenth century onward. Troubled social observers like Thomas Carlyle or Matthew Arnold, abetted by a small troop of tendentious historians and "crowd psychologists"— Hippolyte Taine, Gabriel Tarde, Gustave LeBon, and, later, Wilfred Trotter—worried over the democratization of modern culture as a growing threat to the orderly conduct of public business and the rational solution of social problems. They never failed to offer in evidence the ugly passions unleashed in the excited, sanguinary *journées* of the French Revolution as a somber caution against the savage and irrational eruptions of angry and aggrieved masses. Freud's analysis, though it begins as a commentary on LeBon's once commanding work on the psychology of the crowd, significantly enlarged the field of inquiry to explore the hidden grounds of collective conformity in so disciplined an organization as the Roman Catholic Church.[5] His results were tentative and partial, but, in persuasively linking the individual to his emotional neighbors, Freud's *Group Psychology and the Analysis of the Ego* contains some welcome informal proposals that may serve to improve the not wholly satisfactory relations between biography and history.

It is almost proverbial that every historian is something of a biographer; every biographer, something of a historian. Yet there are marked divergencies between the two pursuits, and their commerce, though flourishing, is often tense. Ill-defined as the frontiers between them may be, some biographies are unmistakably the work of a historian, others not. This is not a matter of quality. It seems beside the point to suggest that had he been more of a historian, Lytton Strachey's feline assaults on Victorian worthies would have been more just to their subjects. They would have been less of a caricature if he had been more of a biographer. Nor is the difference between history and biography measurable by the relative allocation of space. The distinction is subtler than this: the historian brings to the life he is writing, or to the biographical passages he fits into his narrative or his analysis, a commitment to the relevant social environment, an informed, trained sensitivity to

5. In his judicious introduction to LeBon's *The Crowd* (1895; tr. 1896, ed. 1960), Robert K. Merton notes that Freud was less than wholly fair to LeBon's reach (though not his grasp); Freud used LeBon's little classic as a stimulus to his own thought. For the crowd psychologists, see Susanna Barrows, *Distorting Mirrors: Visions of the Crowd in Late Nineteenth-Century France* (1981). Robert Bocock's lucid *Freud and Modern Society: An Outline and Analysis of Freud's Sociology* (1976) is congruent with my own views.

the worlds in which his subject had moved. He is expected to possess, and deploy, a firm, professionally cultivated sense of place and time, of public possibilities and constraints. He obviously cannot use a psychology that would leave him mired in esoteric realms of unfathomable drives and mysterious mental closet dramas. But psychoanalytic psychology, though one might at times wonder, is actually anything but that.

Freud constructed the pathways linking biography to history from the most fundamental of human materials: love and hate. These alone, he believed, enable groups to force the solid bonds that make its members compliant, energetic, and intolerant. LeBon, Freud suggested, had astutely observed and cleverly described the characteristic demeanor of crowds, but failed to detect the causes of their cohesion. Students of society, not excluding imaginative writers, had, of course, long known that in groups, individuals can fall back into primitive states of mind, yield their will to leaders, discard restraints and the sensible skepticism that education had so painfully fostered in them. There are pages in Tolstoy's *War and Peace* that illustrate some of these mechanisms to perfection: young count Nicholas Rostov, along with his fellows, falls in love with Tsar Alexander I at first sight: "Rostov standing in the front lines of Kutuzov's army which the Tsar approached first, experienced the same feeling as every other man in that army: a feeling of forgetfulness, a proud consciousness of might, and a passionate attraction to him who was the cause of this triumph." Rostov, almost beside himself, "felt that at a single word from that man all this vast mass (and he himself an insignificant atom in it) would go down through fire and water, commit crime, die, or perform deeds of highest heroism, and so he could not but tremble and his heart stand still at the imminence of that word." To be near that emperor was true happiness for the young enthusiast. "He was happy as a lover when the longed for moment of meeting arrives." Tolstoy, in fact, is quite explicit about Rostov's emotions: "He really was in love with the Tsar and the glory of the Russian arms and the hope of future triumph." Nor—and this is most significant—was he "the only man to experience that feeling during those memorable days preceding the battle of Austerlitz; nine-tenths of the men in the Russian army were then in love, though less ecstatically, with their Tsar and the glory of the Russian arms."[6] One can see why Freud should have said that he envied the novelists and the poets for arriving, through sheer intuitive virtuosity, at psychological insights it took him years to tease out of his patients.

Yet what Freud did in analyzing these phenomena in the light of his late ego psychology was not merely to find a new vocabulary for familiar scenes. He explained them. "In the togetherness of mass individuals, all individual inhibitions fall away and all the cruel, brutal, destructive instincts which lie dormant in each person as relics of the primitive era, are awakened for free drive-gratification."[7] Hunting with the pack provides the kind of pleasure that such surrender of inhibitions usually gives; it generates a feeling of safety and skirts the danger of placing oneself into opposition to the powerful. Freud saw this abandonment of adult controls and perspectives as a luxuriant saturnalia of regression. But, for all its seductive pleasures, such an affect-laden

---

6. Tolstoy, *War and Peace* (1868–69; tr. Louise and Aylmer Maude, 1922–23; ed. in two vols., continuously paginated, 1983), I, 256, 265, 268 [Book I, part 3].
7. Freud, *Massenpsychologie, St.A.,* IX, 73; *Group Psychology, S.E.,* XVIII, 79.

moral holiday is rarely destined to be permanent. After prolonged reverses or in moments of panic, the libidinal ties holding the crowd together can weaken and the group may then splinter and disintegrate.

Group formation, Freud argued, involves two sets of unconscious identifications: the members of the group identify with one another and, collectively, with the leader. This was not invariably a return to utterly primitive modes of feeling and conduct: the leader need not be a person; he can be an idea. Moreover, groups, bound together by invisible bonds of loving loyalty and unquestioning faith, can live by moral standards higher than those its members could reach by themselves. And "as far as intellectual achievement is concerned," Freud wrote, "it remains indeed true that the great decisions of the work of thought, the consequential discoveries and solutions of problems, are possible only to the individual, laboring in solitude. But even the mass mind is capable of mental creations of genius, as proved above all by language itself, as well as by folk song, folklore and the like. Beyond that," Freud added, in one of those reasonable asides in which he joins, once again, individual and social psychology, "it remains unsettled just how much the individual thinker or creative writer owed to the stimulus of the crowd among which he lives, whether he is more than the completer of mental work in which the others had participated at the same time."

Unlike other social psychologists of his age, Freud respected the sheer difficulty of his material. "If one surveys the life of the individual man of today," he wrote, almost resigned to failure, "keeping in mind the mutually complementing accounts of writers on crowd psychology, one may, considering the complications that here emerge, lose the courage for a comprehensive exposition." After all, in modern times, "each individual is a component part of many crowds, tied in manifold ways by identifications, and has constructed his ego ideal on the most varied models." He belongs to his race, his class, his religion, his nation, to stable groupings less conspicuous perhaps than those spectacular transient crowds that make most of the noise but no less significant for his mental formation. Earlier, in his paper on narcissism, Freud had already made the same point from a different perspective. "From the ego ideal," he wrote there, "a significant path leads to an understanding of crowd psychology," for this ego ideal, which he would later call the superego, has "in addition to its individual also a social component" since it "is also the common ideal of a family, an estate, a nation."[8]

The intense attachments that build up these groupings, small or large, are shot through with resentment and rage. Family quarrels can become as bitter as quarrels between clans; carefully buried intimate hostility matches the hatred that often animates a group facing outsiders. "Every religion," Freud writes, is "a religion of love for all those it embraces, and each is disposed toward cruelty and intolerance against those who do not belong to it."[9] Like love, hate begins at home and does not end there.

In propounding such a pessimistic social theory, Freud was writing in a great tradition of social theorists who had long before him glimpsed these portentous truths. Thomas Hobbes, the most fiercely consequent of his intellectual ancestors, had already argued more than two hundred years earlier that "the state of man can never be without some incommodity or other," and inveighed against "the disso-

8. Ibid., *St.A.*, IX, 78, 120, *S.E.*, XVIII, 83, 129; "Narzissmus," *St.A.*, III, 68, "Narcissism," *S.E.*, XIV, 101.
9. Ibid., *St.A.*, IX, 93; *S.E.*, XVIII, 98.

lute condition of masterless men" in the anarchy of civil war, a condition Hobbes described in a matchless, memorable string of potent adjectives, as "solitary, poor, nasty, brutish, and short." In Freud's own time, in 1901, the perceptive English political economist and social critic J. A. Hobson would restate this bleak assessment in language revealing how closely psychoanalytic ideas could parallel the advanced sociological thinking of its times: "it is the chief aim of civilization and of government to repress" the "lusts of blood and physical cruelty."[10] Freud's distinctive contribution was to supply the psychological rationale for this rather bleak perception of man in society and society in man. Civilization, as he saw, is many things: an arena for the creation of art, the pursuit of science, the cultivation of affections, the making of money. But it is also, and decisively, a collective defense against murder and incest, each culture doing the defending in its own way and adapting its style to changing conditions.

For, as historians have particular reason to know, institutions cannot remain immune to the pressures of time and power. One need only read Oliver MacDonagh's informative *Early Victorian Government,* or Alfred Chandler's splendid history of American management, *The Visible Hand,* to recognize that they continually grope for new solutions, emancipate themselves from their primitive origins in unconscious psychological needs to acquire a momentum, and serve interests, of their own. Marxist historians have not been alone in pointing out that institutions can be captured by special interests, corrupted by dominant classes, and dis-

---

10. Hobbes, *Leviathan* (1651; ed. Michael Oakeshott, 1947), 120, 82; Hobson, *The Psychology of Jingoism* (1901), 29.—I shall discuss cultural defense system later, pp. 163–67.

torted by self-serving rhetoric. Still, as I have shown, the pursuit of rational self-interest has its nonrational components. In 1850, Prussia's new constitution contained the notorious three-class electoral law, which grouped voters by the amount of direct taxes due from each of them. This meant that those who, together, paid one third of Prussia's direct taxes elected as many deputies as those who paid the second and those who paid the last third. The consequences, as the eminent German historian Hajo Holborn has put it bluntly, was "an outright plutocratic system."[11] It secured a near-monopoly of political power to Junkers and other landowners, practically guaranteeing these closely allied interest groups all the rewards that a political system can provide. Now, this bit of electoral chicanery elevated into a constitutional principle was, at the same time, an astute defensive device. Sensitive to possible threats from self-confident middle-class citizens and the slowly awakening political awareness of urban working classes, sensitive to intimations of democracy abroad and of revolution at home, the authors of the three-class electoral law helped to exorcise the anxieties of rich and influential Prussians. It will not do simply to dismiss this political stratagem as a cynical, wholly conscious defense of cherished privileges. A way of life, of traditional, once secure domestic and social pleasure, seemed at stake. To neglect the policy by concentrating on the anxiety is to reduce history, unduly, to a mere psychodrama; to neglect the anxiety by concentrating on the policy—which is far more likely to happen with historians—is to flatten, unduly, one's perception of the past.

---

11. Holborn, *A History of Modern Germany,* vol. III, *1840–1945* (1969), 79.

2 | THE SOCIAL SHARE

The discovery just how deeply private emotions are invested in public life is only one way in which Freud's theories can move history beyond sheer biography. In the preceding chapter on human nature I have already indicated some of the others. The basic ingredients making up possible experience, I said there, are strictly limited. This essential economy holds even though component drives, like the libidinal urges, will coalesce in each person in their own particular rhythm and with their distinctive cohesive force. Each undergoes its unique evolution, engendering those impressive variations in conduct and culture that are at once delightful, frightening, and far from predictable, and are the stuff of history. With his acerbic, leering wit, the cartoonist Peter Arno once documented this human unity amid human diversity by showing a bevy of pneumatic beauties individualized by sashes proclaiming them to be "Miss Sweden," or "Miss Tasmania"; displaying themselves in bathing suits, they are parading past their lecherous judges, one of whom says confidentially to another: "A thing like this shows you people are pretty much the same all over."[12] They are—and they are not.

In short, human experiences, though rich and fascinating, tend to observe developmental timetables that bear striking resemblances to one another. Every historian working with rank orders, religious denominations, or entire cultures knows implicitly that he can afford to group the clusters he is studying *as* clusters without necessarily violating the individuality of their members. He is sure to be aware that collective names like "Roman Catholic" or "bour-

---

12. Arno, *The Man In The Shower* (1944), n.p.

geois" or "Norwegian" are capacious, often leaky vessels to be filled with discretion and with a fine feeling for their limited usefulness. He finds it salutary to recall that every Catholic, every bourgeois, every Norwegian is not precisely like all the others gathered under the same rubric. At best, all such labels are shorthand statements of probabilities: individuals identifiable as members of any entity are likely to share moral convictions and religious beliefs, expectations of success and fears of failure, with their fellows. If they do not, the historian has some interesting rebels before him. Class, as E. P. Thompson put it in the much-quoted preface to his *Making of the English Working Class,* is not a thing, not a tight box into which one can squeeze men and women only to forget their individuality. Rather, class is a relationship that "must always be embodied in real people and in a real context." Class "happens when some men, as a result of common experiences (inherited or shared), feel and articulate the identity of their interests as between themselves, and as against other men whose interests are different from (and usually opposed to) theirs." Class is an experience that masses of men undergo in the "productive relations" into which they "are born—or enter involuntarily."[13] And like class, we may add, other institutions incarnate feelings in rules, buildings, emblems.

An instructive fable that Sigmund Freud told in his Introductory Lectures at the University of Vienna in 1917 demonstrates that there is nothing in psychoanalysis to obstruct the recognition of such collective experiences in the life histories of individuals. Freud imagined two little girls living in the same house, one the daughter of the caretaker, the other that of the landlord. The two, little bourgeoise

---

13. Thompson, *The Making of the English Working Class* (1963), 9.

and little proletarian, play freely with one another, and their games soon take an erotic turn. The excitement generated by their highly charged make-believe, usually initiated by the caretaker's daughter who has seen far more of life than her playmate, is bound to eventuate in masturbation. But after that, the sexual histories of the two friends will diverge, and the divergence is predictable to anyone familiar with the class nature of morality. The proletarian girl will continue to masturbate without guilt feelings and later give up the practice; she will perhaps go on the stage, have an illegitimate child, marry an aristocrat. But whatever her eventual career, "she will, at all events, fulfill her life undamaged by the premature activation of her sexuality, free from neurosis." The landlord's daughter, though, will struggle with her "vice," laden with guilt, and will probably come to turn away from sexual information with real, if "unexplained" revulsion, only to acquire, as a young adult, a full-fledged neurosis, the pathetic reward of her middle-class repressions.[14] The reputation of psychoanalysis as responsible for a static and undifferentiated model of human nature, visualizing actors, whether in loin cloths, togas, or business suits, reciting the same boring lines about illicit loves and unconscious hatreds is wholly undeserved. For Freud, experience governed by the passage of time, the stigmata of class, and the accidents of events, molds the ingredients of human nature into dramatic, never wholly repeated, configurations.

Although psychoanalysts are at times rather cavalier about the relevance of the outside world to their work, psy-

---

14. Freud, *Vorlesungen zur Einführung in die Psychoanalyse* (1916–17), *St.A.*, I, 346; *Introductory Lectures on Psycho-Analysis, S.E.,* XVI, 353–54.

choanalytic theory firmly acknowledges that in the making of the individual's mental history, cultural experience must always claim a sizable share. This acknowledgment reinforces Freud's argument that individual and social psychology are, for all practical purposes, identical, and this in turn prompts me to take a brief excursion through the psychoanalytic model of human development, which plots that work of culture along the path of personal maturation. It is no secret that from the moment of its birth, the infant is in uninterrupted commerce with the world of others. It may be convenient, and has long been conventional, to liken human life history to a river rising as a thin trickle, widening and deepening as it picks up tributaries along the way. But the metaphor, though attractive, fails to do justice to the masses of social experience jostling the infant from the outset. Streams of culture come pouring in upon it. That infant, at first a mere bundle of needs, wholly devoted to sleeping, nursing, eliminating, has no way of sorting out its little self from its caretakers. But then the pathetically dependent infant grows visibly into a child, month by month and, at times, day by day; it learns to separate itself from parents, siblings, strangers, and, as it were, to shrink personal boundaries. Reluctantly and with incomplete success, it gives up its almost hallucinatory sense of omnipotence in favor of a self-perception roughly resembling its actual dimensions. But this retreat from fantasy to a measure of realism does not entail a diminution of its engagement with its surroundings. On the contrary, the child's very progress toward mastery—its gradual acquisition of motility, of speech, of confidence in the persistence of loved persons, of stormy passions for others and of defenses against pain—enmeshes it with external realities more irrevocably than ever. The "ego," as Freud summed up his thought in his last book, undergoes a "special development," and does so "under the influence of the real external world around us."[15] The length of nursing, the severity of weaning, the mode of toilet training, the style of manifest parental pleasure and displeasure, and a host of subtler clues are all forceful messages from the outside world, kneading malleable living materials into recognizable little aristocrats, Protestants, or Spaniards. The child's parents, after all, generally the dominant influence on the construction of character, are not hermits. Their manner of rearing their young is, to be sure, insensibly molded by their personal habits and neuroses: much education, as Freud would insist, is the vibrating of one unconscious with the unconscious of another. Whether parents sing to their child or handle it in silence, deal with it consistently or capriciously, admit it to their bedroom or banish it, largely depends on lessons they themselves had absorbed, quite unwittingly, when they in turn were young. At the same time, their style of pedagogy owes quite as much, perhaps more, to the religious, social and cultural worlds in which they have been steeped all their lives. In modern times, at least, and often before, the nuclear family has acted as the chosen agent of culture; it has transmitted and distorted social imperatives, defined the boundaries of the permissible, dictated social norms. It is the child's first, normally decisive, culture, its school, state, and religion.

The oedipal phase fits into this pattern without a seam. It enacts both the essential kinship of all private human experience and its fundamentally social nature. The family triangle is a small society in action, complete with assertions

---

15. Freud, *Abriss der Psychoanalyse* (1940), *Gesammelte Werke*, XVII, 68; *An Outline of Psychoanalysis*, S.E., XXIII, 145.

of authority and attempts at rebellion; the way the parents manage to deal with their child's intemperate and often puzzling emotions is at bottom a social decision made largely by forces behind their back. And the superego emerges from an even more visible interaction between a growing, learning individual and the social forces that press in on it in the shape of adult surrogates. The child absorbs its parents' commands and prohibitions, their often unconscious desires and anxieties, and translates them into exigent demands for conformity and acceptable patterns of conduct, no matter how incomprehensible or even unjust they may appear. Obedience itself becomes a value, a source of rewards and a protection against punishment. Fitting the child into its society by means of authoritative directives at home, at play, in church, begins early and only intensifies as the parents judge their offspring ready for control and discipline. By the time the youngster toddles off to school, he is thoroughly acclimated to the social space that he, his parents, neighbors, and playmates naturally, unself-consciously occupy.

Freud painted a rather somber picture of the cost that socialization is likely to exact from the young. He would have heartily endorsed Gibbon's "protest against the trite and lavish praise of the happiness of our boyish years, which is echoed with so much affection in the world."[16] Childhood no doubt has its intense delights: the warmth of motherly love, the security offered by parental care, the joy of discovering competence and real, instead of illusory, power over segments of the environment. But in the main, it is a sobering school for life, filled with disappointments, renunciations, and conflicts. The Yes of the mother's nurturing

---

16. Gibbon, *Autobiography,* ed. Dero A. Saunders (1961), 68.

breast is inseparable from the No of the mother's punishing hand. External authorities make claims on the child that thwart its natural desire for immediate and unrestrained gratification. To hold in urine and feces until the designated place for disposal is reached but then to hold them in no longer, to postpone feeding until set mealtimes, to give up the pleasurable sensation of touching one's genitals, to moderate the passion for one parent are only some, though surely the worst, among the deprivations that loving parents or nursemaids find themselves compelled to impose and enforce. The stern demand to obey, to be silent when adults speak, to study when one wants to play are sophisticated derivatives of the essential rules that fence in the child almost from its birth, rules it learns to assimilate, though not without protest. To make its assignment all the more irksome and unpalatable, adults ask the child not just to delay or do without cherished gratifications; they insist that it accept their canon gracefully, as just and right, and to see its infringement as an offense, perhaps as the way to hell and perdition which, to most children, means the loss of their parents' love. The child is forced to internalize culture; it learns only too soon that what it wants most is impermissible, probably wicked. To civilize a child is to check it at point after point. That is why it drives its wishes, its lusts and rages, underground into the unconscious; it represses them and stores them up, paving the way for later difficulties in its erotic, professional, or political life.

I have drawn this developmental sketch to underscore my conviction that a sociology of the unconscious is now a realistic possibility.[17] Such a sociology—and history—will not

---

17. The call was first issued by that eccentric psychoanalyst Wilhelm Reich. See the valuable pages in Bocock, *Freud and Modern Society*, 8–17.

slight those external seductions and terrors that bombard the individual as he confronts his parents, siblings, school mates, fellow workers, to say nothing of priests and politicians, all of them acting upon him. My sketch should confirm that culture is not man's superficial drapery, but integral to the very definition of his humanity.[18]

Doubtless the most interesting building blocks for such a history are what Anna Freud called the mechanisms of defense. They are so interesting because, though deeply personal psychological maneuvers, they are chiefly developed in response to collective external realities, and remain in continuous and close touch with them. Ubiquitous, versatile, inventive, these unconscious stratagems make civilization possible and bearable.[19] Seated in the ego, increasing in range and effectiveness as the child grows into its culture, the defenses ward off pain or danger from external even more than from internal sources.[20] They act to reduce, or evade, the anxieties aroused by others, by situations or events, that awaken—or better, reawaken—forbidden im-

---

18. This explains the abysmal failure of every attempt to isolate quintessential human nature before the indelible paint of culture has been applied—that nostalgic research project which goes back to Herodotus and eventuated in the widespread fascination with "wild boys" and "wolf children" right into the age of Freud.

19. The most lucid, still most often cited, summary remains Anna Freud's classic *The Ego and the Mechanisms of Defence* (1936; tr. Cecil Baines, 1937).

20. "The infant and child, equipped at birth only with certain automatic mechanisms for maintaining himself in equilibrium with the environment, increasingly becomes confronted with external conditions of an extremely complex nature. These complex external conditions . . . are not merely sets of 'biological' events, but events of different orders of integration which we call psychological, cultural, social." Hans W. Loewald, "The Problem of Defense and the Neurotic Interpretation of Reality" (1952), *Papers on Psychoanalysis* (1980), 21–22.

pulses, intolerable memories, terrifying fantasies, or pitiless guilt feelings. The repertory of defensive strategies evolves, after some years, into an almost impenetrable coat of armor. Defenses drive conflicts and potential distress out of awareness or deny their existence, tame primitive urges to serve elevated cultural activities, convert aggression into affection, saddle others with ugly feelings to which one dare not confess. They seek to guarantee the integrity, the very survival of the individual, and thus reach into the core of human experience. But, though face- and life-saving, they are also a most inconvenient and inconstant ally. Again and again, they generate more problems than they resolve: much mental suffering can be traced to defenses gone wild.[21] Responding to unnecessary alarms, treating normal erotic or aggressive impulses as though they were actual and heinous crimes, the defenses can erect protective walls that come to be confining prisons of phobias, obsessive gestures, or paralyzing inhibitions.

The same troubling inconsistencies haunt the defenses deployed in, and through, culture. Strictly speaking, to be sure, the defenses are mobilized by individuals, and in their service. Typically, in fact, one source of distress against which the individual defends himself is the exigent demands of culture, which importunes him to perform unpalatable labor and to postpone or surrender many of his cherished desires. As Freud never tired of saying, "Every individual is vir-

---

21. "The ego's defense mechanism" are "protective devices against disruption and disorganization, protections that often overshoot their mark or continue to function when no longer necessary and thus become pathological, interfering with the further organization of the self and the world of objects." Loewald, "Ego-Organization and Defense," *Papers on Psychoanalysis,* 177.

tually an enemy of culture."[22] But institutions, adversaries and oppressors of the individual, are also designed and with the passage of time elaborated to work in his behalf. Freud, we know, had postulated a single "dynamic source" for the achievements of individuals and societies alike, and found that source in what he considered the principal task of the mental apparatus, which is to "relieve the person from the tensions which his needs create in him."[23] The most satisfying mode of relieving these tensions is surely to master the world, to extract from it the gratifications that individuals crave, by founding universities and laboratories, devising banking systems and patent laws. Another mode—and this is the proper business of the cultural defenses—is to arrange tenable compromises, temporary but renewable truces, between unremitting wishes and the fears that these wishes generate, in oneself and in others. To this end, cultural defenses build up legal codes, moral injunctions, religious rituals, marriage customs, and police forces.

Social institutions are agents of satisfaction; they mobilize energies for the sake of securing domination and holding rival claimants at bay. But they also provide defensive cover to ease the lives of the individuals who live under their aegis by constructing forbidding fortifications of honor and indignation, brimming moats of shame and self-reproach—so many stratagems serving to contain the invasion of disorderly, possibly destructive passions. More positively, these defensive institutions license passions that would, without their imprimatur, be profoundly anxiety-provoking; they

22. Freud, *Die Zukunft einer Illusion* (1927), *St.A.*, IX, 140; *The Future of an Illusion, S.E.*, XXI, 6.
23. See above, p. 144.

provide interpretations of the world that lend it a reassuring semblance of order and stability; they give house room to eccentrics whom their contemporaries would, without such refuge, stigmatize as criminals or madmen. The institution of war makes killing praiseworthy; religion rewards ecstasy; chains of command at once control and liberate the urge to exercise power over others. Inevitably, like the individual's defenses, social or cultural defensive systems may fulfill their assignment too well and exacerbate the very anxieties they were presumably created to disarm. But appropriate or not, rational or irrational, the cultural defenses steadily work to define and redefine areas of freedom within which individuals navigate their way.[24]

Here, I strongly suspect, may lurk (to speak with William Langer) the historian's next assignment. To write a history of the defenses, to trace their origins, analyze their personal and social transformations, allocate to each epoch and class the defenses it has found most suitable, would be a noble task. It is striking to see that a few historians, without being psychohistorians, have in fact begun to canvass

---

24. The most interesting work on cultural defense mechanisms has so far been done by English Kleinians. See Elliott Jaques, "Social Systems as Defence against Persecutory and Depressive Anxiety: A Contribution to the Psycho-Analytical Study of Social Processes," Melanie Klein et al., *New Directions in Psycho-Analysis* (1955), 478–98, and a splendid pamphlet by Isabel E. P. Menzies, *The Function of Social Systems as a Defence Against Anxiety: A Report on a Study of the Nursing Service of a General Hospital* (1970), which examines the way an institution (the rules under which nurses deal with patients) can indeed manage to stimulate the anxieties it is devised to assuage. As a treatment of cultural and individual factors, this essay is exemplary. See also, from a quite different perspective, Melford E. Spiro, "Religious Systems as Culturally Constituted Defense Mechanisms," in Spiro, ed., *Context and Meaning in Cultural Anthropology* (1965), 100–13.

defensive activity as valuable clues to the past. I take, as the best instance I know, Keith Thomas's *Man and the Natural World,* a study in changing English attitudes toward animals, fellow humans, trees, and grass. In a half-dozen fascinating, beautifully documented chapters, Thomas traces a marked shift from one cultural style to another— from the haughty posture that man, privileged possessor and ruler of all nature, may do with inferior beings as he will, to the more modest and generous sense of himself as the steward of all he surveys. This shift in social defense systems, largely enacted between the seventeenth and the nineteenth centuries, meant a progressive enlargement of human responsibility for animate and inanimate nature, a lowered threshold of disgust, and a more exacting feeling of compassion. The most wanton cruelty to animals, as Thomas demonstrates, was quite unthinking, permitted not merely by the proud conviction of undisputed overlordship, but also by the convenient notion that the beasts and birds have no feelings and therefore cannot suffer. Gradually, Englishmen learned to discriminate among their legitimate aggressions against animals: only those forming part of the human diet or raiding hen-houses could be slaughtered without a twinge of uneasiness. The once passionately defended practice of torturing and killing animals for sport, as in cock-fighting and bear-baiting, came to seem gratuitous, coarse, indecent, inhuman.

Thomas traces this massive reorientation of the traditional English sensibility by offering an array of telling instances. But he does not fail to propose a series of causes: the spread of scientific knowledge, the incipient secularization of world views, and the emergence of the eighteenth-century cult of feeling. These impulses toward humanitarianism, which came to include animals along with starving humans, prisoners, children, and remote natives within the embrace of tearful sympathy, were supported by practical developments. Industrialization made working animals less necessary than ever before; the rising self-confidence and political maturity of the industrious English middle classes gave strong impetus to anti-aristocratic propaganda directed against hunting, that privileged and cruel sport of rich idlers. By the nineteenth century, the age of pets, of wildlife refuges, of vegetarianism, was at hand—not, Thomas concludes, without burdening Englishmen with a dilemma still troublesome today: "how to reconcile the physical requirements of civilization with the new feelings and values which the same civilization had generated." The modern exploitation of nature has produced a civilization ill at ease with itself, and with a technological inventiveness that generates comforts and spreads prosperity. "A mixture of compromise and concealment," Thomas notes, "has so far prevented this conflict from having to be fully resolved. But the issue cannot be completely evaded and it can be relied upon to recur."[25] In describing civilization as a perplexing dilemma in which no solutions are permanent and every advance exacts its price, Keith Thomas sounds much like Sigmund Freud.

Would Thomas's book have been very different if he had accepted Freud more explicitly than this? The question obtrudes itself, and the answer will speak to issues larger than those raised in this chapter. It is tempting to suggest that the gain of introducing psychoanalytic categories into his tightly argued study would have been marginal at best and probably outweighed by a certain loss of elegance and clar-

---

25. Thomas, *Man and the Natural World: Changing Attitudes in England 1500–1800* (1983), 301, 303.

ity. Actually (and I trust I do not sound patronizing about a magisterial historical work), Thomas in this volume has been speaking Freud without knowing it. He cites Freud just once, and his chosen auxiliary science, we know, is not psychoanalysis but anthropology, of which he had already made inspired use in his *Religion and the Decline of Magic,* published in 1971. Moreover, he has explicitly denied that he has consciously resorted to the psychoanalytic dispensation.[26] But Thomas scatters evidence of being very much at home in Freud's domain. We all live in that domain, more or less, as I have shown, but Thomas makes as much as possible of his unchosen habitat. He employs such psychoanalytic concepts as obsessiveness and projection, guilt and defensiveness; he analyzes the symbolic freight that cockfighting carries by recognizing the sexual *double entendre* underlying the manifest attractions of that bellicose bird.[27]

Still, there is a difference between visiting the country of psychoanalysis and taking out citizenship in it. The alert

26. "I have never set out self-consciously to apply psychoanalytic concepts to history. As a young man I read a good deal of Freud (I think that *Civilisation and its Discontents* was the book that interested me most) . . . But my admiration for Freud himself has always been heavily qualified. I felt that he was very much the child of his time and have never been convinced that his insights have universal validity, though they are a powerful stimulus to the imagination. This is not to say that I haven't been influenced, partly in ways of which I am barely aware . . . . But my *conscious* use of psychoanalytic theory has been minimal." Personal communication, March 31, 1984.

An important text, very much in the psychoanalytic ambiance, is, of course, Norbert Elias's work on the growth of modern manners, first written in the 1930s but reaching general notice only in the mid-1960s. *The Civilizing Process,* 2 vols. (1976; tr. Edmund Jephcott, vol. I, *The Development of Manners* [1978], II, *Power and Civility* [1982]).

27. *Man and the Natural World,* 50, 183.

reader will not have failed to notice that the Freudian vocabulary I have introduced offers a series of redescriptions.
But descriptions can contain explanations, and Freudian
categories can serve as so many pointers to deep diagnoses
of individuals and social groups; they are cues to hidden
dimensions of unconscious motives and repressed conflicts.
A psychoanalytically engaged historian working with the
materials that Keith Thomas has unearthed would go further along the analytic path on which Thomas had already
taken the first steps. Such a historian would wonder about,
and try to find evidence detailing, the fantasy life of English
grammar school boys tying a rooster to a stake and then
pelting it to death, or of huntsmen shooting down tame
deer that gamekeepers had driven within range of their
guns. He would suspect that the suave, self-congratulatory
stance letting well-bred Englishmen condescend to colonial
peoples exhibited traces of primitive psychological stratagems. He would, moving to the nineteenth century, discover
the defensive maneuver of reaction formation—the energetic
unconscious denial of sadism through the exaggerated practice of the opposite—in the virulent and intolerant antivivisectionist. He would (one hopes prudently and with due
respect for the ambiguities of human development) detect
significant resemblances between the increasingly influential
scientific world view, which sees nature not as man's servant
but as quite indifferent to him, and the painful process of
psychological maturation in which the growing child learns
to separate itself from its caretakers and to retreat from its
treasured, wholly fantastic sense of omnipotence. The age
of candid violence and cruelty bears resemblances to a phase
in which aggressive impulses are given free rein in part because so many live on the margin of subsistence and therefore cannot afford to sublimate their hatreds, while the few

who live superbly as warriors do not need to sublimate them. The age of greater humanity and kindness, when affluence is diffused and aristocratic values are under fire, is one in which sublimation becomes both possible and necessary.[28] Such parallels would doubtless have encouraged the psychoanalytic historian to reflect on the share of social forces in mental representations, which Thomas has so skillfully explored in his own way.

3 | THE STUBBORN SELF

The argument proclaiming man's cultural nature enshrines an important truth, but, as Freud asserted over and over, not the whole truth. Psychoanalysts have never withdrawn their attention from the individual's uniqueness, from his brave wrestling for integrity. Their case for the stubborn self has been energetically argued in recent decades in some distinguished essays, and I have buttressed that case in my discussion of the drives and their fates. But since historians

---

28. These psychoanalytic speculations are not intended as props to complacency. The historian is not a moral judge, though there is, of course, no reason why he should not welcome the spread of decency and humanity. But, whatever the historian's proper place in ethical inquiry, it is at any event true, as Thomas does not fail to observe, that sublimation may go wrong, maturity be less appealing than youth. The shift in English attitudes toward animals was by no means an unambiguous blessing. Self-restraint and preoccupation with the suffering of others exacted its price in a certain censoriousness, a measure of prudishness, and in what Charles Dickens derisively called, in *Bleak House,* telescopic philanthropy—the lavishing of pious charitable attentions on distant, often unresponsive tribes while neglecting the poor nearer to home. Psychoanalysts could only agree: Freud, no enemy to civilization or the sublimation of instinctual drives, firmly believed that nineteenth-century middle-class culture had in fact driven its self-control and sexual asceticism to the point of neurotic disease—an argument I qualify in my *Education of the Senses.*

have stood aside from the debate in which these essays have participated, it will be appropriate to rehearse their argument here. Probably the most provocative among these approaches toward a just—and for the historian, eminently usable—appraisal of human nature in culture has been a paper of 1961 by the sociologist Dennis Wrong on "the oversocialized conception of man" that he detected among his colleagues. His title, which has added a term to the vocabulary of contemporary social science, sufficiently indicates the point it so persuasively makes: while there have been some articulate dissenters from orthodoxy, the reigning sociological theory of our age, best exemplified in the writings of Talcott Parsons, has tried to explain the existence of social order by man's capacity to internalize the norms of his culture. Man, on this view, is wholly molded by the institutions that surround and overwhelm him. Naturally he responds to external forces, to the police power of authorities that inspire him with fear and impel him toward compliance; but more than that, he takes society's rules into himself. Hence, were he to disobey them, he would feel guilty.[29]

But in this oversocialized conception of man, Wrong complains, the psychological process of "internalization has imperceptibly been equated with 'learning,' or even with 'habit-formation' in the simplest sense." This disastrous

---

29. Dennis H. Wrong, "The Oversocialized Conception of Man in Modern Sociology" (1961), in *Skeptical Sociology* (1976), 31–46, at 37. See also Wrong's "Postscript 1975" and his companion essay "Human Nature and the Perspective of Sociology" (1963), ibid., 47–54, 55–70. Wrong has noted a little sadly that the first of these essays, with its catchy title, has attracted far more attention than anything else he has written. There is some reason for this (doubtless galling) selectivity: his paper on the oversocialized conception of man is a significant corrective for every sociologist—and historian.

oversimplification discards "the whole stress" of psychoanalysis "on inner conflict—on the tension between powerful
impulses and superego controls." For Freud, Wrong argues,
this conflict is of crucial importance, and has proved far
subtler, far closer to human experience, than that advocated
by the sociologists whom Wrong criticizes. They see the individual who conforms feeling at peace; but psychoanalysis
has demonstrated that such an individual may suffer far
more exquisitely than the nonconformist, defiant dissenter.
"To Freud, it is precisely the man with the strictest superego, he who has most thoroughly internalized and con-
formed to the norms of his society, who is most wracked
with guilt and anxiety."[30]

This dark, ironic psychological reality is inaccessible to
social scientists unduly impressed with the capacity of culture to integrate its diverse components. Hence the pervasiveness of conflict both in society and in the individual
must remain a mystery to them, to be denigrated or explained away. Indeed, what Freud saw, and what these sociologists do not see, is that conflict is normal, not just
deviant. They have almost willfully closed their eyes to the
pressures of unconscious needs, to the importunities of
the pleasure principle. The "most fundamental insight" of
psychoanalysis is "that the wish, the emotion, and the fantasy are as important as the act in man's experience." By insisting on man's malleability, on his hunger for approval
from others, most social scientists have dropped the stubborn self from view. And so, Wrong concludes, "When
Freud defined psychoanalysis as the study of the 'vicissitudes of the instincts,' he was confirming, not denying, the
'plasticity' of human nature insisted upon by social scien-

30. Ibid., 36, 37.

tists. The drives or 'instincts' of psychoanalysis are not fixed dispositions to behave in a particular way; they are utterly subject to social channeling and transformation and could not reveal themselves in behavior without social molding." There can be no doubt that for "psychoanalysis man is indeed a social animal; his social nature is profoundly reflected in his bodily structure." But the differences between the Freudian view and that of most sociologists remain profound. "To Freud man is a *social* animal without being entirely a *socialized* animal. His social nature is itself the source of conflicts and antagonisms that create resistance to socialization by the norms of any of the societies which have existed in the course of human history."[31] What makes the sociological misreading of human nature so particularly grating is that it is a misreading of psychoanalysis, a violation of Freud in the name of Freud, whom most of these social scientists think they have studied with care and profit.

Some six years before Dennis Wrong registered his pointed, highly effective protest against a theory of man that would simply drown the individual in his social ambiance, Lionel Trilling arrived at the same conclusions from a literary perspective. Ruminating over Freud's prominent role in defining the modern idea of culture, Trilling celebrates Sigmund Freud's commitment to biology, which he sees as offering unmatched assistance to the threatened individual. Certainly, Trilling writes, Freud "made plain how the culture suffuses the remotest parts of the individual mind, being taken in almost literally with the mother's milk." But, while Freud describes the person as pervaded by his culture to his very marrow, "there is in what he says about culture an unfailing note of exaspera-

---

31. Ibid., 45.

tion and resistance." His "view of culture is marked" by a powerful *"adverse* awareness," an "indignant perception," a "tragic regret." Although the self, for Freud, is "formed by its culture," he "also sees the self as set against the culture, struggling against it, having been from the first reluctant to enter it."[32] Culture, in short, is indispensable and stifling at the same time. What may rescue the individual from its fatal embrace are his instinctual urges; Freud's insistence on the drives' unremitting search for pleasure, which is anchored in his essential endowment, is "so far from being a reactionary idea that it is actually a liberating idea. It proposes to us that culture is not all-powerful. It suggests that there is a residue of human quality beyond the reach of cultural control." The thirst for community that bedevils even the educated, their consuming need to be "all non-conformists together," must be corrected by firm resistance to this "cultural omnipotence."

This resistance draws strength from the Freudian reflection that "somewhere in the child, somewhere in the adult, there is a hard, irreducible, stubborn core of biological *reason,* which culture cannot reach and which reserves the right, which sooner or later it will exercise, to judge the culture and resist and revise it."[33] This is more than elegant

---

32. Trilling, *Freud and the Crisis of Our Culture* (1955), 36, 38–39.
33. Ibid., 48, 52–52, 53–54. See also the autobiographical essay by Melford E. Spiro, "Culture and Human Nature," in George D. Spindler, ed., *The Making of Psychological Anthropology* (1978), 330–60, in which Spiro reports his gradual emergence from the dogmatic cultural determinism fashionable among anthropologists to the far subtler determinism he found in Freud, a determinism that assigns a prominent and indeed indelible role to the permanent elements in human nature. For a devastating account of the cultural determinism that Spiro managed to overcome, see Derek Freeman's rather too vigorous but informative dissection of Margaret Mead's

and emphatic; as an exposition of Freud's settled convictions about the dialectical interplay between the individual and his culture, it is precisely right. One need only read Freud's case histories to acknowledge the justice of Lionel Trilling's—and Dennis Wrong's—appraisal of Freud's thought on human nature: all of the analysands Freud thought worth writing about were at once recognizably themselves and representative of widely shared experiences; they were at the same time the victims of others and of themselves.

Precisely like psychoanalysts, though for professional reasons of their own, historians find themselves tracing the thread of individuality in the tapestry of society. However uncertain a historicist the modern historian may be, he is bound to be committed to individualism, to seek out what is unique in each historical personage, each historical event, each historical epoch. The rest, he will say, is sociology. But his individualism is under persistent challenge; his need to generalize, to assume and exhibit the reality of larger entities—clans, professions, classes—is steadily upon him. It is at this point that the shared experiences of which I have spoken clamor for recognition and collective description.[34] Even the comparative historian, casting his trained comprehensive glance at the diverse materials before him, must be quite as concerned with what the various elements in his

---

field work, *Margaret Mead and Samoa: The Making and Unmaking of an Anthropological Myth* (1983).

34. Reflecting on this matter, the distinguished ancient historian Chester G. Starr has written: "When one links a mass of events in different places or times by a connective tissue of generalization, the uniqueness of such historical events is thereby limited, for generalization is possible only if we can establish the presence of valid similarity." "Reflections upon the Problem of Generalization," in Louis Gottschalk, ed., *Generalization in the Writing of History* (1963), 3.

comparisons have in common as with showing what differentiates them from one another. Doubtless, the historian finds generalizations a convenience; they save energy in research and ease communication of results. But if they are to be more than rhetorical devices, they must rest on the conviction that they have captured substantial similarities, even partial identities, and, at the same time, a continuous—and discoverable—interaction between the individuals making up the collectivity and that collectivity itself.

It would be only too tempting to dismiss such historiographical preoccupations as play with banal issues that each historian can resolve almost intuitively for himself by calling on his professional experience. But the problems are genuine enough, no less pressing for being generally ignored. They arise with particular insistence in the analysis of common beliefs or dominant ideals. Certainly the pervasive reality of dominant notions about man, nature, and destiny, and their intrusive impact on the men who have imbibed them as cues from culture from their first sentient moments onward, seems beyond denying: the current vogue of the French term *mentalité,* which is only *Zeitgeist* brought up to date, testifies to that. The distinctive contribution of psychoanalysis to the study of *mentalité*—a generalization if there ever was one—is its discovery of hidden conflicts and invisible pressures bearing on the making of men's minds. Shared beliefs, the psychoanalyst will say, are at least in part shared illusions and shared fantasies.[35]

The issues that this discussion raises are so delicate and so important, that I want to review the ways that scientists of man and society may shuttle profitably between indi-

---

35. See D. W. Winnicott, "Transitional Objects and Transitional Phenomena" (1951), in *Through Paediatrics to Psycho-Analysis* (1958; ed. 1975), 229–42.

vidual and social psychology. The historian may elaborate and clarify the fairly rudimentary Freudian social psychology that explains group coherence and group actions by mutual identifications, by the liberating effect sheer collective existence has on impulses normally held in check, and by the way groups free themselves from their original purposes to pursue purposes of their own. He may, next, appeal to the psychoanalytic perspective of human nature which sees that nature as offering an impressively varied but strictly limited repertory of possible wishes, feelings, and anxieties, thus enabling the historian to predict—prudently, always alert to deviations—how collectivities are likely to think and act together. He may, too, follow the Freudian developmental schedule that analyzes how the individual internalizes social mores, social beliefs, social prohibitions, and how his culture, principally acting through the mediation of his intimates, provides directions for his raw drives, hidden wishes, and floating anxieties. He may, in addition, follow the procedures first devised and popularized by Erik Erikson in his *Young Man Luther:* to concentrate on the character and fortunes of an influential personage who, the author will assume, reflects and articulates the deepest tensions of his time and the underlying temper of his contemporaries with exemplary lucidity or with neurotic but instructive intensity.

This Eriksonian style of analysis, in which the historian reads culture through an individual, has its risks and its opportunities; its efficacy hinges far more on a careful historical exploration of the great personage's social world than on the diagnosis of his character structure. One of the more perceptive of these ventures is, in my judgment, Arthur Mitzman's *Iron Cage,* which undertakes a historical and psychoanalytic interpretation of Max Weber. According to

Mitzman's reading of Weber's tormented psychological life, which included a painful rebellion against his father and a lengthy psychotic breakdown, his innermost dilemmas reflected the dilemmas of his rigid and repressive culture which, at least to a restless, probing intellect like Weber's, at once invited radical disobedience to authority and punished it pitilessly. Finally, the psychoanalytic historian in search of a social psychology may trace the culture in the individual and the individual in his culture by exploring the defenses that help him, and his culture, to get through life.[36]

I have quoted a Freud, confident that his discoveries opened the way to an understanding of society by offering explanations of individual minds at work. He said so once again near the end of his life, in the postscript he added in 1935 to the brief autobiography he had published ten years earlier. He was nearly eighty, and could look back on half a century of seminal thinking about man in his culture. "After the lifelong detour through the natural sciences, medicine and psychotherapy," he wrote, "my interest returned to those cultural problems which had once fascinated the youth scarcely awakened to thinking." As early as 1912,

---

36. Arthur Mitzman, *The Iron Cage: An Historical Interpretation of Max Weber* (1970). For another, prudent instance of this procedure, see Thomas A. Kohut, "Kaiser Wilhelm II and his parents: an inquiry into the psychological roots of German policy towards England before the First World War," in John C. G. Röhl and Nicolaus Sombart, eds., *Kaiser Wilhelm II: New Interpretations* (1982), 63–89. For a bolder and hence more vulnerable effort to derive foreign policy from the character of governing politicians, see Judith M. Hughes, *Emotion and High Politics: Personal Relations in Late Nineteenth-Century Britain and Germany* (1983). The issue in general is discussed by John E. Mack, "Psychoanalysis and Historical Biography," *J. Amer. Psychoanal. Assn.* XIX (1971), 143–79.

he recalled, he had investigated the origins of religion in *Totem and Taboo* from a psychoanalytic angle of vision; in the 1920s, he had carried this work further in *The Future of an Illusion* and *Civilization and its Discontents*. He had been helped by "recognizing, more and more clearly, that the events of human history, the interactions between human nature, cultural development, and the precipitates of primeval experiences—as whose representative religion thrusts itself forward—are only the mirror of the dynamic conflicts between the ego, the id and the superego which psychoanalysis studies in the individual, the same events repeated on a larger stage."[37] Freud never doubted that the road from couch to culture is open. The sympathetic historian, retracing Freud's steps, will agree, but he is bound to add that the psychoanalysts have left him much work to do. Their road is neither completely paved nor adequately mapped. What the historian has at his disposal is a suggestive sketch that he must fill out with his own researches, using his own skills. Perhaps it is enough for his morale to know that the Freudian dispensation has supplied him with the map and the means and that, in the difficult boundary area where individual and social psychology meet and merge, psychoanalysis has managed to hold in healthy balance the social share in the individual's mind on the one hand, and the stubborn and unique self on the other.

---

37. Freud, "Selbstdarstellung; Nachschrift 1935" (1936), *Gesammelte Werke*, XVI, 32; "An Autobiographical Study; Postscript (1935)," *S.E.*, XX, 72.

6

The Program in Practice

1 | THOUGHTS ON THE RECORD.

One brave pocket of resistance remains to fire on the Freudian assailant after all the historians' defensive fortifications have been leveled and their commonsense fortress invaded: the proposal to integrate psychoanalysis into historical research and interpretation may prove, after all, impracticable. Even the historian professing himself fully persuaded by the preceding chapters has good reasons to hold this final doubt in reserve. He may acknowledge that his discipline can profit from a dependable psychology; that psychoanalysis is precisely such an auxiliary discipline; that the psychoanalytic perception of human nature is ultimately compatible with his own largely tacit views; that psychoanalysis can sharpen his sensitivity not only for tradition-bound and irrational thought and conduct, but also for rational self-interest; and that the proverbial individualism of psychoanalysis, rather than frustrating, can inform the historian's investigation of collective phenomena. Yet, conceding all this, he may persist in recalling once again his favorite and (he believes) devastating reservation: one cannot, when all is said, psychoanalyze the dead.

I have granted from the outset that this is more than just a clever obstructive demurrer. The past, individual or collective, is not a patient. Clio on the couch does not respond to interpretations, does not develop transferences on her analyst. She just lies there. We find the disheartening implications of her obstinate, frustrating passivity spread across the pages of psychohistorical writings. It is certainly undeniable that the record Freudian historians, beginning with Freud himself, have compiled is less than confidence-inspiring. David Stannard was shrewd to devote the opening chapter of his assault on psychohistory—and psychoanalysis—to Freud's essay on Leonardo da Vinci. The shortcomings of that frankly exploratory paper have been sufficiently exposed: in analyzing the single, tantalizing memory of his early childhood that Leonardo confided to his notebooks, Freud made much of a mistranslated pivotal word. The bird that, Leonardo would recall many years later, had come to him when he was a little boy in his cradle, opened his mouth with its tail, beating him in his lips many times, was not a vulture, as Freud supposed, but a kite. This unraveled part of Freud's intricate skein of reasoning about Leonardo's psychological development: the vulture, a bird associated in Egyptian mythology with motherhood and androgyny, had led Freud into some far-reaching speculations; the kite was just a bird. And in drawing intimate biographical inferences from Saint Anne's youthful appearance in Leonardo's celebrated painting of the Virgin with mother and child, he did less than justice to the artistic convention of blooming Saint Annes available in Leonardo's time.

All this has given critics of psychohistory some welcome ammunition. But while Freud was piqued into writing a paper on Leonardo by the fascinating and mysterious inner history of an artist he greatly admired, its originating impulsions stemmed from his interest in character formation and the origins of homosexuality. "Leonardo da Vinci and a Memory of his Childhood" does not pose as a psychobiography and is therefore far from being a conclusive test of the uses to which the historian may put psychoanalysis.[1] Still, it is a less than promising beginning.

Nor have later ventures by psychoanalysts been calculated to silence all doubts. Erik Erikson's pace-setting psychobiography of Luther which, as I noted earlier, really founded psychohistory in the mid-1950s, is a moving piece of wisdom literature; Erikson offered his mature reflections on one adolescent, young man Luther, from the perspective of a sympathetic and cultivated analyst professionally engaged in easing the harrowing and inspiring lot of gifted, profoundly disturbed youngsters. Surely the program for a working alliance between psychoanalyst and historian that Erikson sets out in his opening chapter is a model of its kind. At the same time, Martin Luther was a less than

---

1. "Where Freud has misinterpreted Leonardo, and he admits more than once in his book how speculative his attempt is, it was in part because he ignored or misread certain facts. His false conclusions do not imply that psychoanalytic theory is wrong; the book on Leonardo, a brilliant *jeu d'esprit,* is no real test of this theory, which here has been faultily applied." Meyer Schapiro, "Leonardo and Freud: An Art-Historical Study," *Journal of the History of Ideas,* XVII, 2 (April 1956), 178. Schapiro's brilliant and respectful critique provoked the psychoanalyst Kurt Eissler into a substantial, far from impertinent if excessively angry (and hence anxious) rejoinder, *Leonardo da Vinci: Psycho-Analytic Notes on the Enigma* (1961). For a lucid discussion of Freud's paper, including the kite-vulture debacle, see the "Editor's Note" to "Leonardo" in Freud, *S.E.,* XI (1957), 59–62.

happy choice, though a compelling one, to exemplify that program: we cannot be sure that Luther's critical episodes, on which his psychoanalytic biographer has principally drawn, happened in the way they were recorded later, or whether they ever happened at all.[2] Moreover, Erikson's assiduous epigones have, for the most part, lacked his intellectual energy and his gift for graceful exposition.

To make the work of Freudian historians more problematic still, and keep skeptical historians skeptical, psychoanalysts' unconvincing forays into psychoanalytic history have been matched by historians' incursions into the same dark and dangerous terrain. There is little point in launching a critique of psychohistorical writings since the mid-1950s; they add up to very varied performances and are, in sum, by no means wholly depressing. To advert, even glancingly, to the fiascos of psychohistory is not to yield the ground but to clear it. For their own part, historians have been only too pleased to find this literature provoking enough to keep their resistance alive. In their jaundiced reading, psychohistorians have been guilty of explaining away carefully marshalled political theories as sheer reflections of ambiguous sexual identifications, or of degrading significant shifts in family relationships into orgies of oedipal combat. In actuality, these psychohistories are rarely quite so blatant, rarely quite so vulgar, as their irritated and impatient reviewers have liked to complain. Still, while psychohistorians have earnestly disclaimed any leaning toward reductionism,[3] their

---

2. See Roger A. Johnson, ed., *Psychohistory and Religion: The Case of "Young Man Luther"* (1977), which includes, among other articles, Roland Bainton's extensive and devastating review of Erikson's book.
3. Thus Isaac Kramnick writes, in the preface to his *The Rage of Edmund Burke: Portrait of an Ambivalent Conservative* (1977): "It

monographs and syntheses have too often succumbed to that temptation. Reductionism appears so besetting a defect of psychohistories that historians have seen it woven into their very fabric, an ineradicable and fatal flaw.

But reductionism is an accident of psychoanalytic history rather than of its essence. It is the most palpable among the growing pains of a discipline that has been young for some time now but may continue to claim the latitude open to a discipline still in the exploratory phase. Admittedly, psychoanalytic history is singularly susceptible to plagues of enthusiasts. Its more unfortunate products have many causes, like those perpetrated in other branches of history. But, as critics have fairly if rather maliciously insisted, too many psychohistorians have yielded to the attractions of simplicity and symmetry, to seductions that historians wielding a new and exciting interpretative instrument have found peculiarly irresistible. Still, we have adequate theoretical and practical antidotes to immunize the historian against such lures.

This confident (some might say, complacent) assertion calls for some comment. "Reductionism" is, as we know, a term of abuse. Yet reduction, the reasoned enterprise of dissolving one scientific theory in a larger, more comprehensive theory, is a thoroughly respectable scientific procedure.[4] It

---

is the relationship between Burke's life, personality, and social thought that will be studied here." And Bruce Mazlish, introducing his *James and John Stuart Mill: Father and Son in the Nineteenth Century* (1975), 8, insists: "John Stuart Mill is not a patient, and psychohistory, as we seek to practice it, does not wish to treat him as one." The reader may be forgiven for wondering if these praiseworthy intentions have been fully carried through. (See my *Education of the Senses*, 465).

4. Reduction is "an undeniable and recurrent feature of the history of modern science. There is every reason to suppose that such reduc-

derives its legitimacy from the rule of parsimony, Occam's razor, which instructs the scientist not to multiply laws and theories needlessly. To the extent that conscious thoughts and palpable events may be exhaustively explained by largely unconscious wants or conflicts, psychoanalytic reduction is not reductionist. The issue is wholly concrete: in historical practice, we can decide whether an interpretation crosses the line of acceptable economy into the forbidden terrain of naiveté only after the fact, and instance by instance. There is nothing inherently implausible about a historical explanation that assigns primacy to psychological factors. Like other scientists, the historian longs to offer one explanation where there had been two explanations before, and this in face of historians' carefully cultivated commitment to diversity. It has been their search for a neat and perspicuous explanatory scheme that has driven psychohistorians toward a deliberately primitive id psychology insensitive to the reality-testing work of the ego, and to demote adult historical actors to bundles of persistent, unresolved childhood symptoms. They have, in short, acted contrary to Whitehead's apt piece of advice to the investigator to seek simplicity and distrust it. Freud was not of their persuasion: he aimed at subsuming individual character and conduct under overarching psychological laws and, at the same time, establishing the uniqueness of each person. Far from spoiling the celebration of human variety and historical specificity, he would have supplied champagne for it.

He would have done so in the name of overdetermination. Critics have sometimes read that cardinal psychoanalytic principle as a prudent evasion of responsibility. But then, those determined to find fault with Freud will find it. Hence they have not scrupled to accuse him of being a single-minded simple-minded dogmatist selling one predictable ubiquitous causal agent, sexuality, and at the same time of taking refuge, in his bewilderment at the human drama, behind the glittering vagueness of multiple causation. Overdetermination is in fact nothing more than the sensible recognition that a variety of causes—a variety, not infinity— enters into the making of all historical events, and that each ingredient in historical experience can be counted on to have a variety—not infinity—of functions.[5] The historian, working with a wealth of causal agents subtle and gross, immediate and remote, intent on scanting none of them and on subjecting them to order, can only agree and applaud. Seek complexity, the historian and the psychoanalyst can say in unison, seek complexity and tame it.

2 | WAYS AND MEANS

In moments of good-natured self-denigration, psychoanalysts have sometimes wryly cautioned themselves against drawing rash inferences: "Do not generalize from one case," they will say, "generalize from two cases." Fortunately, recent historical literature offers more than two instances of how psychoanalytic perceptions may act as aids to discovery and interpretation. The array of Freudian in-

---

5. "It should be emphasised that overdetermination does not mean that the dream or symptom may be interpreted in an infinite number of ways." Nor, for that matter, "does overdetermination imply the independence or the parallelism of the different meanings of a single phenomenon." J. Laplanche and J.-B. Pontalis, *The Language of Psychoanalysis* (1967; transl. Donald Nicholson-Smith, 1973), 292–93.

struments is, after all, finely graded and remarkably versatile. I have learned in my own work that the historian may enlist Freudian perceptions to discover themes of critical moment but long marginal to historical scholarship—the hidden agendas that almost imperceptibly dominate childhood, the family, and culture as a whole, and the libidinal or aggressive currents that stealthily but irresistibly invade social and political life. He may attend to the metaphors that color cultural discourse. He may observe the passsionate, scarcely concealed rages that leave their deposits in play and in festivals ranging from the gross hostility of charivaris to the oblique messages of initiation rites. Beyond that, he may analyze society's reverberating and revealing silences. For the psychoanalytic historian, as for Sherlock Holmes, the dog that did not bark in the night may be called to testify as a reluctant but knowing witness. Psychoanalysis offers ideas and, in the right setting, with proper self-restraint, even some techniques that may provide un-hoped-for access to popular fantasies, to dreams and slips and other symptomatic acts, and to the defensive tactics that individuals and institutions quite unwittingly employ. It alerts the historians to documents that are useless, silent, and unmeaning without its theories.

Analyzing anxious campaigns against prostitution for my study of love in nineteenth-century culture, I was struck by the widespread desire to rescue "fallen women" and reclaim them for a pure and respectable life. The commitment to such rehabilitation was intense and, for most reformers, conscious. It animated the committees of experts formed in large cities across Western civilization late in the nineteenth century as it did earlier organizers of halfway houses and Magdalen shelters; it engrossed the quick sympathies of Charles Dickens and, more notoriously, of William Ewart

Gladstone who would cruise the nocturnal streets of London to accost young whores with tracts, well-meant speeches, and invitations to meet his wife at home. All these benevolent efforts fit into the improving mentality of the nineteenth-century middle classes whether pious or secular. But I became convinced that they drew much of their energy from an unconscious idea, the rescue fantasy, the wish to rehabilitate strangers, a disguise for the far more potent wish to restore the purity of the mother who, though officially an angel, does mysterious and terrible things with father behind closed bedroom doors. Had I not studied Freud, I would neither have seen the rescue fantasy in action, nor stumbled on how much heavy duty it does in a culture ready for compassion.

Other psychoanalytic insights and practices have enabled me to follow up clues I would never have recognized, and commended interpretations I could never have imagined, without their aid. Reading entries in private journals as though they were chains of associations—the kind of untrammeled meandering that every analysand is bidden to undertake on the couch—I saw myself treating abrupt leaps from theme to theme not as casual digressions or accidental swervings of attention but as patterns of coherent, surprisingly legible, mental processes. Diary keeping and journal writing, especially in the nineteenth century enjoined by parents and teachers, have long had their conventions; health, the weather, and deep thoughts about love or religion were almost obligatory topics. They, too, can become revealing symptoms for a society much preoccupied with the state of one's body or one's soul. But beyond that, the often curious twists in the succession of private observations and confessions revealed more, with their unconscious linkages, than the writer himself could ever reveal intentionally.

Again, studying the dreams that diarists or letter writers have thought interesting enough to record and, in their own amateurish way, to interpret, I could tease out of their latent dream thoughts well-camouflaged erotic and aggressive material of which the blander surfaces of their other surviving testimony had left no inkling whatever. Moreover, the clusters of manifest dream symbols or other details that seem to recur most frequently in certain cultures at certain moments offered me valuable, in some ways induplicable clues to little-noticed but very general conflicts. Similarly, to give but one more instance, I was made aware how freely aesthetic documents of a given society—its novels, poems, or paintings—disclose, under the psychoanalytic lense, the manner in which that society attempts to resolve, or refuses to acknowledge, issues it finds too delicate to discuss candidly. The all too human inclination to incest, the perils and promises of the exposed human body, men's underlying (as distinct from their overt) fear of women, or women's fear of men, all grist to the analyst's mill, can become informative material for historians.[6]

In the last several decades, a handful of biographers and historians has successfully integrated this way of reading into their accustomed, time-tested methods. They have not always mentioned Freud's name: Edmund Morgan, for one, has suggested that had he not occupied himself with Freud as he was writing his dissertation on Puritan family life in seventeenth-century Massachusetts, he would have written a far different book.[7] At times, though, the debt has been ex-

---

6. Detailed applications in Peter Gay, *The Bourgeois Experience: Victoria to Freud,* vol. I, *Education of the Senses* (1984), and vol. II, *The Tender Passion* (forthcoming 1986).

7. Personal communication, October 15, 1983.

plicitly acknowledged, never more instructively than in E. R. Dodds's magisterial *The Greeks and the Irrational.*[8] His procedure, no less than his results, will repay attention here.

Dodds opens his book with an intriguing, somewhat tendentious account of how he came to write it: as an organic enterprise in which Freudian propositions do not function as applied, chic decorations, but, held ready in the preconscious, serve to organize perceptions of past experience and bring dusty scholarly knowledge to life. One day, Dodds remembered, looking at the Parthenon sculptures in the British Museum, he happened upon a young man who was looking at the same sculptures but—unlike Dodds—was visibly unmoved. The two fell into conversation, and Dodds asked the young man if he could define his cool response. "Well," he ventured, after reflecting a bit, "it's all so terribly *rational,* if you know what I mean." Dodds thought he knew. It set him thinking: "Were the Greeks in fact quite so blind to the importance of non-rational factors in man's experience and behavior as is commonly assumed both by their apologists and by their critics?" Dodds's most eminent fellow classicists, including Gilbert Murray and Maurice Bowra, were inclined to dismiss the dramatic irrationality of Greek religion as sheer playfulness, as mere literature. Thus, this chance meeting, juxtaposed with the refusal of scholars to take Greek religion seriously, defined for Dodds

---

8. See above, pp. 40–41. The reviews were highly appreciative and extremely numerous, both in classical and historical journals. But while Dodds's reviewers extravagantly admired his masterpiece, they have shown little interest in following its lead, another instance just how resistant our profession is to psychoanalytic history, even when someone demonstrates that it can be done well.

"the question out of which this book grew."[9] The book was his answer.

It is always risky for readers to substitute their genetic guesses for those of the author—he, after all, was there. But I submit that Dodds's splendid study of Greek experience did not simply grow out of a question—or, at least, the question did not stand at the beginning of the inquiry. It had a weighty history behind it.[10] The professional investigator, after all, approaches his chosen task equipped with tested techniques, articulated points of view, copious information, and some ideas about the frontiers of controversy in his discipline. However tentatively he may put it, even to himself, he will fantasize about finding a new fact, developing a new line of reasoning, perhaps generating a new theory that will bring him, if not fame, money, and the love of beautiful women, at least the notice of his peers. The prod of self-discipline, the habit of throwing unsettling doubts at his most prized notions and his most meticulously honed epigrams, and confronting them with the evidence as it emerges—all that comes later.

Dodds's exploration, as he formulated it after his chance encounter, implied some conclusions he had developed, with a scholar's patience and a scholar's fund of information, after decades of work in ancient texts. An exigent though by no means malevolent demon had accompanied his career: a fascination with the irrational side of human experience. In his beautiful autobiography, published in 1977, two years before his death, he describes this "recurrent element" that had run "for more than sixty years like a separately coloured

9. Dodds, *The Greeks and the Irrational* (1951), 1.
10. For the best known and most persuasive formulation of this point, see Karl Popper, *Conjectures and Refutations: The Growth of Scientific Knowledge* (1962).

thread through the patchwork" of his life, as "the attempt to observe and if possible understand some few of that vast range of peculiar phenomena which occupy the disputed territory between science and superstition." Luckily, he had learned to use the occult without the occult using him; he defined himself as a sober "psychical researcher" attracted to unexplained facts, because "he believes that they can and should be explained, being as much part of nature as any other facts." The "long-term objective" of the "psychical researcher," Dodds noted, "is not to glorify the 'occult' but to abolish it by bringing its true significance to light and fitting it into its place in a coherent world picture. Far from wishing to pull down the lofty edifice of science, his highest ambition is to construct a modest annexe which will serve, at least provisionally, to house his new facts with the minimum of disturbance to the original plan of the building."[11]

This passage could have been written by Sigmund Freud. Much like Freud, Dodds took a passionate interest in beliefs, practices, and modes of conduct that fellow rationalists were dismissing as superstitions, as symptoms of derangement, or as imaginative play picturesquely concealing the reasonable thought beneath. Much like Freud, Dodds took dreams, madness, and trance seriously, and succeeded in

---

11. Dodds, *Missing Persons* (1977), 97–98. A year before this autobiography was published, I said of Freud that "he had no use whatever for the celebration of irrational forces, or for the primitivism that would evade the dialectic of civilization by abandoning civilization altogether. He had not labored in the sickroom of the human mind to join the party of disease; he had not descended to the sewer of human nature to wallow in what he had found there." Dodds belonged to this school of thought. "Introduction: Freud. For the Marble Tablet," *Berggasse 19: Sigmund Freud's Home and Offices, Vienna 1938; The Photographs of Edmund Engelman* (1976), 41.

uncovering aspects of the Greek mind that his predecessors had quite literally not seen. It permitted him to recognize the Greeks' habit of ascribing their states of mind to divine intervention, not as a conventional excuse or a flight from responsibility, but as a form of projection, "the pictorial expression, of an inward monition"; it was from such inner feelings, pinned on the gods, that "the divine machinery developed." Then some time late in the fifth century B.C., this projection, in which "unsystematised, nonrational impulses, and the acts resulting from them, tend to be excluded from the self and ascribed to an alien origin" gradually gave way to a "nascent demand for social justice," a certain " 'internalising' of conscience."

Dodds's resort to technical terminology enabled him to make two closely related points. He took antique projective activity as a cue to archaic styles of thinking, not as some mysterious, accidental tic. And, by recognizing the translation of undesirable impulses into the mischievous interventions of capricious deities as a defensive mechanism, he could rise above moralizing. What other scholars, less trained in psychoanalytic ways of thinking, would have seen as a calculated piece of sophistry—if they had seen it at all— Dodds could interpret as a mental activity almost wholly unconscious in nature. With characteristic circumspection, Dodds did not venture a complete explanation for this shift from "Shame-culture to Guilt-culture." He cites Malinowski's theory that irrational beliefs occupy the space into which rational human control has not ventured, or from which it has retreated; and he alludes to pervasive social upheavals that might have "encouraged the reappearance of old culture-patterns." But as a good Freudian, he finds such explanations incomplete, and suggests that historians take a closer look at Greek domestic life. "The family situation in ancient Greece" had given "rise to infantile conflicts whose echoes lingered in the unconscious mind of the adult." After all, "the psychologists have taught us"—and for "the psychologists" read "Freud and his followers"— "how potent a source of guilt-feelings is the pressure of unacknowledged desires, desires which are excluded from consciousness save in dreams or daydreams, yet are able to produce in the self a deep sense of moral uneasiness." Rounding out the argument, he notes how "closely" the Homeric Zeus was "modelled on that of the Homeric pater-familias."[12]

"The psychologists" sharpened Dodds's perception of the Greeks and the irrational in other decisive ways. He sees Dionysiac rites and the cult of Apollo as opposite and equally necessary pendants to one another: "each ministered in his own way to the anxieties characteristic of a guilt-culture," for, while Apollo "promised security," Dionysus "offered freedom."[13] Again, he recognizes in Plato's "Eros a precursor of Freudian libido," a filiation on which Freud himself had commented earlier.[14] Or he interprets both the reasonableness of reported dreams, and the astonishing inappropriateness of remembered feeling, with a vocabulary, and perceptions, he had drawn from *The Interpretation of Dreams:* the first, Dodds suggests, was an instance of "secondary elaboration," the second an "inversion of affect." Finally, he accounts for the renewal of antique superstitions during the decline of the classical age, that new, yet so old, desperate resort to magical healing, by invoking regression,

---

12. Dodds, *Greeks and the Irrational,* 14, 17, 32, 37, 44–45, 47.
13. Ibid., 76–78.
14. Ibid., 213, 218; see Freud, "Preface to the Fourth Edition" (1920) *Three Essays on Sexuality, S.E.,* VII, 134, and *Group Psychology and the Analysis of the Ego* (1921), *S.E.,* XVIII, 91.

which led in the end to still cruder regressions, to the incantation of magical curses designed to destroy enemies.[15]

Regression, of course, involves a return to earlier phases of mental organization, and Dodds accepted Freud's metaphor describing the mind as a geological deposit that preserves the archaic under more recent layers. "A new belief-pattern," Dodds writes, echoing both Gilbert Murray and Freud, "very seldom effaces completely the pattern that was there before: either the old lives on as an element in the new—sometimes an unconfessed and half-conscious element—or else the two persist side by side, logically incompatible, but contemporaneously accepted by different individuals or even by the same individual."[16] In concrete instances, then, as in sweeping interpretations, Freud gave Dodds a way of seeing and of finding surprising readings for familiar texts.

On occasion, psychoanalysis has not just unriddled historical mysteries but discovered the mystery to be intriguing and pregnant with explanatory possibilities. Maynard Solomon's biography of Ludwig van Beethoven is an example of such imaginative detective work. Beethoven went through life obstinately believing, and wasted valuable energy trying to prove, that he had not been born in December 1770, but rather in December 1772. His baptismal certificate, which he asked his friends to procure for him over and over, unequivocally declared the earlier date, 1770, to be correct. But Beethoven refused to accept the plain evidence before him. In 1977, Solomon, a musicologist thoroughly versed in

---

15. Dodds, *Greeks and the Irrational*, 114, 123, 193–94.
16. Ibid., 179.

Freudian ways of thinking, resolved this conundrum with a psychoanalytic insight called the family romance. This fantasy, very widespread especially among the young, imagines one's parents to be only stepparents, or one's father only a stepfather, and one's real parentage, distinguished and exalted. The psychological function of this partially unconscious fiction is to give the imprimatur to the child's aggressive impulses and, especially when the victim is the parent of the same sex, to grant access to the other, adored parent, if only in the largely repressed imagination. Previous biographers of Beethoven had certainly not overlooked his irrational campaign to establish an imaginary birthdate for himself, and had tried out a variety of superficial and implausible explanations. Solomon, equipped to work with sharper intellectual instruments, linked Beethoven's tenacious defense of his fantasy to his dismaying childhood, marred by his father's irresponsibility, dishonesty, and alcoholism. Beethoven, one might think, had good conscious grounds for detesting his father. But his fantasy, which became a permanent and active ingredient in his character, went far beyond rational criticism or disappointment to link up with concealed wishes and hatreds that Beethoven could never satisfy or exorcise. Thus Solomon's Freudian perceptions make poignant sense of what had seemed to his precursors an odd delusion or a self-serving mystification.[17]

With equal penetration, Solomon succeeded in unraveling an unsavory, extremely puzzling domestic drama that shadowed Beethoven's later years: his indefatigable efforts to secure the guardianship over, virtually to kidnap, his

---

17. See Solomon, *Beethoven* (1977), esp. 3–6, 21–22. For an admirable attempt to come close to the soures of creativity, see Mary M. Gedo, *Picasso: Art as Autobiography* (1980).

nephew Karl, son of his late brother Caspar. He slandered Johanna van Beethoven, the boy's mother, to his friends and to the authorities; he went to court several times, exposing himself in the process to embarrassing and trying interrogations, all to gain possession of Karl. Repeatedly, he would speak of himself as if he were the boy's father, as though reiteration would convert the metaphor into a literal truth. Johanna van Beethoven, far less well connected than her famous brother-in-law, and as an occasionally unchaste woman vulnerable to charges of somewhat willful morality, fought back with her son very much on her side. This strange family duel went on for years and was punctuated by Karl's escapes from his smothering uncle culminating, not long before Beethoven's death, in an attempt to commit suicide.

This distressing affair has generated much earnest moralizing and no less earnest apologetics; it has been taken as proof of Johanna van Beethoven's unsuitability as a mother or, conversely, as a tragic symptom of Ludwig van Beethoven's mental collapse. Solomon, working with the psychoanalytic dictum that excessive passion signals an underlying conflict in which an opposite passion is secretly in play, persuasively argues that Beethoven was defending himself against strong erotic desires for his sister-in-law and masked hostility against his nephew. These proposals, and others punctuating Solomon's biography, considerably enrich our sense of Beethoven's tempestuous inner life and skillfully reach beyond his deafness to exhibit some of the obscure causes making him that unpredictable, rude, disorganized, unkempt bear so familiar to his indulgent and awestruck contemporaries. Solomon modestly enough never professes to do more than touch on Beethoven's supreme secret, his genius as a composer. But he gives us a Beethoven more believable, more truly human, than his idolatrous, and even his most scholarly, biographers had done before him.

Another psychoanalytic biography belongs in my catalogue of successes, Frederick Crews's study of Hawthorne, *The Sins of the Fathers,* published in 1966. Crews sets out his argument by "chiding" earlier biographers of Hawthorne for relying on "a simplistic psychology that looks only at surfaces," largely in the service of making Hawthorne into a respectable, "boring" moralist or pious believer. He concedes that one might cite passages supporting "what might be called a rudimentary Christianity." But, he adds, as a good Freudian, "the biographer is responsible for his subject's contradictions as well as his uplifting statements." Crews's Hawthorne is haunted by the "doubting habit" and ridden by "ambivalence." What makes Hawthorne interesting, he argues, is not some implausible transcendental explanation, but the fact that he was "self-divided, tormented."[18] Crews reads the neatness and piety, the apparent innocence of Hawthorne's literary surfaces as defensive stratagems, at once cultural in shape and personal in origins.

The gain in such a reading is marked. Crews remains true to Hawthorne's texts and clarifies much that has baffled other scholars. While he is too scrupulous a writer to fall into jargon and uses technical language sparingly,[19] he borrows his intellectual weapons entirely from the psychoanalytic arsenal, from Freud above all, and from Sandor Ferenczi, Karl Abraham, and the Erik Erikson of *Young*

---

18. Frederick C. Crews, *The Sins of the Fathers: Hawthorne's Psychological Themes* (1966), 6–10.
19. I note among others, "return of the repressed," "displacements," and "sublimations," ibid., 17; "Inhibition," 24; "censorship," 25; "anxiety," 34; "projection," 46; "ego," 74; "repression," 150.

Man Luther. This is psychoanalytic biography at its most felicitous.[20] It discovers precisely what Hawthorne had in mind when he called himself a writer "burrowing, to his utmost ability, into the depths of our common nature, for the purposes of psychological romance," intending to "reach the terrible core of man's being."[21] It is instructive how often Crews proclaims his intention of taking seriously the texts he is exploring, or the most minute clues that Hawthorne has left for his readers to ponder. This is another legacy of Freud, sensitively applied: to look closely, to overlook nothing.

One critical matter that Crews does not overlook is that Hawthorne was too anxious to realize his program without hesitations and frequent betrayals. "His penetration into secret guilt is compromised not only by his celebrated ambiguities of technique but by reluctance and distaste." It could not have been otherwise: drawing in his work "largely upon his own nature" and "disturbed by what he found,"[22] Hawthorne felt compelled to resist, or smooth out, his terrifying discoveries.

---

20. *Sins of the Fathers* is not flawless. Crews's facility tempts him into some rash deductions, and to overlook some psychoanalytic clues. Moreover, he betrays a certain credulity about "Victorian" culture. Hawthorne's wife, Sophia, was neither so angelic or aseptic as he makes her out to be, nor was the Hawthornes' culture quite so mendacious and prudish: the oft-repeated tale of the American ladies draping the legs of their piano in modest little skirts (a tale he accepts without cavil [see p. 14]), has been shown up as legend or a unique incident. See Carl N. Degler, "What Ought to Be and What Was: Women's Sexuality in the Nineteenth Century," *American Historical Review*, LXXIX, 5 (December 1974), 1467–90, and Peter Gay, *The Bourgeois Experience: Victoria to Freud*, vol. I, *Education of the Senses* (1984).

21. Ibid., 10–11.

22. Ibid., 11.

Thus equipped, taking "modern psychological theories seriously," Crews reinterprets "The Maypole of Merry Mount," one of "Hawthorne's most familiar and seemingly shallow tales." Far from being "banal" or "obvious," it proves in Crews's analysis a most uncomfortable erotic tale in which "the denied element surreptitiously reappears in imagery and innuendo," a tale awash in "suggestions of impotence and castration," while the "surface narrative remains conventionally 'pure.'" This well-known and innocuous story, then, provides access to the "inmost configuration" informing his plots, which explore, nearly all, "a definable, indeed classic, conflict of wishes."[23] We recognize this classic conflict as nothing else than the Freudian family drama driven into the unconscious only to resurface, stylized and its passions disguised, in Hawthorne's fictions.

In later chapters, Crews works out these insights with impressive panache. He clears away the generally accepted interpretation of Hawthorne as a celebrant, mildly critical but largely chauvinistic, of his New England ancestors. His preoccupation with colonial Massachusetts "is only a special case of his interest in fathers and sons, guilt and retribution, instinct and inhibition." What pervades his historical tales, Crews shows, is "the sense of symbolic family conflict writ large." The " 'Puritans' are the repressive side of Hawthorne."[24] Seeking to expose his ancestors, it turns out, Hawthorne has exposed mainly himself.

Crews pursues Hawthorne's ever-repeated act of self-exposure in a roughly chronological analysis of his tales and novels. He demonstrates Hawthorne's overriding preoccupations with incest between brother and sister as well as

23. Ibid., 16, 17–20, 24–26.
24. Ibid., 29, 60, 31.

incest vaguely Lesbian in connotation; with sadomasochistic entanglements; with the search for the idealized father; with the compulsive workings of a vengeful, pitiless super-ego punishing impious death wishes.[25] All this in an atmosphere of ambiguity, of sexual curiosity and longing held in check by sexual fear.[26] These unconscious conflicts do not, of course, lie casually side by side. They are essential ingredients in the oedipal triangle, which Crews finds to be dominating Hawthorne's characters throughout his career as a writer.

Hawthorne's enduring masterpiece, *The Scarlet Letter,* yields a very similar reading; Crews sees it as a novel in which libidinal desire coexists with feelings of guilt, and must forever wrestle them to the death.[27] *The Scarlet Letter* "has chiefly sprung, not from Puritan society's imposition of false social ideals on the three main characters, but from their own inner world of frustrated desires." Hawthorne leaves his readers "with a tale of passion through which we glimpse" a tragic truth, "the terrible certainty that, as Freud put it, the ego is not master in its own house." This is not to say that Crews slights the cultural in favor of the psychological world; what interests him most as he rehearses the hidden elements in Hawthorne's art is in fact "the conjunction of sexual and social themes." He moves, throughout, skillfully between biography and history, mind and culture. Crews's vision of man as the cultural animal equipped both with a potent unconscious and, at the same time, an equally potent capacity to learn from, and try to master, the world,

25. In order: ibid., chs. III, VI, VII; IV; V.
26. Ibid., chs. VI, VII, XII.
27. See ibid., 79.

is congruent with the psychoanalytic theory of mind that I
have developed in these chapters.[28]

The most systematic, most intensely cultivated attempt
to make the psychoanalytic persuasion work for history, at
once insisting on particularity and comprehensiveness, is
probably John Putnam Demos's *Entertaining Satan,* a study
of witchcraft in seventeenth-century New England. The delusions from which the witches, their victims, and their
judges suffered found social, institutionalized expression,
and drew on beliefs generally held and rarely questioned.
Yet the mental conflicts that gave rise to suspicions, accusa-
tions, and confessions, to acts of retribution and expiation,
were experiences of individuals. Demos skillfully works to
segregate and, at the same time, to blend, these personal
and public domains, the respective impress of intimate
neurosis and of communal strains that, together, constitute
his theme. To exhibit and dramatize this necessary multiplicity of vantage points, Demos has divided his book into
four sections: biography, psychology, sociology, and, in the
end, history, to plot the chronology of mental and public
events as a rising and declining arc of persecution.[29]

Demos's study rests solidly on his confident control over
the traditional ways of doing American Colonial history.
But it is, of course, his innovative psychoanalytic commitments, shifting somewhat eclectically among several over-
lapping psychoanalytic schools, that have caused the most
lively discussion and are of particular interest to these

28. Ibid., 142, 153, 180. The later history of Crews's engagement with
psychoanalysis is curious and to my mind a bit sad. See below pp.
234–35.
29. For the reception of Demos's book, see above, pp. 16–17.

pages. Never moving away from his cast of characters, Demos plays over them psychoanalytic searchlights like conversion hysteria, adolescent conflicts, exhibitionistic tendencies, narcissistic rage, projection or related defenses against troubling impulses, to account for behavior that appeared to contemporaries as simply deviant and very dangerous. And, with great effectiveness, he turns these lights on the witches' victims and persecutors. In one respect, in assigning to psychology only one section out of four, Demos's even-handed strategy works against him. It is arguable that he might have found a more elegant formal solution, but what matters most is that psychology informs all the four aspects of early Massachusetts history he has chosen to examine. The first two contain substantial and searching psychological profiles of witches, and in his last two sections, devoted to collective experience across space and time, Demos conscientiously returns to individual cases, to those fragments of culture at once unique and typical. "Biography, psychology, sociology, history," so he concludes his programmatic remarks, "four corners of one scholar's compass, four viewpoints overlooking a single field of past experience. Each captures part, but not all, of the whole," but together, though the connections are far from smooth and the labor "toilsome," the total historical experience emerges into view: "To see all this from *different* sides is to move at least some way toward full and final comprehension."[30] This, it seems to me, attractively and

---

30. Demos, *Entertaining Satan: Witchcraft and the Culture of Early New England* (1982), 15. One need only read Demos's book in tandem with H. R. Trevor-Roper's well-known compendious essay on "The European Witch-craze of the Sixteenth and Seventeenth Centuries" (*Religion, the Reformation and Social Change and Other Essays* [1967], 90–192) to recognize the advantage of the psychoana-

prudently hints at the ambition appropriate to psychoanalytic history, at its potential share in the historian's pursuit of the whole.

3 | TOTAL HISTORY

The aspiration toward total history is older by many centuries than its first express formulation. The ingredients of any program for seizing the rounded essence of the past, synthesizing the circumscribed scholarly findings of many monographs and in many archives, must naturally vary with each historian's definition of what matters most and what, in that light, deserves to be included in his copious scenario. Whether he believes the world principally moved by the hand of Providence, the force of technological innovation, the pressures of the unconscious, will determine the contours of his total history and the materials he will ultimately find worthy of inclusion. Certainly the ideal cannot rationally imply the exhaustively detailed presentation of every minute component of an event or an era, all aspects of its environments, and all its preconditions back into the mists of unrecorded time. A total history of the Battle of Waterloo that records the feelings, actions, and fates of

lytic cast of mind in explaining the elusive phenomenon of witch-persecutions. Trevor-Roper is nothing if not sophisticated; he links the "witch-craze" to a number of sociopsychological causes such as general misery, social malaise, the need to make enemies, and he recognizes that it was not torture alone that elicited those horrendous, often obscene confessions on which the witch-burners built their case. He writes with a sense of the contribution that the study of psychopathology can make to an understanding of these persecutions. But the precision, the firm grasp on inner dynamics, that characterizes Demos's psychoanalytic study is only vaguely present in, often absent from, Trevor-Roper's suave presentation.

every soldier (even presuming that such an account could ever be physically possible) would fall into the absurdities typical of the obsessive collector: a catalogue, no matter how exhaustive, does not add up to a comprehensive, let alone a comprehending history.

Rather, the call for a total history has been, for over two centuries, a critique of official historical practice, a call for light and air in a pedantic, stifling atmosphere. Voltaire, arguing that "a lock on the canal that joins the two seas, a painting by Poussin, a fine tragedy," are "a thousand times more precious than all the court annals and all the campaign reports put together," was following his instinct for the meatiness of life, as he urged historians to step away from hagiography, genealogy, and the higher gossip.[31] A century after him, Jacob Burckhardt found room in his epoch-making portrait of Renaissance Italy for the conduct of festivals, the revival of scholarship, the position of women, the careers of literati, and the vagaries of personality. His near-contemporary, Thomas Babington Macaulay, offered, in the celebrated third chapter of his *History of England,* a breathtaking survey of the culinary and the traveling habits of Englishmen in 1685, of polite manners, the public health, attitudes toward the poor, signs on inns. The battle cry of total history, as we have come to use it, expresses a certain impatience with historians who continue to cling to the glittering and memorable surfaces of events, to politics, diplomacy, and the lives of great men. To be sure, the social historians who have dominated the profession for well over a quarter of a century forcefully demon-

---

31. J. Brumfitt, *Voltaire Historian* (1958), 46; see Peter Gay, *The Enlightenment, An Interpretation,* vol. II, *The Science of Freedom* (1969), 393.

strate that the days of exclusive concentration on dates and dynasties are definitively over. But while their work has forced new materials on the serious attention of their fellow historians, it would be a mistake to claim that in consequence we are all total historians now. A transfer of concerns is not the same as their expansion. The search for total history goes on, and in this search, psychoanalytic history has much work to do.

In 1966, in his massive exploration of Languedoc from the beginning of the sixteenth to the beginning of the eighteenth century, Emmanuel Le Roy Ladurie first gave this rallying cry wide currency. He had "risked," he wrote, "the adventure of a total history." His path had been smoothed by two powerful exemplars, Marc Bloch and Lucien Febvre, whose influence had outlived them in the work of such admiring legatees as Fernand Braudel and through the journal, the *Annales,* they had founded more than three decades earlier. Le Roy Ladurie intended his thesis to place the "circumscribed framework of a human group" into all its worlds, not forgetting the prevailing climate and the region's principal crops, patterns of migration and population shifts, rare wealth and endemic poverty, stolid endurance and devastating moments of explosive discontent. In some inspired pages, notably those he devotes to that sanguinary uprising of 1580, the Carnival of Romans, Le Roy Ladurie even touches, lightly, on "historical psychoanalysis,"[32] to hint at the unconscious sources of the savagery that sometimes broke out among the Languedoc peasantry upon prolonged provocation. Following Marc Bloch's splendid *Société féodale,* he cunningly sets his *cadre*

---

32. Le Roy Ladurie, *Les paysans de Languedoc,* 2 vols. (1966), II, 399.

limité in motion to plot his account along the chain of time. Plainly, at least in those days, Le Roy Ladurie did not wholly share his colleagues' contempt for *l'histoire événementielle:* structure does not drive out development; analysis is compatible with narration. In *Les paysans de Languedoc,* a total historian has cast a wide net.

Had they lived to read his book, Le Roy Ladurie's intellectual fathers would have found it a realization of their fondest wishes. Marc Bloch, after all, had already ventured into closely analogous domains of experience: in *Les rois thaumaturges,* he had transformed a specialized, far from promising monographic subject in medical mythology (the English and French kings' presumed ability to cure scrofula by touching the sufferer) into an absorbing history of mental styles. Later, in *La Société féodale,* that unsurpassed synthesis, he left conventional legal and political medievalists behind as he reconstructed the feudal world with concise essays on its kinship system, its peculiar sense of history and of time, its folklore as preserved in epic poetry, and drew rich, unsuspected information from linguistic habits and place names. Meanwhile Lucien Febvre, the polemical partner in this harmonious pair of innovative historians, would bully his colleagues with exclamatory persistence to scrap parochial historical specialties which, he thought, only impeded the comprehension of past experience. He would lament his profession's failure to write histories of love and death, of pity, cruelty, and joy. Emotional, melodramatic, always the self-conscious fighter for a new history, Febvre wanted his profession to bathe in the past.[33] At his bidding, more than one historian would take the plunge.

---

33. For a brief account of the *Annales* school and its two founders, see H. Stuart Hughes, *The Obstructed Path: French Social Thought*

But the waters, though turbulent and bracing, have proved, when all is said, not quite so deep as Febvre's adventurous followers have supposed. After all, what one historian hails as the admirable realization of total history another may qualify as an exercise in comparative prudence. The historian of historiography must record his gratitude to Bloch and Febvre and the *Annales* school they founded: after their intrepid expeditions, our profession will never be the same. Yet in the end, they stopped short. I have already quoted Marc Bloch as calling on the historian to explore men's "secret needs of the heart," but defining those needs as lodged in "human consciousness."[34] This is the point where psychoanalytic history may enter to expand our definition of total history decisively by annexing the unconscious, and the incessant traffic between mind and world, to the historian's legitimate territory of inquiry.

One of the most untoward consequences of the reductionism that has dogged too many psychohistorians' steps is that it has obscured the promise inherent in Freudian history. For it has, much in the manner of the new social historians, only shifted the profession's horizons without appreciably enlarging them. To neglect the ego in favor of the id is of a piece with neglecting the bourgeoisie for the proletariat. Nor has the cause of psychoanalytic history been advanced by its reputation for providing emergency relief in moments of bafflement. There are those who see the Freudian historian as the expert of last resort, called to the bedside of the past only after all other diagnosticians have confessed their inability to make sense of the clinical picture. Even histo-

in the Years of Desperation 1930–1960 (1968), ch. 2, "The Historians and the Social Order," esp. pp. 44, 60.
34. See above, p. 7.

rians reluctant to acknowledge the value of psychoanalysis as an auxiliary discipline have found uses for it as they fail to discover rational causes for panics or riots, for outbursts of bigotry or self-destructive behavior. But while the historian who has gone to school to Freud would be churlish to refuse assistance in sorting out what his colleagues have thought an impenetrable tangle, he has credentials to aspire to greater things than this specialist's niche. Psychohistorians have been justly criticized for leaping to conclusions, but, paradoxically, they have been guilty far less of arrogance than of unwarranted modesty.[35] Precisely in fastening on psychopathology, in converting their subjects into neurotic specimens, they have passed up the supreme opportunity to which Freud's work toward a general psychology has invited them.

Psychoanalytic history, then, is at its most ambitious an orientation rather than a specialty. I cannot reiterate often enough that psychoanalysis offers the historian not a handbook of recipes but a style of seeing the past. That is why Freudian history is compatible with all the traditional genres—military, economic, intellectual—as well as with most of their methods. It is bound to provoke conflicts only with historians openly distrustful of Freud's insights or firmly committed to behaviorist psychologies. Psychoanalysis should inform other auxiliary sciences, other techniques; it should enrich, without disturbing, paleography, diplomatics, statistics, family reconstruction. Nor need it be reductionist. To be steeped in Freud does not compel historians to see only the child in the man; they can also observe

---

35. In this paragraph, and the next, I am drawing on ideas, and formulations, I first advanced some years ago in *Art and Act: On Causes in History—Manet, Gropius, Mondrian* (1976), esp. 21–32.

the man developed out of the child. The historian who persists in stressing the causal impact of economic motives, technological innovations, or class struggles need not yield up these objective influences on action to the specious argument that they are trivial and superficial phenomena. Life, as the historian studies it whether in the individual or the group, in single events or long sweeps of time, is a series of compromises in which the irrepressible drives, the warning signals of anxiety, the stratagems of defense, the persecutions of the superego, all play a leading but not an exclusive role. History is more than a monologue of the unconscious, more than a dance of symptoms.

In saying all this, I am not proposing to discount, or in any way minimize, the radical quality of the psychoanalytic way of thought, and its unique, subversive perspective. Any attempt to assimilate, let alone merge, the world of psychoanalysis and of history would only compromise the characteristic contributions each has to offer. The point is, rather, to ease the traffic between them, to dismantle the barriers of distrust and self-imposed ignorance that have prevented the historian from feeling, if not comfortable, at least reasonably safe in the analyst's realms. The historian, I wrote in 1976, "collects, and, at best, corrects, the public memory."[36] In this daunting task, psychoanalysis can be of momentous assistance, for it does not merely analyze what people choose to remember, but uncovers what they have been compelled to distort, or forget.

Nothing is more seductive than to draw unwarranted analogies between psychoanalysis and other, rather different disciplines. Both history and psychoanalysis are sciences of memory, both are professionally committed to skepticism,

---

36. Ibid., 2.

both trace causes in the past, both seek to penetrate behind pious professions and subtle evasions. History and psycho-analysis thus seem destined to collaborate in fraternal search for the truth about the past. Yet fraternity, it is necessary to reiterate, is not identity. The anxiety that invades historians faced with the Freudian presence is perfectly justified. They have excellent reasons for suspecting that to embrace psychoanalytic ideas is to plunge them into a strange world. It is a world of ambivalences, repressions, and conflicts, where little is certain, less is reassuring, and everything is immune to conclusive proof and open to contradictory interpretations. Yielding to the persuasions of Freud will necessarily force historians to change, often drastically, the way they do history, force them to dispense with prized convictions and to revise their favorite conclusions. The risks are formidable, the prospects of failure ominous, the promises of reward uncertain. But what stands beckoning at the end of the hazardous journey may prove worth it all: a grasp, firmer than ever, on the totality of human experience.

Bibliography

For the sake of clarity and convenience, I have grouped the titles in this bibliography by chapters, listing, with a few exceptions, each entry in the chapter in which it first appeared. I have added a few other interesting titles that I did not have an opportunity to discuss in the text. Need I add that these listings make no claim to completeness?

CHAPTER 1: Secret Needs of the Heart

In the rapidly growing contentious literature about Freud, the man and his work, David E. Stannard, *Shrinking History: On Freud and the Failure of Psychohistory* (1980) deserves particular attention, since it has shaped the way many historians think, and talk, about psychoanalysis as a possible auxiliary discipline. Well-served by economy of expression, fluency of style, and a scrupulous abstention from personal vilification, this effort to devastate Freud's creation is, however, compromised by tendentiousness. It is unreliable in its proof texts: thus, Stannard quotes a substantial passage from the influential English philosopher Gilbert Ryle to discredit the Freudian unconscious. In his witty *The Concept of Mind* (1949), Ryle had indeed inveighed against traditional mind-body dualism by tilting at what he called "the dogma of the Ghost in the Machine." Now, drawing upon this critique, Stannard explicitly says that Ryle "has referred to the psychoanalytic idea of the unconscious" and enlists Ryle in his own cause as dismissing all this stuff as a "logical howler" (Stannard, 55). Yet Ryle did not have the psychoanalytic view of the unconscious in mind at all but Descartes's dualism, and in fact he calls Freud "psychology's one man of genius" (Ryle, 324), a tribute for which one is not prepared by Stannard's pages. Again, Stannard will cite articles, like Anne Parsons' long, sympathetic comparative essay on the Oedipus complex and refer to it as a "very perceptive treatment" (Stannard, 172, n.15) without either integrating it into his argument, or telling his readers what Parsons had in fact said. Again, in trying to deny psychoanalysis any scientific standing, Stannard relies on the authority of George Klein, without informing his readers that in context the passage he quotes is not critical of Freud at all, or that Klein was a discriminating Freudian psychologist. (Stannard, 137; see George S. Klein, *Perception, Motives, and Personality* [1976].) No balanced attempt to do justice to the complexities of psychoanalytic research and experimentation can be expected from Stannard's pages.

For the controversy over Woodrow Wilson, see above all Alexander L. George and Juliette L. George, *Woodrow Wilson and Colonel House: A Personality Study* (1956; ed. 1964). The Georges are prudent and somewhat eclectic, and their deliberate avoidance of technical language (see p. 317) makes the precise identification of their psychoanalytic point of view difficult; it permits the inference that they have seasoned their classical Freudian approach with a dash of Adler's ideas about compensation for feelings of inadequacy. The tantalizing material they present might have permitted a more radical psychoanalytic reading than they have chosen to give it, but that would certainly have further increased the risk of rejection by the historical fraternity. The struggle among historians over Woodrow Wilson's troubled career is highly instructive. Avid to deny any psychological etiology for Wilson's at least partly self-induced failures as President of Princeton University and, later, in an almost pathetic replay, as President of the United States, the most eminent Wilson scholars have found it necessary to saddle their man with a series of strokes—as though it were somehow more respectable for Wilson to have blundered into disaster as a consequence of physical rather than mental causes. See Edwin A. Weinstein, James William Anderson, and Arthur S. Link, "Woodrow Wilson's Political Personality, a Reappraisal," *Political Science Quarterly*, LXXXXIII, 4 (Winter 1978–79),

585–98, and the Georges' persuasive reply, "Woodrow Wilson and Colonel House: A Reply to Weinstein, Anderson, and Link," ibid., LXXXXVI, 4 (Winter 1981–82), 641–65. Undeterred, Dr. Weinstein has expanded his stroke thesis in a book, *Woodrow Wilson: A Medical and Psychological Biography* (1981) which, in my judgment, does not particularly strengthen his case. See in addition, Juliette L. George, Michael F. Marmor, and Alexander L. George, "Research Note/Issues in Wilson Scholarship: References to Early 'Strokes' in the Papers of Woodrow Wilson," with a rejoinder by Arthur S. Link and three of his coeditors on the Wilson Papers, and a reply to that by the Georges and Marmor, *The Journal of American History*, LXX (1984), 845–53, 945–56.

Barzun, Jacques, *Clio and the Doctors: Psycho-History, Quanto-History & History* (1974).

Bloch, Marc, *The Historian's Craft* (1949; tr. Peter Putnam, 1954, ed. 1964).

Bouwsma, William J., "Anxiety and the Formation of Early Modern Culture," in Barbara C. Malament, ed., *After the Reformation: Essays in Honor of J. H. Hexter* (1980), 215–46.

Bowlby, John, *Attachment* (1969; 2nd ed., 1982).

———, "Psychoanalysis and Child Care" (1958), "The Making and Breaking of Affectional Bonds" (1976–77), "Effects on Behaviour of Disruption of an Affectional Bond" (1967–68), "Separation and Loss within the Family" (1968–70), in *The Making and Breaking of Affectional Bonds* (1979).

Carr, E. H., *What Is History?* (1960).

Cioffi, Frank, "The Cradle of Neurosis" [a review of Masson (see below), *The Assault on Truth*], *The Times Literary Supplement* (July 6, 1984), 743–44.

Cobb, Richard, *Reactions to the French Revolution* (1972).

———, *Paris and Its Provinces, 1792–1802* (1975).

Crews, Frederick, "The Freudian Way of Knowledge," *The New Criterion* (June 1984), 7–25. (See entries on Crews in Chapter 6.)

Cunliffe, Marcus, "From the Facts to the Feelings" [review of

Joseph F. Byrnes, *The Virgin of Chartres: An Intellectual and Psychological History of the Work of Henry Adams,* and Charles K. Hofling, *Custer and the Little Big Horn: A Psychobiographical Inquiry*], in *The Times Literary Supplement* (October 23, 1981), 1241–42.

Demos, John P., *Entertaining Satan: Witch-Craft and the Culture of Early New England* (1982).

Dodds, E. R., *The Greeks and the Irrational* (1951).

Elton, G. R., *The Practice of History* (1967).

Erikson, Erik H., *Young Man Luther: A Study in Psychoanalysis and History* (1958).

Fischer, David Hackett, *Historians' Fallacies: Toward a Logic of Historical Thought* (1970).

Freud, Sigmund: I am citing both the German edition, *Studienausgabe* [henceforth *St.A.*], ed. Alexander Mitscherlich et al., 11 vols. (1969–1975), and, in English, the *Standard Edition of the Complete Psychological Works of Sigmund Freud* [henceforth *S.E.*], tr. and ed. James Strachey et al., 24 vols. (1953–1975).

――――, *Drei Abhandlungen zur Sexualtheorie* (1905), *St.A.*, V, 37–145; *Three Essays on the Theory of Sexuality, S.E.*, VII, 125–243.

――――, "Zur Dynamik der Übertragung" (1912), *St.A.*, *Ergänzungsband,* 157–68; "The Dynamics of Transference," *S.E.*, XII, 97–108.

――――, "Die Verdrängung" (1915), *St.A.*, III, 103–18; "Repression," *S.E.*, XIV, 141–58.

――――, "Triebe und Triebschicksale" (1915), *St.A.*, III, 75–102; "Instincts and their Vicissitudes," *S.E.*, XIV, 109–40.

――――, "Aus der Geschichte einer infantilen Neurose" (1918), *St.A.*, VIII, 125–232; "From the History of an Infantile Neurosis," *S.E.*, XVII, 1–122.

――――, *Das Ich und das Es* (1923), *St.A.*, III, 273–337; *The Ego and the Id, S.E.*, XIX, 1–66.

――――, *Das Unbehagen in der Kultur* (1930), *St.A.*, IX, 191–270; *Civilization and its Discontents, S.E.*, XXI, 59–145.

Gay, Peter, "Rhetoric and Politics in the French Revolution," *American Historical Review,* LXVI, 3 (April 1961), 664–

76. [Slightly revised for Gay, *The Party of Humanity: Essays in the French Enlightenment* (1964), 162–81.]

———, "Freud and Freedom," in Alan Ryan, ed., *The Idea of Freedom: Essays in Honour of Isaiah Berlin* (1979), 41–59.

———, "On the Bourgeoisie: A Psychological Interpretation," in John M. Merriman, ed., *Consciousness and Class Experience in Nineteenth-Century Europe* (1979), 187–203.

———, *The Bourgeois Experience: Victoria to Freud,* vol. I, *Education of the Senses* (1984).

Gittings, Robert, *The Nature of Biography* (1978). Lectures by a seasoned biographer with some side swipes at psychobiography.

Gottschalk, Stephen, "Mrs. Eddy Through a Distorted Lense" [review of Julius Silberger, Jr., *Mary Baker Eddy*] *Christian Science Monitor* (July 2, 1980), 17.

Halévy, Elie, *England in 1815* (1913; tr. E. I. Watkin and D. A. Barker, 1949).

Harrison, Brian, *Peaceable Kingdom: Stability and Change in Modern Britain* (1982). A collection of essays on politics, rhetoric, and reform movements by a historian whose work shows how much one can accomplish without Freud.

Hexter, J. H., *The History Primer* (1971).

Hughes, Judith M., *Emotion and High Politics: Personal Relations at the Summit in Late Nineteenth-Century Britain and Germany* (1983).

Kitson Clark, G., *The Critical Historian* (1967).

Langer, William L., "The Next Assignment," *American Historical Review,* LXIII, 2 (January 1958), 283–304. [Available in Langer, *Explorations in Crisis: Papers in International History,* ed. Carl E. and Elizabeth Schorske (1969), 408–32.]

Lefebvre, Georges, "Foules Révolutionnaires" (1934), in *Etudes sur la Révolution Française* (1954), 271–87.

———, "Le Meurtre du comte de Dampierre (22 Juin 1791)" (1941), ibid., 288–97.

Loewenberg, Peter [review of Barzun, *Clio and the Doctors*], *Clio: An Interdisciplinary Journal of Literature, History, and the Philosophy of History,* V, 1 (Fall 1975), 123–27. A rather severe but just assessment.

———— [review of Stannard, *Shrinking History*], *Bulletin of the Southern California Psychoanalytic Institute,* No. 63 (Winter 1982), 36–38. Critical but fair.

————, *Decoding the Past: The Psychohistorical Approach* (1983). A varied collection of essays, polemical, biographical and historical, by a professional historian and practicing psychoanalyst.

Lowe, Donald M., *History of Bourgeois Perception* (1982).

Lynn, Kenneth S., "History's Reckless Psychologizing," *The Chronicle of Higher Education* (January 16, 1978), 48.

Macfarlane, Alan, "Difficult Women" [review of Demos, *Entertaining Satan*], *The Times Literary Supplement* (May 13, 1983), 493.

Malcolm, Janet, *Psychoanalysis: The Impossible Profession* (1981).

————, *In the Freud Archives* (1984).

Masson, Jeffrey Moussaieff, *The Assault on Truth: Freud's Suppression of the Seduction Theory* (1984).

Mitzman, Arthur, "Psychohistory Besieged" [review of Stannard, *Shrinking History*], *Theoretische Geschiedenis,* IX, 1 (1982), 37–54.

Olsen, Donald J., *The Growth of Victorian London* (1976).

Ricoeur, Paul, *Freud and Philosophy: An Essay on Interpretation* (1965; tr. Denis Savage, 1970).

Saussure, Raymond de, "Psychoanalysis and History," in Géza Róheim, ed., *Psychoanalysis and the Social Sciences,* II (1950), 7–64. Astonished analyst, wondering at historians' neglect of Freud, attempts to remedy this (a little naively) with instances.

Stone, Lawrence, *The Family, Sex and Marriage in England, 1500–1800* (1977).

————, "Children and the Family" (1966), rev. in Stone, *The Past and the Present* (1981).

Thomis, Malcolm I., *Responses to Industrialization: The British Experience 1780–1850* (1976).

Trumbach, Randolph, *The Rise of the Egalitarian Family: Aristocratic Kinship and Domestic Relations in Eighteenth-Century England* (1978).

Weber, Eugen, *Peasants into Frenchmen: The Modernization of Rural France 1870–1914* (1976).

Wehler, Hans-Ulrich, "Zum Verhältnis von Geschichtswissenschaft und Psychoanalyse," *Historische Zeitschrift,* CCVII (1969), 529–54. [Somewhat revised in Wehler, *Geschichte als Historische Sozialwissenschaft* (1973), 85–123.]

———, "Geschichtswissenschaft und 'Psychohistorie,' " *Innsbrucker Historische Studien,* I (1978), 201–13, translated as "Psychoanalysis and History," *Social Research,* XXXXVII, 3 (Autumn 1980), 519–36.

Weinstein, Fred, and Gerald M. Platt, *Psychoanalytic Sociology: An Essay on the Interpretation of Historical Data and the Phenomena of Collective Behavior* (1973).

CHAPTER 2: The Claims of Freud

For Herbert Silberer's and Otto Pötzl's path-breaking experiments, see the generous excerpts in David Rapaport, ed., *Organization and Pathology of Thought* (1951), 195–233; Rapaport also prints long passages from other classic experiments and annotates them exhaustively. For Silberer, a fascinating and deeply neurotic polymath who committed suicide in 1922 at the age of forty, see Wilhelm Stekel, "In Memoriam Herbert Silberer," *Fortschritte der Sexualwissenschaft und Psychoanalyse,* I (1924), 408–20. Pötzl's "The Relation Between Experimentally Induced Dream Images and Indirect Vision" is conveniently available in Charles Fisher, ed., *Preconscious Stimulation in Dreams, Associations, and Images; Classical Studies, Psychological Issues,* Monograph 7 (1961), 41–120; it should be read in conjunction with the important paper by Rudolf Allers and Jakob Teler, "On the Utilization of Unnoticed Impressions in Associations" (1924), ibid., 121–50, and the critical introduction by Fisher (1–40). The most comprehensive exposition of Fisher's own pioneering experiments is his "Psychoanalytic Implications of Recent Research on Sleep and Dreaming," *J. Amer. Psychoanal. Assn.,* XIII (1965), 197–303.

The literature on psychoanalytic experimentation is by now substantial and growing steadily. Among the most rewarding reports is Martin Mayman, ed., *Psychoanalytic Research: Three Approaches to the Experimental Study of Subliminal Processes, Psychological Issues,* Monograph 30, esp. Mayman, "Introduction: Reflections on Psychoanalytic Research" (1–10), Lester Luborsky, "Forgetting and Remembering (Momentary Forgetting) During Psychotherapy: A New Sample" (29–55), Philip S. Holzman, "Some Difficulties in the Way of Psychoanalytic Research: A Survey and a Critique" (88–103), and Paul E. Meehl, "Some Methodological Reflections on the Difficulties of Psychoanalytic Research" (104–17).

For an attempt to integrate predictions into the process of psychoanalytic proof, see Helen D. Sargent, Leonard Horwitz, Robert S. Wallerstein, and Ann Appelbaum, *Prediction in Psychotherapy Research: A Method for the Transformation of Clinical Judgments into Testable Hypotheses, Psychological Issues,* Monograph 21 (1968). By far the most satisfactory, most thoroughgoing review and evaluation of the experimental literature is Paul Kline, *Fact and Fantasy in Freudian Theory* (1972; 2nd ed., 1981). Seymour Fisher and Roger P. Greenberg, *The Scientific Credibility of Freud's Theories and Therapy* (1977) is even more complete in its coverage of modern research than Kline, but less discriminating. Fisher and Greenberg, eds., *The Scientific Evaluation of Freud's Theories and Therapy* (1978) is a fair-minded anthology. Among the skeptics, Adolf Grünbaum has proved most formidable in a long series of articles needing no separate citation here because he has summarized his position in *The Foundations of Psychoanalysis: A Philosophical Critique* (1984). It is only right to note that Grünbaum singles out Freud's "brilliant theoretical imagination" (p. 278) for praise. The most powerfully argued defense taking Grünbaum into account is Marshall Edelson, "Is Testing Psychoanalytic Hypotheses in the Psychoanalytic Situation Really Impossible?" *PSC,* XXXVIII (1983), 61–109. See also Edelson, *Hypothesis and Evidence in Psychoanalysis* (1984) and his earlier "Psychoanalysis as Science, Its Boundary Problems, Special Status, Relations to Other Sciences, and Formalization," *The Journal of Nervous and Mental Diseases,* CLXV (1977), 1–28. B. A. Farrell, *The Standing of Psychoanalytic Theory* (1981) assesses the experimental material with some carefully reasoned reservations. See also Barbara

Von Eckardt, "The Scientific Status of Psychoanalysis," in Sander L. Gilman, ed., *Introducing Psychoanalytic Theory* (1982), 139–80, the impressive paper by Donald McIntosh, "The Empirical Bearing of Psychoanalytic Theory," *Int. J. Psycho-Anal.*, LX (1979), 405–31, and the astute comments in Saul Friedländer, *History and Psychoanalysis: An Inquiry into the Possibilities and Limits of Psychohistory* (1975; tr. Susan Suleiman, 1978).

Abraham, Karl, "Über eine besondere Form des neurotischen Widerstandes gegen die psychoanalytische Methodik" (1919), *Gesammelte Schriften in zwei Bänden*, ed. Johannes Cremerius (1971; ed. 1982), I, 276–83.

Breuer, Josef, and Sigmund Freud, *Studien über Hysterie* (1895); *Studies in Hysteria*, in Freud, *S.E.*, II.

Conkin, Paul, and Roland N. Stromberg, *The Heritage and Challenge of History* (1971).

Cosin, B. R., C. F. and N. H. Freeman, "Critical Empiricism Criticized: The Case of Freud," in Richard Wollheim and James Hopkins, eds., *Philosophical Essays on Freud* (1982), 32–59.

Fenichel, Otto, "A Critique of the Death Instinct" (1935), in *The Collected Papers of Otto Fenichel*, First Series, collected and edited by Hanna Fenichel and David Rapaport (1953), 363–72.

Freud, Sigmund, *Traumdeutung* (1900), *St.A.*, II; *The Interpretation of Dreams*, *S.E.*, IV–V.

———, "Bruchstück einer Hysterie-Analyse" (1905), *St.A.*, VI, 83–186; "Fragment of an Analysis of a Case of Hysteria," *S.E.*, VII, 1–122.

———, *Der Witz und seine Beziehungen zum Unbewussten* (1905), *St.A.*, IV, 9–219; *Jokes and their Relation to the Unconscious*, *S.E.*, VIII.

———, "Charakter und Analerotik" (1908), *St.A.*, VII, 23–30; "Character and Anal Erotism," *S.E.*, IX, 167–75.

———, "Über 'wilde' Psychoanalyse" (1910), *St.A.*, *Ergänzungsband*, 133–41; "'Wild' Psychoanalysis," *S.E.*, XI, 219–27.

———, "Aus der Geschichte einer infantilen Neurose ('Der Wolfsmann')" (1918), *St.A.*, VIII, 125–232; "From the History of an Infantile Neurosis," *S.E.*, XVII, 1–122.

————, "Die Verneinung" (1925), *St.A.*, III, 371–77; "Negation," *S.E.*, XIX, 235–39.

————, "Hemmung, Symptom und Angst" (1926), *St.A.*, VI, 227–308; "Inhibitions, Symptoms, and Anxiety," *S.E.*, XX, 77–172.

————, *Neue Folge der Vorlesungen zur Einführung in die Psychoanalyse*, *St.A.*, I, 448–608; *New Introductory Lectures on Psychoanalysis*, *S.E.*, XXII, 3–182.

————, "Konstruktionen in der Analyse" (1937), *St.A.*, *Ergänzungsband*, 392–406; "Constructions in Analysis," *S.E.*, XXIII, 255–69.

Gay, Peter, *Art and Act: On Causation in History—Manet, Gropius, Mondrian* (1976).

————, "Sigmund Freud: A German and His Discontents," in *Freud, Jews and Other Germans: Masters and Victims in Modernist Culture* (1978), 29–92.

————, "Six Names in Search of an Interpretation: A Contribution to the Debate over Sigmund Freud's Jewishness," *Hebrew Union College Annual*, LIII (1982), 295–307.

Gill, Merton M., and Philip S. Holzman, *Psychology versus Metapsychology: Psychoanalytic Essays in Memory of George S. Klein, Psychological Issues*, Monograph 36 (1976).

Glover, Edward, "Research Methods in Psycho-Analysis" (1952), in *On the Early Development of Mind* (1956), 390–405.

Glymour, Clark, "Freud, Kepler, and the Clinical Evidence" (1974), in Richard Wollheim and James Hopkins, eds., *Philosophical Essays on Freud* (1982), 12–31.

Hilgard, Ernest R., "Psychoanalysis: Experimental Studies," *International Encyclopedia of the Social Sciences*, David L. Sills, ed., 17 vols. (1968), XIII, 37–45.

Hook, Sidney, "Science and Mythology in Psychoanalysis," in Hook, ed., *Psychoanalysis, Scientific Method and Philosophy: A Symposium* (1959), 212–24.

Hughes, Stuart H., "History and Psychoanalysis: The Explanation of Motive," in *History as Art and As Science: Twin Vistas on the Past* (1964), 42–67.

Jones, Ernest, *The Life and Work of Sigmund Freud*, vol. III, *1919–1939: The Last Phase* (1957).

Kanzer, Mark, and Jules Glenn, eds., *Freud and His Patients* (1980).

Masur, Gerhard, *Prophets of Yesterday: Studies in European Culture, 1890–1914* (1961).

Medawar, Sir Peter, *The Art of the Soluble* (1967).

———, *Induction and Intuition in Scientific Thought* (1969).

———, *Pluto's Republic* (1982). Incorporates both previous titles.

Nagel, Ernest, "What is True and False in Science" [review of Medawar, *Art of the Soluble*], *Encounter*, XXIX (September 1967), 68–70.

Patze, Adolf, *Ueber Bordelle und die Sittenverderbniss unserer Zeit. Eine medicinalpolitische Abhandlung* . . . (1845).

Popper, Sir Karl, "Philosophy of Science: A Personal Report," in C. A. Mace, ed., *British Philosophy in Mid-Century* (1957), reprinted in Popper, *Conjectures and Refutations: The Growth of Scientific Knowledge* (1963; 2nd ed., 1965), 33–65.

Rapaport, David, *The Structure of Psychoanalytic Theory: A Systematizing Attempt, Psychological Issues,* Monograph 6 (1960).

Shakow, David, and David Rapaport, *The Influence of Freud on American Psychology* (1964).

Sherrill, Robert, "How Reagan Got That Way" [review of Robert Dallek, *Ronald Reagan: The Politics of Symbolism* (1984)], *The Atlantic,* CCLIII, 3 (March 1984), 127–31.

Stone, Leo, "Reflections on the Psychoanalytic Concept of Aggression," *The Psychoanalytic Quarterly,* XL (April 1971), 195–244.

Sulloway, Frank J., *Freud, Biologist of the Mind: Beyond the Psychoanalytic Legend* (1979).

Wallace, Edwin R., IV, *Historiography and Causation in Psychoanalysis: An Essay on Psychoanalytic and Historical Epistemology* (1985).

Watkins, J. W. N., "Ideal Types and Historical Explanation," in Herbert Feigl and Mary Brodbeck, eds., *Readings in the Philosophy of Science* (1953), 723–43.

Chapter 3: Human Nature in History

Among Freud's many texts on the Oedipus complex, starting with *The Interpretation of Dreams* (*S.E.*, IV, 261–66), *The Ego and the Id* (*S.E.*, XIX, 3–62, passim) is probably the most important. See also his case of Little Hans, "Analysis of a Phobia of a Five-Year-Old Boy" (1909), *S.E.*, X, 3–149. For the varieties that the complex assumed in Freud's thought, see esp. the short paper of 1924, "The Dissolution of the Oedipus Complex," *S.E.*, XIX, 173–79. And see Géza Róheim, "The Oedipus Complex, Magic and Culture," in Róheim, ed., *Psychoanalysis and the Social Sciences*, II (1950), 173–229. On aggression in the oedipal phase, there is Leo Rangell, "Aggression, Oedipus, and Historical Perspective," *Int. J. of Psycho-Anal.*, LIII (1972), 3–12. From the sizable psychoanalytic literature on the "nuclear complex," I single out René Spitz and K. M. Wolf, "Autoeroticism—Some Empirical Findings and Hypotheses on Three of Its Manifestations in the First Year of Life," *PSC*, III–IV (1949), 85–120; Heinz Hartmann, "Problems of Infantile Neurosis," in *Essays on Ego Psychology: Selected Problems in Psychoanalytic Theory* (1964), 207–14; and a series of comments in various papers by Anna Freud, gathered in *Indications for Child Analysis and Other Papers, 1945–1956* (1969).

William N. Stephens, *The Oedipus Complex: Cross-Cultural Evidence* (1962) is a carefully reasoned and documented essay in comparative cultural anthropology which comes to the conclusion that, making allowances for the largely indirect nature of the ethnographic testimony, "the massive evidence leaves a rather small margin for doubt. The probability is high that this hypothesis [Freud's Oedipus complex], embodying several of the core-assumptions of psychoanalytic theory, is approximately valid" (p. 185). The six papers that Seymour Fisher and Roger P. Greenberg have selected for their eclectic reader, *The Scientific Evaluation of Freud's Theories and Therapy* (1978), deliberately chosen to represent a spectrum of opinions, tend to contradict one another, and to leave the issue open. But in his fine survey, *Fact and Fantasy in Freudian Theory* (1972; 2nd ed. 1981), Paul

Kline concludes that the evidence for Freud's theory is quite strong (esp. ch. 6, and 290–95). Hans W. Loewald's witty and incisive paper, "The Waning of the Oedipus Complex" (1979), in *Papers on Psychoanalysis* (1980), 384–404, is indispensable, both on the fading interest in the complex in the psychological profession (unjustified) and in the developing individual (desirable). Melford E. Spiro, *Oedipus in the Trobriands* (1982) is a brilliant refutation of Malinowski's claim that the Trobriand islanders do not show an Oedipus complex.

The issue of self-interest deserves far more examination from a psychoanalytic perspective than it has had. There is, in addition to the Hartmann paper on the psychoanalytic theory of the ego cited in the text (above, p. 106), Edith Jacobson, *The Self and the Object World* (1964), which has shrewd observations, esp. 75–93, 136–55, 205–8. See also Mark Kanzer, "Ego Interest, Egoism and Narcissism," *J. Amer. Psychoanal. Assn.*, X (1962), 593–605, and M. Eagle, "Interests as Object Relations," *Psychoanalysis and Contemporary Thought*, IV, 4 (1981), 527–65. In a most thoughtful essay, *The Passions and the Interests: Political Arguments for Capitalism before Its Triumph* (1977), Albert O. Hirschman has shown that when the idea of interest first emerged in the Renaissance, it was seen as a powerful counterweight to man's passions. (Part One, "How the Interests Were Called Upon to Counteract the Passions.") Hirschman also demonstrates that the emergence of "economic advantage" as the "core meaning" of interests was a relatively late development; it is not how Machiavelli or Spinoza used the term (esp. 32). Milton L. Myers, *The Soul of Modern Economic Man: Ideas of Self-Interest, Thomas Hobbes to Adam Smith* (1983) is informative.

Beard, Charles A., *An Economic Interpretation of the Constitution of the United States* (1913; with new Introduction, 1935).

Bentham, Jeremy, *Introduction to the Principles of Morals and Legislation* (1789).

Bullitt, William, and Sigmund Freud, *Thomas Woodrow Wilson: A Psychological Study* (1967).

Cochran, Thomas C., "Economic History, Old and New," *American Historical Review*, LXXIV (June, 1969), 1561–72.

Dodds, E. R., "The Misunderstanding of 'Oedipus Rex' " (1966), in *The Ancient Concept of Progress and Other Essays on Greek Literature and Belief* (1973), 64–77.

Eliot, T. S., "Tradition and the Individual Talent" (1919), *Selected Prose,* ed. John Hayward (1953), 21–30.

Ellenberger, Henri F., *The Discovery of the Unconscious: The History and Evolution of Dynamic Psychiatry* (1970).

Febvre, Lucien, *Life in Renaissance France,* ed. and tr. Marian Rothstein (1977).

Fenichel, Otto, *The Psychoanalytic Theory of Neurosis* (1945).

Freud, Sigmund, "Zur Geschichte der psychoanalytischen Bewegung" (1914), *Gesammelte Werke,* X, 44–113; "On the History of the Psycho-Analytic Movement," *S.E.,* XIV, 3–66.

———, "Zur Einführung des Narzissmus" (1914), *St.A.,* III, 37–68; "On Narcissism: An Introduction," *S.E.,* XIV, 67–102.

———, "Die Verdrängung" (1915), *St.A.,* III, 103–18; "Repression," *S.E.,* XIV, 141–58.

———, "Das Unbewusste" (1915), *St.A.,* III, 119–73; "The Unconscious," *S.E.,* XIV, 159–215.

———, "Triebe und Triebschicksale" (1915), *St.A.,* III, 75–102; "Instincts and their Vicissitudes," *S.E.,* XIV, 109–40.

———, *Vorlesungen zur Einführung in die Psychoanalyse* (1916–17), *St.A.,* I, 34–445; *Introductory Lectures on Psychoanalysis, S.E.,* XV, XVI.

———, "Das Fakultätsgutachten im Prozess Halsmann" (1931), *Gesammelte Werke,* XIV, 541–42; "The Expert Opinion in the Halsmann Case," *S.E.,* XXI, 251–53.

———, *Abriss der Psychoanalyse* (1940), *Gesammelte Werke,* XVII, 63–138; *An Outline of Psychoanalysis, S.E.,* XXIII, 141–207.

Gay, Peter, *The Enlightenment: An Interpretation,* vol. II, *The Science of Freedom* (1969).

———, *Style in History* (1974).

Goethe, Johann Wolfgang, *Faust, Der Tragödie Zweiter Teil* (1832).

Halévy, Elie, *The Growth of Philosophic Radicalism* (1901–4; tr. Mary Morris, 1928).

Hartmann, Heinz, "Comments on the Psychoanalytic Theory of the Ego" (1950), in *Essays on Ego Psychology: Selected Problems in Psychoanalytic Theory* (1964), 113–41.

Hofstadter, Richard, "The Pseudo-Conservative Revolt" (1954), in *The Paranoid Style in American Politics and Other Essays* (1963), 41–65.

———, *The Progressive Historians: Turner, Beard, Parrington* (1968).

James, William, *The Letters,* ed. Henry James, 2 vols. (1920).

Johnson, Christopher H., "The Revolution of 1830 in French Economic History," in John M. Merriman, ed., *1830 in France* (1975), 139–89.

Kehr, Eckart, *Schlachtflottenbau und Parteipolitik, 1894–1901* (1930).

Liddell Hart, B. H., *History of the First World War* (1930; ed. 1972).

Macaulay, Thomas Babington, "James Mill's Essay on Government: Utilitarian Logic and Politics" (originally in *Edinburgh Review,* No. XCVII [March 1829]), in Jack Lively and John Rees, eds., *Utilitarian Logic and Politics* (1978).

Meinecke, Friedrich, *Die Entstehung des Historismus,* 2 vols. (1936).

Neumann, Franz, *Behemoth: The Structure and Practice of National Socialism, 1933–1944* (1942; 2nd ed., 1944).

Pares, Richard, "The Historian's Business" (1953), in *The Historian's Business and Other Essays,* ed. R. A. and Elizabeth Humphreys (1961), 1–10.

Smith, Page, *The Historian and History* (1964).

Strickland, Geoffrey, *Stendhal: The Education of a Novelist* (1974).

Taylor, A. J. P., Review of Bullitt and Freud, *Thomas Woodrow Wilson,* in *The New Statesman and Nation* (May 12, 1967), 653–54.

Tilly, Charles, *From Mobilization to Revolution* (1978).

CHAPTER 4: Reason, Reality, Psychoanalysis
and the Historian

On the vexed, much debated, question of the place of reality in mental representations, see, in addition to the titles by George Devereux and Sandor Ferenczi cited in the text, David Beres and Edward D. Joseph, "The Concept of Mental Representation in Psychoanalysis," *Int. J. Psycho-Anal.*, LI (1970), 1–9; Roy Schafer, "The Psychoanalytic Vision of Reality," ibid., 279–97; Joseph Sandler and Bernard Rosenblatt, "The Concept of the Representational World," *PSC,* XVII (1962), 128–45; Sigmund Freud's terse fragment, "Internal World," *An Outline of Psycho-Analysis,* (1940), *S.E.,* XXIII, 205–7; and one of D. W. Winnicott's most imaginative papers, "The Location of Cultural Experience," *Int. J. Psycho-Anal.,* IIL (1966), 368–72. G. R. Elton, *The Practice of History* (1967), has some effective polemical passages in defense of the historian's ability to grasp reality—a sensible position by no means universally shared in the historical craft. The most vigorous defense of the role that reality plays in the mind comes in the critiques of Kleinian ideas on the part of "orthodox" Freudians. See esp. Otto F. Kernberg, "A Contribution to the Ego-Psychological Critique of the Kleinian School," *Int. J. Psycho-Anal.,* L (1969), 317–33, with most helpful bibliography.

Besançon, Alain, *Histoire et expérience du moi* (1971).

Davidson, Donald, "Paradoxes of Irrationality," in Richard Wollheim and James Hopkins, eds., *Philosophical Essays on Freud* (1982), 289–305.

Devereux, George, *Dreams in Greek Tragedy* (1976).

Duby, Georges, "Histoire des mentalités," in Charles Samaran, ed., *Encyclopédie de la Pléiade* (1961), 937–66.

Erikson, Erik H., "The Strange Case of Freud, Bullitt, and Woodrow Wilson, I," *The New York Review of Books,* VIII, 2 (February 9, 1967), 3–6.

Ferenczi, Sandor, "Stages in the Development of the Sense of Reality" (1913), in *First Contributions to Psychoanalysis,* tr. Ernest Jones (1952), 213–39.

Freud, Anna, *The Ego and the Mechanisms of Defence* (1936; tr. Cecil Baines, 1937).

Freud, Sigmund, "Eine Kindheitserinnerung des Leonardo da Vinci" (1910), *St.A.*, X, 87–159; "Leonardo da Vinci and a Memory of his Childhood," *S.E.*, XI, 59–137.

————, "Psychoanalytische Bemerkungen über einen autobiographisch beschriebenen Fall von Paranoia (Dementia Paranoides)" (1911), *St.A.*, VII, 133–203; "Psychoanalytic Notes on an Autobiographical Account of a Case of Paranoia (Dementia Paranoides)," *S.E.*, XII, 3–82.

————, "Formulierungen über die zwei Prinzipien des psychischen Geschehens" (1911), *St.A.*, III, 13–24; "Formulations on the two Principles of Mental Functioning," *S.E.*, XII, 213–26.

————, "Zur Einleitung der Behandlung" (1913), *St.A., Ergänzungsband*, 181–203; "On Beginning the Treatment," *S.E.*, XII, 121–44.

————, " 'Ein Kind wird geschlagen' (Beitrag zur Kenntnis der Entstehung sexueller Perversionen)" (1919), *St.A.*, VII, 229–54; " 'A Child is Being Beaten.' A Contribution to the Study of the Origin of Sexual Perversions," *S.E.*, XVII, 175–204.

————, "Über einige neurotische Mechanismen bei Eifersucht, Paranoia und Homosexualität" (1922), *St.A.*, VII, 217–28; "Some Neurotic Mechanisms in Jealousy, Paranoia and Homosexuality," *S.E.*, XVIII, 221–32.

————, "Der Realitätsverlust bei Neurose und Psychose" (1924), *St.A.*, III, 355–61; "The Loss of Reality in Neurosis and Psychosis," *S.E.*, XIX, 183–87.

————, *The Origins of Psycho-Analysis: Letters to Wilhelm Fliess, Drafts and Notes: 1887–1902*, ed., Marie Bonaparte et al. (1950; tr. Eric Mosbacher and James Strachey, 1954).

Gay, Peter, "A revisionist view of Freud in retreat" [review of Masson, *The Assault on Truth*], *The Philadelphia Inquirer*, "Books/Leisure" (February 5, 1984), 1, 8.

Hartmann, Heinz, "Notes on the Reality Principle" (1956), in *Essays on Ego Psychology: Selected Problems in Psychoanalytic Theory* (1964), 241–67.

Hofstadter, Richard, "The Strange Case of Freud, Bullitt, and Woodrow Wilson, II," *The New York Review of Books,* VIII, 2 (February 9, 1967), 6–8.

Hollingshead, August B., and Frederick C. Redlich, *Social Class and Mental Illness* (1958).

Israëls, Han, *Schreber, Father and Son* (1981).

Landes, David S., and Charles Tilly, eds., *History as Social Science* (1971).

Le Goff, Jacques, *Time, Work, and Culture in the Middle Ages* (1977; tr. Arthur Goldhammer, 1980).

Le Roy Ladurie, Emmanuel, *Les Paysans de Languedoc,* 2 vols. (1966).

Niederland, William, *The Schreber Case* (1974).

Pears, David, *Motivated Irrationality* (1984). Technical but rewarding.

Schafer, Roy, *Aspects of Internalization* (1968).

Schur, Max, *The Id and the Regulatory Principles of Mental Functioning* (1966).

Sterba, Richard F., "The Fate of the Ego in Analytic Therapy" (1934), *Int. J. Psycho-Anal.,* XV, 117–26.

Thompson, E. P., *The Making of the English Working Class* (1963).

Weber, Max, *The Protestant Ethic and the Spirit of Capitalism* (1904–5; tr. Talcott Parsons, 1930).

CHAPTER 5: From Couch to Culture

Arno, Peter, *The Man in the Shower* (1944).

Barrows, Susanna, *Distorting Mirrors: Visions of the Crowd in Late Nineteenth-Century France* (1981).

Bocock, Robert, *Freud and Modern Society: An Outline and Analysis of Freud's Sociology* (1976).

Brodie, Fawn M., *The Devil Drives: A Life of Sir Richard Burton* (1967). Psychoanalytically oriented biography.

Elias, Norbert, *Über den Prozess der Zivilisation. Soziogenetische und Psychogenetische Untersuchungen,* 2 vols. (1939; tr.

Edmund Jephcott, vol. I, *The Development of Manners* [1978]; vol. II, *Power and Civility* [1982].)

Ellmann, Richard, "Freud and Literary Biography," *The American Scholar,* LIII, 4 (Fall 1984), 465–78. Thoughtful reflections.

Freeman, Derek, *Margaret Mead and Samoa: The Making and Unmaking of an Anthropological Myth* (1983). (But see, for a very different perspective and necessary corrections, Mary Catherine Bateson, *With A Daughter's Eye: A Memoir of Margaret Mead and Gregory Bateson* [1984]).

Freud, Sigmund, *Totem und Tabu* (1912–13), *St.A.,* IX, 287–444; *Totem and Taboo, S.E.,* XIII, 1–161.

———, "Das Interesse an der Psychoanalyse" (1913), *Gesammelte Werke,* VIII, 390–420; "The Claims of Psycho-Analysis to Scientific Interest," *S.E.,* XIII, 165–90.

———, *Massenpsychologie und Ich-Analyse* (1921), *St.A.,* IX, 61–134; *Group Psychology and the Analysis of the Ego, S.E.,* XVIII, 67–143.

———, *Die Zukunft einer Illusion* (1927), *St.A.,* IX, 135–89; *The Future of an Illusion, S.E.,* XXI, 1–56.

———, "Selbstdarstellung; Nachschrift 1935" (1936), *Gesammelte Werke,* XVI, 31–34; "An Autobiographical Study: Postscript" (1935), *S.E.,* XX, 71–74.

Garraty, John A., *The Nature of Biography* (1958). Esp. chs. V and VI.

Gay, Peter, "Liberalism and Regression," *PSC,* XXXVII (1982), 523–45.

Gibbon, Edward, *Autobiography,* ed. Dero A. Saunders (1961).

Hobbes, Thomas, *Leviathan* (1651; ed. Michael Oakeshott, 1947).

Hildesheimer, Wolfgang, *Mozart* (1977; tr. Marion Faber, 1983). Brilliant biographical meditation indebted to psychoanalysis.

Hobson, J. A., *The Psychology of Jingoism* (1901).

Holborn, Hajo, *A History of Modern Germany,* vol. III, *1840–1945* (1969).

Jaques, Elliott, "Social Systems as Defence against Persecutory and Depressive Anxiety: A Contribution to the Psycho-Analytical Study of Social Processes," Melanie Klein et al., *New Directions in Psycho-Analysis* (1955), 478–98.

Kohut, Thomas A., "Kaiser Wilhelm II and his parents: an inquiry into the psychological roots of German policy towards England before the First World War," in John C. G. Röhl and Nicolaus Sombart, eds., *Kaiser Wilhelm II: New Interpretations* (1982), 63–89.

Lasch, Christopher, *The Culture of Narcissism: American Life in An Age of Diminishing Expectations* (1978). Ambitious psychocultural diagnosis.

LeBon, Gustave, *The Crowd* (1895; tr. 1896, ed. with introduction by Robert K. Merton, 1960).

LeVine, Robert A., *Culture, Behavior, and Personality* (1973). An excellent study of the "personality and culture" problem.

Liebert, Robert S., *Michelangelo: A Psychoanalytic Study of His Life and Images* (1983). A psychoanalyst's biography.

Loewald, Hans W., "The Problem of Defense and the Neurotic Interpretation of Reality" (1952), *Papers on Psychoanalysis* (1980), 21–32.

———, "Ego-Organization and Defense" (Panel contribution, 1973), ibid., 174–77.

Mack, John E., "Psychoanalysis and Historical Biography," *J. Amer. Psychoanal. Assn.,* XIX (1971), 143–79.

Marvick, Elizabeth Wirth, *The Young Richelieu: A Psychoanalytic Approach to Leadership* (1983).

Menzies, Isabel E. P., *The Function of Social Systems as a Defence Against Anxiety: A Report on a Study of the Nursing Service of a General Hospital* (1970). A psychoanalytical pamphlet that deserves to become a classic.

Meyer, Bernard C., *Joseph Conrad: A Psychoanalytic Biography* (1967).

Meyer, Donald B. [review of Erikson, *Young Man Luther*], *History and Theory,* I, 3 (1961), 291–97.

Mitzman, Arthur, *The Iron Cage: An Historical Interpretation of Max Weber* (1970).

Moore, Burness E., Panel report "Psychoanalytic Knowledge of Group Processes," *J. Amer. Psychoanal. Assn.,* XXVII (1979), 145–56.

Seigel, Jerrold, *Marx's Fate: The Shape of a Life* (1978). An ambitious "psychological biography."

Shore, Miles F., "A Psychoanalytic Perspective" [on modern biography], *Journal of Interdisciplinary History*, XII, 1 (Summer 1981), 89–113.

Spiro, Melford E., "Religious Systems as Culturally Constituted Defense Mechanisms," in Spiro, ed., *Context and Meaning in Cultural Anthropology* (1965), 100–13.

———, "Culture and Human Nature," in George D. Spindler, ed., *The Making of Psychological Anthropology* (1978), 330–60.

Starr, Chester G., "Reflections upon the Problem of Generalization," in Louis Gottschalk, ed., *Generalization in the Writing of History* (1963), 3–18.

Strozier, Charles B., *Lincoln's Quest for Union: Public and Private Meanings* (1982). Both a psychoanalytic biography and a historical interpretation.

Thomas, Keith, *Man and the Natural World: Changing Attitudes in England 1500–1800* (1983; American subtitle, *A History of the Modern Sensibility*).

Thomas, Robert David, *The Man Who Would Be Perfect: John Humphrey Noyes and the Utopian Impulse* (1977). Persuasive Freudian life.

Tolstoy, Leo, *War and Peace* (1868–69; tr. Louise and Aylmer Maude, 1922; ed. in two vols. continuously paginated, 1983).

Trilling, Lionel, *Freud and the Crisis of Our Culture* (1955).

Winnicott, D. W., "Transitional Objects and Transitional Phenomena" (1951), in *Through Paediatrics to Psycho-Analysis* (1958; ed., 1975), 229–42.

Wrong, Dennis H., "The Oversocialized Conception of Man in Modern Sociology" (1961), in *Skeptical Sociology* (1976), 31–46.

———, "Postscript 1975," ibid., 47–54.

———, "Human Nature and the Perspective of Sociology" (1963), ibid., 55–70.

CHAPTER 6: The Program in Practice

I have already cited Dodds's magisterial *The Greeks and the Irrational* (1951), but want to cite it again here. Of the enthusiastic reviews, see among many others, James A. Notopoulos, in *The Classical Journal,* IIL (1952–53), 273–79; W. Edward Brown, *Yale Review,* XXXXI (1951–52), 47–74; or the references to Dodds in W. J. W. Koster, *Le mythe de Platon, de Zarathoustra et des Chaldéens. Etude critique sur les relations intellectuelles entre Platon et l'Orient,* in *Mnemosyne,* Supplementum Tertium (1951). Dodds's Wiles Lectures for 1962–63, *Pagan and Christian in an Age of Anxiety* (1965) are less epoch-making but show, once again, how deeply a sure-footed and superbly informed student of the past can probe with Freudian instruments. Dodds's concise autobiography, *Missing Persons* (1977), is a moving supplement to his scholarship.

As for Frederick Crews: in 1970, he edited a substantial anthology, *Psychoanalysis and Literary Process,* which he introduced with an energetic defense of Freud against, among others "[René] Wellek and [Austin] Warren's icy and confused chapter on 'Literature and Psychology' " (p. 8) in their *Theory of Literature* (1949). He was no less severe with critics who "season a conventional argument with references to Freud" (p. 7), or those who offer only too facile "rhetorical" refutations of Ernest Jones's controversial *Hamlet and Oedipus* (p. 16n). He justly acknowledged that "Freud's achievement is entangled in an embarrassingly careless scientific tradition" (p. 17) and that psychoanalytic literary scholars have done some problematic work. Yet he remained, firmly and explicitly, a "Freudian critic" (p. 17). He did not shift from that stance for some years. In an ingratiating collection of partly confessional essays dating from 1967 to 1975, *Out of My System* (1975), he reaffirmed his Freudian allegiances, though with some—eminently reasonable—reservations. He objects to what he calls "relatively 'ideological' " as opposed to "relatively 'scientific' " strands in psychoanalytic thought. He has difficulties with Norman O. Brown's apocalyptic version of psychoanalysis. But even in the last paper he includes, "Reductionism and its Discontents," with all its prudent, sensible, cautions against the "hazards of reduction-ism" (p. 167), he flatly declares himself to be one who believes "that principles of Freudian psychoanalysis can be usefully applied to literary criticism" (166). I should note that I fully share these objections, difficulties, and cautions. Then something happened. In 1980, Crews published "Analysis Terminable," a vehement assault on psychoanalysis as a therapy in the pages of *Commentary* (July), and, in 1984, an even more uninhibited broadside, "The Freudian way of knowledge," *The New Criterion* (June), 7–25, in which he blasts Freud as a liar, a monomaniac, a crackpot, a drug addict, and concludes with the hope that a later generation may be "able to understand more fully how, in the topsy-turvy moral atmosphere of our century, we came to befuddle ourselves with the extraordi-nary and consequential delusion of Freudian thought" (p. 24). (It is, incidentally, highly instructive to read an article by Henri F. Ellenberger ["The Story of 'Anna O': A Critical Review with New Data," *Journal of the History of the Behavioral Sciences,* VIII, 3 (July 1972), 267–79] to which Crews appeals, but which tells a quite different, far less anti-Freudian story than Crews's use—or abuse—of it would intimate.) Crews's only allusion to his own extensive Freudian past—"People who fall under that spell, as I myself once did" (p. 24)—is far too casual to account for the decade and more of his psychoanalytically committed publications. The stridency of his attacks, their prosecutor's vigor, their tenden-tious over-interpretations—to say nothing of their misinterpreta-tions—make one long for the elegance and rationality of his earlier writings. Nor does Crews's tramp to Canossa discredit his *Sins of the Fathers* (1966) any more than Tolstoy's repudiation of his liter-ary works can detract from the stature of *War and Peace* or *Anna Karenina.* Crews's psychoanalytic exploration of Hawthorne's fic-tion retains its value as a study in its own right, and as evidence in behalf of applied psychoanalysis. I cannot help wondering, though, how the Crews of 1984 would review the Crews of 1966, 1970, or 1975.

Brumfitt, J., *Voltaire Historian* (1958).

Degler, Carl N., "What Ought to Be and What Was: Women's Sexuality in the Nineteenth Century," *American Historical Review,* LXXIX, 5 (December 1974), 1467–90.

Dekker, Rudolf M., and Herman W. Roodenberg, "A Suitable Case for Treatment? A Reappraisal of Erikson's Young Man Luther," *Theory and Society*, XII (1983), 775–800.

Demos, John, *A Little Commonwealth: Family Life in Plymouth Colony* (1970). (And see again Demos, *Entertaining Satan: Witch-Craft and the Culture of Early New England* [1982]).

Eissler, Kurt, *Leonardo da Vinci: Psycho-Analytic Notes on the Enigma* (1961).

Freud, Sigmund, "Vorwort zur vierten Auflage" [to *Drei Abhandlungen zur Sexualtheorie*] (1920), St.A., V, 45–46; "Preface to the Fourth Edition" [to *Three Essays on Sexuality*], *S.E.*, VII, 133–34.

Gay, Peter, "Introduction: Freud. For the Marble Tablet," *Berggasse 19: Sigmund Freud's Home and Offices, Vienna 1938; The Photographs of Edmund Engelman* (1976), 13–54.

————, *Art and Act: On Causes in History—Manet, Gropius, Mondrian* (1976).

Gedo, Mary M., *Picasso: Art as Autobiography* (1980).

Hughes, H. Stuart, *The Obstructed Path: French Social Thought in the Years of Desperation 1930–1960* (1968).

Johnson, Roger A., ed., *Psychohistory and Religion: The Case of "Young Man Luther"* (1977).

Kramnick, Isaac, *The Rage of Edmund Burke: Portrait of an Ambivalent Conservative* (1977).

Laplanche, J., and J.-B. Pontalis, *The Language of Psychoanalysis* (1967; tr. Donald Nicholson-Smith, 1973).

Mazlish, Bruce, *James and John Stuart Mill: Father and Son in the Nineteenth Century* (1975).

Nagel, Ernest, *The Structure of Science: Problems in the Logic of Scientific Explanation* (1961).

Popper, Sir Karl, *Conjectures and Refutations: The Growth of Scientific Knowledge* (1962).

Schapiro, Meyer, "Leonardo and Freud: An Art-Historical Study," *Journal of the History of Ideas*, XVII, 2 (April 1956), 147–78.

Solomon, Maynard, *Beethoven* (1977).

Splitter, Randolph, *Proust's Recherche: A Psychoanalytic Interpretation* (1981).

[Strachey, James], "Editor's Note," to Freud's "Leonardo," in Freud, *S.E.*, XI (1957), 59–62.

Trevor-Roper, H.R., "The European Witch-Craze of the Sixteenth and Seventeenth Centuries," in *Religion, the Reformation and Social Change and Other Essays* (1967), 90–192.

Volkan, Vamik D., and Norman Itzkowitz, *The Immortal Atatürk: A Psychobiography* (1984). Interesting collaboration between a psychoanalyst and a specialist on the Near East.

Wurgaft, Lewis D., *The Imperial Imagination: Magic and Myth in Kipling's India* (1983). Psychobiography and psychohistory.

Acknowledgments

Since I have been working on this book, off and on, from about 1974, in close conjunction with *The Bourgeois Experience: Victoria to Freud* (vol. I, 1984; vol. II forthcoming, 1986) and have incurred debts to institutions and individuals, I am gratefully recording them in my acknowledgments for those volumes. They bought me time, gave me attention, supplied me with material, and commented on my argument and my style.

My earliest attempt to rehearse some of the themes to become *Freud for Historians,* outside of my graduate and undergraduate classes at Yale, goes back to an address on overdetermination I delivered before the New York State Association of European Historians at Ithaca College, Ithaca, New York, in 1967. In 1974, I presented two lectures at the University of Cincinnati on historiography and causation and, in the same year, spoke at Hamline University, St. Paul, Minnesota, on the tricky issue of representativeness. In the following year, 1975, I talked at Colorado College, Colorado Springs, on cultural history, emphasizing the possible relevance of psychoanalysis. In 1977, I helped to inaugurate a new president at the College of Wooster, Wooster, Ohio, with an address on the historian as the scientist of memory, and, in the same year, lectured on overdetermination to the Kanzer Seminar at Yale, at Hunter College, New York City, and before the Berkeley College Fellowship at Yale. Then, in 1978, I took the occasion of the Gallatin Lecture at the Institute for the Humanities at New York University to speak about "An Arsenal for Amateurs," an early version of what has become Chapter 1. In the same year, I first adumbrated what has developed into Chapter 4 of this book at Kenyon College, Gambier, Ohio, speaking on "Reason, Reality, the Psychoanalyst and the Historian." Later that year, I broadened my focus in talking about history and psychoanalysis at Smith College, Northampton, Massachusetts, and on "Human Nature in History," a draft for Chapter 3, at Antioch College, Yellow Springs, Ohio. In the Benjamin Rush Lecture that I delivered to the American Psychiatric

Association in Chicago on "Reductionism" in the spring of 1979, I rehearsed the problems of the psychohistorian facing his intractable human materials. A revised version of that theme became my lecture at Stetson University, Deland, Florida. In April 1979, I spent a most enjoyable and instructive weekend at Colgate University, Hamilton, New York, discussing the tense relations of psychoanalysis and history with interested faculty. Finally, later that year, I spoke at Syracuse University in upstate New York, on "From Biography to History," an experimental version of what has become Chapter 5.

The New York Psychoanalytic Society provided an exciting and welcoming critical forum for my ideas in January 1980, as I presented a paper on "Objections to Psychohistory." The Ena H. Thompson lectures I inaugurated in April and May 1980 at Pomona College, Claremont, California, were principally on the substance of the history of the nineteenth-century bourgeoisie, but contained substantial passages on methodology that have survived into this book. In June, I gave the keynote address to a conference on leadership at the Michael Reese Hospital and Medical Center, Chicago, again on objections to psychohistory. The following month, I had the honor of being the Jessie and John Danz Lecturer at the University of Washington, Seattle; my three presentations were my first attempt at a coherent and expansive argument. They bore the resounding title, "Psychoanalytic Perspectives on the Past: Freud for Historians," of which the subtitle, of course, eventually became the title of this book. The four Freud Lectures I gave at Yale in the fall of 1980 under the auspices of the Western New England Institute for Psychoanalysis and the Humanities Center at Yale were, like my Ena H. Thompson lectures at Pomona, a mixture of substance and method, though on quite different themes.

In 1981 I was deeply moved to be chosen as the first Arthur M. Wilson Memorial Lecturer at Dartmouth; I remembered my old friend by joining, as best I could, his central interests and mine with "Experience of a Life: Psychoanalytic Thoughts on Biography." Later that year, I ventured among psychoanalysts once again, speaking at the New York Hospital-Cornell Medical Center, Westchester Division at White Plains on "Psychoanalysis and History." In March 1982, I spoke at Arizona State University, Tempe, Arizona, on the same theme. In the following month, I participated in a conference on psychohistory (and psycholiterature) at Swarthmore, where I examined this by now familiar subject from a new angle with a paper on "History, Psychohistory, and Psychoanalytic History." In May, I varied both topics at Stanford University and at San Jose State College, California, returning to psychoanalysis and history. And in the same month, I was given a splendid opportunity to exercise my critical—I trust not hypercritical—capacities in the sixth annual O. Meredith Wilson Lecture in History at the University of Utah, Salt Lake City, with a lecture titled "The Historian as Psychologist"; I have embodied much of that talk, in somewhat different form, in my first chapter.

I spent much of the academic year 1983–84 at the Wissenschaftskolleg zu Berlin—West Berlin, of course—subtitled Institute for Advanced Study, a hospitable "think tank" where I managed to do some lecturing, to my fellow fellows, to the Karl Abraham Institute in psychoanalysis, and the rather more eclectic Arbeitsgruppe Berlin der deutschen psychoanalytischen Gesellschaft, on various aspects of psychoanalysis in history. In June 1984, I took my ideas on the road, leading a day of most stimulating lecture-discussions at the Max-Planck-Institute at Göttingen. In July, I had the opportunity to do the same at the University of Amsterdam. The working conditions at the Kolleg were ideal, and it was there that I gave my manuscript its final revisions, taking into account my critics' comments. It would be invidious to single out too many of those who made my stay in Berlin an ideal one, but I do want to mention particularly the two librarians who found elusive materials for me—Frau Gesine Bottomley and Frau Dorte Meyer-Gaudig, and my secretary, Frau Andrea Herbst, who did prodigious deciphering in a language not her own.

In this last phase of final, final revisions I continued to try out my ideas on students and faculties. I am grateful to Queens College for being chosen their first visiting scholar in a new and ambitious program for the humanities, which gave me a rich week of discussions and formal presentations. As the Ida Beam Lecturer at the University of Iowa, Iowa City, in November, I explored once more the themes that have occupied me for so many years. Finally, in early 1985, I gave the luncheon address at the meeting of the Indiana Historical Society on "Human Nature in History: Bridges Between History and Psychoanalysis," and addressed the psychoanalytic section of the American Psychological Association in New York on "From Couch to Culture: Psychoanalysis for the Historian." As I look back at all these occasions for gratitude, I become keenly aware, once again, of how many audiences I have experimented on and how much I owe to them all.

I have expressed elsewhere, and want to emphasize once more, that I should hardly have been able to write this book—certainly not this way—without the work I did as a research candidate in the Western New England Institute for Psychoanalysis.

Betty Paine turned my manuscript into prose an editor could read. Nancy Lane at Oxford University Press was immensely helpful, and Rosemary Wellner edited the book with a light hand.

An array of friends, colleagues, and acquaintances—I hope I have forgotten none of them!—proved most patient with my inquiries; they made observations and raised objections that have found their way into the text, lent me inaccessible books, sent me offprints I could not easily procure, generously answered letters, and above all talked to me—both supportively and critically. I thank particularly Peter Bieri, Martin and Ridi Bergmann, William Bouwsma, Judy Coffin, Clifford Geertz, Hank Gibbons, Cyrus Hamlin, Jackie and Gaby Katwan, Otto Kernberg, Thomas A. Kohut, Dick and Peggy Kuhns (as always), Weston LaBarre, Carl Landauer, Emmanuel LeRoy Ladurie, Peter Loewenberg, Janet Malcolm, John Merriman, Jerry Meyer, Marc Micale, Arthur Mitzman, Richard Newman, Hank Payne, Ernst Prelinger, Keith Thomas, Henry Turner, and my constant reader Bob Webb.

I have saved my readers to the last. Carl ("Peter") Hempel lent his unsurpassed acumen to the difficult Chapter 2. Stefan Collini, John Demos, Harry Frankfurt, Quentin Skinner, and Vann Woodward went over the whole manuscript, page by page, argument by argument, adjective by adjective, with an affectionate care others save for their own work. My book, risky as its argument remains, is much the better for their nice sense of discrimination, their tact with me and my language, and their willingness to be severe when needed without ever dampening my enthusiasm for my project. My wife Ruth, as usual, did not permit the manuscript to escape to the press before giving it the most thorough perusal. My gratitude to such readers is, I hope, adequate.

PETER GAY

Index